The Long Shadow of Emile Cailliet

The Long Shadow of Emile Cailliet
Faith, Philosophy, and Theological Education

ABIGAIL RIAN EVANS and CLEMENS BARTOLLAS
with
GORDON GRAHAM and KENNETH HENKE

☙PICKWICK *Publications* • Eugene, Oregon

THE LONG SHADOW OF EMILE CAILLIET
Faith, Philosophy, and Theological Education

Copyright © 2011 Abigail Rian Evans and Clemens Bartollas. All rights reserved. Except for brief quotations in critical publications or reviews, no part of this book may be reproduced in any manner without prior written permission from the publisher. Write: Permissions, Wipf and Stock Publishers, 199 W. 8th Ave., Suite 3, Eugene, OR 97401.

Pickwick Publications
An Imprint of Wipf and Stock Publishers
199 W. 8th Ave., Suite 3
Eugene, OR 97401
www.wipfandstock.com
ISBN 13: 978-1-61097-112-6

Cataloging-in-Publication data:

Evans, Abigail Rian.

The long shadow of Emile Cailliet : faith, philosophy, and theological education / Abigail Rian Evans and Clemens Bartollas, with Gordon Woodrow Graham and Kenneth Henke.

xvi + 206 p. ; 23 cm. — Includes bibliographical references.

ISBN 13: 978-1-61097-112-6

1. Cailliet, Émile 1894– 2. Christian philosophers — United States — Biography. 3. Theology — Study and teaching. I. Bartollas, Clemens. II. Graham, Gordan Woodrow. III. Henke, Kenneth. IV. Cailliet, Émile, 1894–

BR102.C12 E93 2011

Manufactured in the U.S.A.

This book is dedicated to all of Emile Cailliet's students,
who both here and abroad, have lived the Christian pattern of life inspired by Cailliet's teaching and Christ's light, which shone through him.

Emile Cailliet in his home on Alexander Street in Princeton (1947–1959) (Photograph by Milt Riviere).

Contents

List of Illustrations / ix
Preface / xi
Acknowledgments / xv

1. The Man: A Journey into Light / 1
2. The Believer: A Christian Centurion / 48
3. The Teacher: The Princeton Years / 76
4. The Christian Scholar: An Evangelical Intellectual / 97
5. The Philosopher: A Christian Philosopher in a Theological Seminary / 123

   Epilogue / 139

APPENDIXES
   A. Emile Cailliet Biographical Chronology / 147
   B. Account of the Wedding of Emile and Vera Cailliet / 150
   C. I Met the Huguenots / 152
   D. A Layman Among Ministers / 159
   E. Where Would Jesus Be? / 170
   F. The Mind's Gravitation Back to the Familiar / 175
   G. This I Believe / 183
   H. Cailliet's Princeton Course Descriptions / 185
   I. The Role of Seminary Education in the Secular Order / 189

Bibliography / 199
Authors / 203

Illustrations

All images taken from Emile Cailliet Collection, Special Collections, Princeton Theological Seminary Library, except where noted.

1. Emile Cailliet in his military uniform during WWI service (1914–1917) as a part of the 44th Infantry Regiment, Fifth Battalion of Sharpshooters. / 11
2. Photo of Emile Cailliet (far left) taken in 1915 after being wounded in action, near the time of his marriage to Vera Brabazon. / 16
3. Vera and Emile Cailliet and dog, crossing the Atlantic en route to the United States on the *Ile de France*, 1930. / 24
4. Emile Cailliet attending a dinner at Scripps College (1931–1941), Claremont, CA. / 25
5. Doris Brunzie, Cailliet's daughter and youngest child, on left with artist Eileen Fabian in front of portrait of Emile Cailliet, now hanging in Stuart Hall, Princeton Theological Seminary. / 44
6. Photograph of Emile Cailliet's first Bible, *La Sainte Bible*, received from Vera Cailliet on December 17, 1917. / 51
7. Faculty of Princeton Theological Seminary, 1958; Cailliet stands front row, third from right. / 84
8. Emile Cailliet, the early scholar. / 98
9. Emile Cailliet's *La Sainte Bible*, received from Vera Cailliet on December 17, 1917; Book of "Apocalypse" (Revelation). / 144
10. Emile and Vera Cailliet in later years. / 145

Preface

THIS BOOK AIMS TO examine the importance of Christian philosophy in theological education through the prism of the life and teachings of Emile Cailliet. The title is a twist on Cailliet's oft-repeated words, "the long shadow of Immanuel Kant." Kant misdirected philosophy and religion, whereas Cailliet's shadow, illuminated by his love for Christ, put them back on the right path. The book's primary focus is on his years of teaching at Princeton Theological Seminary to which all the authors of this book are connected. This work examines Cailliet as a believer, teacher, scholar, and philosopher. The concluding chapter, written by Gordon Graham, one of Cailliet's successors, discusses philosophy's place in theological education, one of Cailliet's primary interests at Princeton Seminary. Cailliet's presence, Christian faith, and philosophical perspectives informed his students' seminary education in regard to Christian philosophy and their understanding of faith.

Although Cailliet wrote over twenty books, none of them articulated his formal position on the nature of theological education. However, it is clear from his teaching at seminary and his writings on philosophy and philosophers, especially Pascal, that he saw philosophy as an integral part of seminary training. In addition, he gave several speeches at faculty meetings (copies of which are in the Princeton Theological Seminary archives) about the proposed new curriculum, which provide insights into his perspectives.

The sources for this book are as follows: (1) The Princeton Seminary archives of Cailliet's papers—correspondence, articles, speeches, and personal items such as French newspapers, his World War I diary, his annotated Bible, etc.; (2) books, articles, and formal lectures by Cailliet and a few secondary unpublished materials about his life and thought; (3) interviews, based on a questionnaire developed by Evans and Bartollas, of approximately 70 of Cailliet's former Princeton Seminary students and teaching assistants from the 1950s, as well as a few remaining friends and family members, including his daughter; (4) genealogy and family information from ancestry.com; and (5) historical material relevant to his life.

There is no historical trail to follow in writing a biography of Cailliet, as this is the first one. Therefore, the book is a collection of impressions, rather like an abstract painting, where the reality is there but not always clearly delineated. Understanding the social and cultural context in which Cailliet lived illuminates his work and his impact on theological education. We do know that he was heavily influenced by the French Huguenots and parachurch groups such as Young Life and the Salvation Army. He came from an Augustinian theology through Pascal and was deeply immersed in the moderate evangelical wing of American Christianity which emphasized the centrality of the Bible and a personal relationship to Christ. However, he also embraced the importance of culture, especially science and philosophy, in conversation with theology.

This book is not strictly a biography but to some degree a distillation of remembrances of those who knew him, as well as insights gained from his own papers. It has become clear in writing this book that it is not possible to integrate neatly the various accounts of Cailliet, the man. The perspectives are often conflicting, as most people knew only one aspect of Cailliet rather than knowing him as a complex and multi-faceted person. We do not wish to shape his legacy to any particular agenda or point of view but present our findings for the reader to draw his/her own conclusions. If we may be so bold, accepting only one perspective of him is rather like trying to read one gospel account rather than understanding each as four different points of view of the same subject.

Another challenge in writing this book was separating fact and hearsay in regard to stories about Cailliet. For example, was "Yippee Cailliet" his nickname or that of his dog? As we discovered and as discussed in the teacher chapter of this book, it was the nickname the students gave the dog, spelled "Yippie-Yi-Yo-Ki-Yay," but some may have also referred to Cailliet in fun with this nickname. Not only are there different versions of the same event, but also some memories shared by individual students with no known resources to corroborate the stories. Cailliet was described as arrogant and distant by some, by others as a warm and caring professor who took a deep interest in his students. He was characterized as a liberal evangelical, which in today's definitions appears an oxymoron.

WHY WE WISH TO DO THIS PROJECT

Since there has never been a biography of Cailliet, we believe his legacy should be preserved and made available to future generations, especially those in seminary education. This book is a modest introduction to his life and thought with the hope that others may be inspired to pursue a more in-depth analysis of his scholarship and contributions. Dr. Emile Cailliet was an outstanding teacher. His course in Christian philosophy was for many students the most interesting course during their first term at Princeton Theological Seminary. For two of the authors, Evans and Bartollas, Princeton Seminary MDiv graduates, class of 1961, it was probably the best course we had at Princeton, as many of our classmates also stated. We both sat near the front of the class. The seats were nearly filled, and there was an intense energy present. Cailliet was widely respected and feared by the students. This large, silver-haired man with a massive brow and thick lens on his glasses, who looked to be in his late 50s, entered the lecture hall. He walked to the front of the class and set forward a reshaping of Western philosophy if it had followed Heraclitus, rather than Parmenides. We would then have believed in a world of perpetual change and becoming.

Students were spellbound by his challenging thoughts which led to discussions far into the night. The way he electrified the first class, as well as those that followed, is also discussed in Chapter 3, "The Teacher: The Princeton Years." The impact of Cailliet's brilliance and insights reached far beyond the walls of Princeton Seminary. Through his speaking and preaching, Cailliet's influence touched local congregations, college audiences, prep schools, and groups of Young Life workers.

Authors Gordon Graham and Kenneth Henke's interest in Cailliet comes from other perspectives. Graham, who now teaches philosophy and ethics at Princeton Seminary, is carving out the place and importance of philosophy in theological education. He finds in Cailliet a kindred spirit based on their shared perspective that philosophy is not simply a handmaiden to theology or subsumed in a mere apologetics role, but an important discipline with a rightful role in seminary education. Kenneth

Henke has had a long interest in Cailliet through his study with Douglas Steere at Haverford College. Professor Steere was a close friend of Emile Cailliet who shared with Cailliet a professional interest in the philosophy of religion and a personal interest in the practice of the Christian devotional life. As an archivist at the Princeton Seminary Library, Henke has also had the opportunity to become familiar at first hand with the treasured original documents about and by Cailliet.

Emile Cailliet was one of the most influential Christians of the twentieth century. Whether in his work on Pascal and his critique of Kant, his evaluation of the contributions of Young Life and the Salvation Army, Cailliet's books and articles that addressed the role of laity in the church, he was a pivotal witness to the Christian faith.

Furthermore, we want to preserve Cailliets work because he was a seminal but neglected thinker whose influence extends from science to literature and from philosophy to spirituality and theology. Other than a PhD dissertation written in 1985, there has been no formal attempt to synthesize his scholarly contributions. Several books on Cailliet were planned shortly after his death, but unfortunately, not one was completed and published. Now that Princeton Theological Seminary is approaching its bicentennial year in 2012, this seems an auspicious time for such a book.

We consider a Cailliet study of major importance because it is so relevant to what is taking place within the Christian church and faith today. Here was a Christian who was comfortable with science, philosophy, literature, culture, and history. He relished debates with those whose perspective was different from his own. He cherished the time he spent with philosophers and scientists.

Our particular focus, or thrust, in this study is: (1) how Cailliet's life and thought influenced his seminary teaching; (2) the story of his conversion and Christian faith (3) why Christian philosophy is an important part of theological education; and (4) an appraisal of Cailliet's enduring legacy, which includes his impact on Princeton Seminary students, faculty, and administrators, and some of his scholarly work. We invite the reader to stand in the long shadow of Cailliet and consider how his life and thought can help us tackle some of the knotty questions which face us today. Our hope is to inspire readers to explore some of Cailliet's important works and therein find wisdom and understanding in their search for meaning and purpose in life. This was Cailliet's goal as he journeyed into the light.

Acknowledgments

It has been over fifty years since we were students of Emile Cailliet at Princeton Theological Seminary. After we decided to write a brief book about Cailliet, we received extensive support and assistance during our years of research. To begin, we want to acknowledge our appreciation for the chapters written by Gordon Graham and Kenneth Henke, which greatly enhance this volume.

We are grateful to the former students of Cailliet who responded to our questionnaire with letters and phone calls about their evaluation of Cailliet in the classroom. We are very appreciative of Rosemary Mitchell, Vice President for Seminary Relations at Princeton Seminary, whose office did the mailings to these Princeton alumni. Most of these students are identified by initials in the footnotes of the book.

We are indebted to Clifford Anderson, chief archivist, and his staff at Princeton Seminary who assisted us and provided free access to Dr. Cailliet's papers. Of special note is the research of Kenneth Henke who found and interpreted so much of the archival material. We are also grateful to the Cailliet family for their gifts of Emile Cailliet's papers to Princeton Theological Seminary, which have allowed us and future scholars to obtain important information about Cailliet's life and thought.

Richard Oman and Charles MacKenzie, former teaching assistants and friends of Cailliet, provided important insights about him. Also helpful were the interviews with Thomas Gillespie, James Armstrong, Eileen Moffett, Donald Stine, and Daniel Theron. Dr. Theron also commissioned and funded the portrait of Cailliet that now hangs at Princeton Seminary. We especially appreciate the kindness of Doris Brunzie, Dr. Cailliet's daughter, for her willingness to respond to our queries about her father.

Acknowledgments

The talents and assistance of friends and colleagues helped us to complete our research and writing on Dr. Cailliet. We especially wish to thank Janice Miller who provided administrative assistance in the early stages of this book; Louise Winfield's translations of several French letters received by Cailliet and Mary Tiebout's excellent assistance with many of the translations and interpretations of Cailliet's archival papers written in French. We are especially indebted to Kristen Hays Berthelotte who provided excellent editorial work on every phase of the manuscript and Diedre Cave who prepared this MMS for the publisher. Finally, we appreciate the editors and staff at Wipf and Stock for their willingness to publish this volume and for their guidance in moving it through the publication process.

—Abigail Rian Evans and Clemens Bartollas

1

The Man

A Journey into Light

OVERVIEW

THIS CHAPTER WILL SKETCH some of the major periods of Emile Cailliet's life which helped to shape who he was. These glimpses of his life help to paint a picture, or better, a tapestry of a rather complex man. As to be expected, most of the material is drawn from family, friends, and colleagues' perspectives and recollections rather than from first-person accounts.

In many ways, Emile Cailliet's life was not easy—fighting for the French in World War I, facing a firing squad, doing missionary work and research in Madagascar, and then emigrating to the United States where he never felt completely at home. He really was a citizen of two countries: France and America. All these experiences were reflected in his rather austere countenance, though there was also a romantic and fun-loving side that his family and close friends came to know. He made a tremendous impact on a generation of students who wrote to seek his counsel years after graduating. We are most interested in focusing on his Princeton years where he states that his decision to come to Princeton Theological Seminary was based on his desire to shape the field of Christian philosophy.[1] Sadly, his last years were partially overshadowed

---

1. Emile Cailliet, notes, May 29, 1947, Emile Cailliet Collection, Special Collections, Princeton Theological Seminary Library, Letter Box 2.

by financial hardship, his wife's illness and death, and his own ailments. The Alzheimer's disease and subsequent death of his beloved wife of fifty-four years and his own lingering illness, accompanied by aphasia, were sad notes to a rich life.

A misunderstanding over sabbaticals and pension from Princeton Seminary caused Cailliet financial hardship since he only received $200 each month,[2] which in 2010 terms translates to $1,500 per month. One person close to Cailliet, Daniel Theron, reported that the seminary later solved the financial issues but no correspondence could be found in that regard. However, personal friendships with John Mackay and James McCord of Princeton Seminary continued, which extended to Cailliet's children. Warm letters exchanged in the late 1960s and in the 1970s expressed affection, regard, and praise for his contributions to the seminary and the high esteem in which he was held by students and faculty from his years in Princeton.[3]

Overarching Cailliet's life was a deep Christian faith which permeated every aspect of who he was from the time of his conversion at age twenty-three until his death. He was an evangelical intellectual grounded in both biblical revelation and modern thought; one might even call him a pious intellectual. The wonderful juxtaposition of these streams, which today strike us as somewhat unlikely, provide an example of how we can transform our current bifurcation of personal piety and intellectual rigor. In the scholarly world, he was best known for his outstanding research and writing on Pascal. Even Andrew Blackwood, Princeton Theological Seminary professor of Homiletics, wrote a letter to Cailliet on the occasion of Pascal's birthday which he obviously believed Cailliet would be observing.[4]

The theme for this chapter is taken from the title of one of Cailliet's last books, *Journey into Light*, which discusses his conversion to Christianity, in 1917, and the ensuing radical shift of his life. At first it seems unlikely that he would become a fervent Christian but one can see God's hand in

---

2. Correspondence between John Mackay and James McCord, October 16, 1959, Emile Cailliet Collection, Special Collections, Princeton Theological Seminary Library.

3. Correspondence with John Mackay and James McCord, Emile Cailliet Collection, Special Collections, Princeton Theological Seminary Library, Box 9, File 226.

4. Andrew Blackwood to Emile Cailliet, May 1, 1948, Emile Cailliet Collection, Special Collections, Princeton Theological Seminary Library, Box 1.

Cailliet's life.⁵ His faith journey was unusual, which should come as no surprise considering his life story and the dramatic shift of his very foundations. Becoming a Christian completely defined who he was as a man. If he were still alive, he would surely be trying to reach people around the globe, urging them to use their intelligence to see and hear the risen Christ at work in our world.⁶ All of his scholarship, research, teaching, and life were put in service to Christ; he retained his love of philosophy and science and integrated them into his faith and teaching. He saw the importance of building on the insights from other disciplines but they, in a sense, were also converted to be viewed under the cross of Christ. This is why we call him an evangelical intellectual.

Cailliet's conversion did not transform him into a saint; in fact, as with all of us, his flaws were very evident. However, in many ways, he lived on a mystical plane and illuminated the inner Christian life as few others have done. This is evident from his tremendous impact both on those who were struggling with their own questions about God, as well as those mature giants of the Christian faith who found in him fresh insights and challenges to reexamine their own walk with God.

FROM ATHEIST TO CHRISTIAN

We will begin this chapter with his conversion, primarily focusing on how this seminal event fundamentally shaped who he was. It is important in understanding his Christian conversion and ministry to remember that he was more or less an agnostic until age twenty-three.⁷ There is no doubt that the seeds of his conversion were planted during World War I when he watched his companion die in front of him. This event, as he later wrote, threw into bold relief the emptiness of naturalistic philosophy, in which he could find no answers and no comfort. However, he writes that his reasons for enlisting to fight in the war were born out of utter pessimism: a

---

5. The title most likely comes from a line in Eugene O'Neill's dedication of his play "Long Day's Journey into Night," which Cailliet saw on Broadway and reviewed. Cailliet, Review of "Darkness over Broadway." O'Neill credited his wife with leading him on a "Journey toward the light."

6. Brossoie, letter to Bartollas, June 16, 2009.

7. Cailliet, *Journey into Light*, 11.

sense of relentless fate and views of determinism.[8] Cailliet also had vainly sought the meaning of life through many books but none seemed to carry the answers he wanted. In this sense he was ripe for the message the Bible would bring to him. This was the instrument of his conversion.

One student notes the parallels of Cailliet's conversion to that of other great Christians. "I would like to add that after my graduation from Princeton Theological Seminary, I read a biography of Dr. Cailliet [*Journey into Light*] and I found some similarity between him and St. Augustine. From the outset he was not a professing Christian. He was a rational, intellectual unbeliever who was converted to Christianity. If my memory does not betray me, his wife, who was a Christian, contributed to his conversion."[9] Many students commented on his dramatic move to Christianity.[10]

We glean, from several of Cailliet's articles and books, his understanding of the radical nature of conversion to the Christian faith. His views, of course, were influenced by his own dramatic turn from naturalism/atheism to a deep and abiding Christian faith and vocation.[11] "With Blaise Pascal the new man in Christ sighs in a tremendous exaltation of his whole being: 'Joy, joy, joy, tears of joy!'"[12]

Before he discovered the Bible, Cailliet attempted to find a philosophy that would speak to him.

> The day came when I put the finishing touch to "the book that would understand me," speak to my condition, and help me through life's happenings. A beautiful, sunny day it was. I went out, sat under a tree, and opened my precious anthology. As I went on reading, however, a growing disappointment came over me. Instead of speaking to my condition, the various passages reminded me of their context, of the circumstances of my labor over their selection. Then I *knew* that the whole undertaking would not work, simply because it was of my own making. It carried no strength of persuasion. In a dejected mood, I put the little book back into my pocket.
>
> At that very moment, my wife—who, incidentally, knew nothing of the project on which I had been working—appeared at the

---

8. Ibid., 13.
9. PCL, letter to author Bartollas, May 13, 2009.
10. CSH, letter to Evans and Bartollas.
11. Cailliet, "Christian Experience," 330.
12. Ibid., 331.

gate of the garden, pushing the baby carriage.¹³ It had been a hot afternoon. She had followed the main boulevard only to find it too crowded. So she had turned to a side street which she could not name because we had only recently arrived in town. The cobblestones had shaken the carriage so badly that she had pondered what to do. Whereupon, having spotted a patch of grass beyond a small archway, she had gone in with the baby for a period of rest . . . it turned out that the patch of grass led to an outside stone staircase which she had climbed without quite realizing what she was doing. At the top, she had seen a long room, door wide open. So she had entered. At the further end, a white-haired gentleman worked at a desk. He had not become aware of her presence. Looking around, she noticed the carving of a cross. Thus she suddenly realized that this office was part of a church building—of a Huguenot church edifice hidden away as they are all, even long after the danger of persecution has passed. The venerable-looking gentleman was the pastor. She walked to his desk and heard herself say, "Have you a Bible in French?" He smiled and handed over to her a copy, which she eagerly took from his hand; then she walked out with a mixed feeling of both joy and guilt.¹⁴

As she now stood in front of me, she meant to apologize . . . But I was no longer listening to her; "A Bible, you say? Where is it? I have never seen one before!" She complied. I literally grabbed the book and rushed to my study with it. I opened and "chanced" upon the Beatitudes! I read, and read, and read—now aloud with indescribable warmth surging [through me] . . . I could not find words to express my awe and wonder. And suddenly the realization dawned upon me: This *was* the Book that would understand me!¹⁵

Of this experience Emile says:

I continued to read deeply into the night, mostly from the Gospels. [Especially the gospel of John through which Christ shone] And lo and behold, as I looked through them, the One of whom they spoke, the One who spoke and acted in them became alive to me. The providential circumstances amid which the Book had found

---

13. The baby was their first daughter Hélène, which Emile noted in the Bible given to him by Vera Cailliet.

14. This seminal day of Vera giving Emile *La Sainte Bible* published in 1913 was December 17, 1917, based on Cailliet's entry in this Bible (Emile Cailliet Collection, Special Collections, Princeton Theological Seminary Library, Box 1).

15. Cailliet, *Journey into Light*, 16–18.

me now made it clear that while it seemed absurd to speak of a book understanding a man, this could be said of the Bible because its pages were animated by the Presence of the Living God and the Power of His mighty acts. To this God I prayed that night, and the God who answered was *the same God* of which it was spoken in the Book.[16]

His daughter Doris confirms Vera's role in Cailliet's introduction to the Bible. "Yes. Even with his Catholic education, he had scarcely been introduced to the Bible. Vera Cailliet *was* instrumental in Dr. Cailliet's becoming a Christian. She presented him with his first Bible. That sacred volume impressed him very much!"[17]

THE EARLY YEARS—GROWING UP IN FRANCE: 1894–1926

Having reviewed Cailliet's dramatic conversion, we return to a glimpse of his early years. Emile Cailliet was born in Dampierre, Marne, France on December 17, 1894, to his parents Adrien and Jeanne (née Courtin) Cailliet.[18] Since there have been no biographies of Emile Cailliet, reconstructing his early life is challenging. His daughter provides some insights into Cailliet's childhood and adolescence. "Regarding my Papa's recollections of his family life, the one that stands out is a remembrance of our grandfather, grandpère Adrien Cailliet, and his outstanding role in the family dealings. No, there wasn't a great deal *said* about Adrien's influence on *Emile* as a child, or on Lucien, for that matter. Lucien was the musical one. The grandpère's influence, which lived on, was a developing passion for music and this touched Lucien chiefly. Papa Cailliet himself, after great success at Scripps, achieved success by publishing."[19] It appears, however, that Emile was also musical since when writing to Vera of their early courtship, he mentions his playing "L'Exilé"[20] on the violin on Christmas Eve 1913.[21]

---

16. Ibid., 18.
17. Brunzie, interview with Evans and Bartollas.
18. The word "cailliet" means "curd" or cream; there is a yogurt drink called "du lait cailliet."
19. Brunzie, letter to Evans and Bartollas.
20. Composed by Auguste Samie and first published in 1859.
21. Emile Cailliet to Vera Cailliet, "Memo from Memsie to Choquie," 1961, Emile

In summary, Emile Cailliet came from a very illustrious French family. His brother Lucien[22] preceded him migrating to the States, settling first in Drexel Hill, Pennsylvania, and later moving to California. Lucien toured the United States with the French Army Band, sailing from Le Havre on March 2, 1915 on the USS *Chicago*, along with many musicians. His wife, Valentine, and son, Marcel, joined him in September of that year.[23] He registered for World War I to fight for the Americans and was disqualified because of a disability.[24] His two sons, René, who went into medicine, and Marcel, who went into music, were a source of pride.[25] Valentine traveled back and forth from France during this period and in 1921, traveled with two children listed as her daughters, Julie and Marguerite, ages six and three, respectively.[26]

Lucien was a renowned musician with the Philadelphia Orchestra, which he joined in 1919, and he conducted several regional orchestras in the greater Philadelphia area. He became a U.S. citizen on January 25, 1923, and moved to Los Angeles fourteen years later, where he composed and performed with various orchestras, playing the clarinet and saxophone, and arranging music for wind ensemble and piano. He married his second and much younger wife, Vera L. Jeffrey,[27] on June 23, 1946, in California. She was a talented musician who worked with her husband arranging, producing and publishing music. Later in his career, he taught at the University of Southern California and wrote many compositions, contributing to over sixty Hollywood films as a composer and arranger between 1938 and 1965.[28] He and Vera had two sons, Paul and Claude, and moved to Wisconsin for retirement.

Cailliet Collection, Special Collections, Princeton Theological Seminary Library.

22. Lucien Cailliet (May 22, 1891–January 3, 1985)
23. Ancestry.com, "Ship manifest, March 1915," accessed March 2011.
24. Ancestry.com, "Military records, Lucien Cailliet," accessed March 2011.
25. Brunzie, interview with Evans and Bartollas.
26. Ancestry.com, "Ship manifest, January 1921," accessed March 2011.
27. Vera L. Cailliet (February 18, 1926–August 17, 2008)
28. "Lucien Cailliet," *Baker's Biographical Dictionary of 20th Century Classical Musicians*.

8 THE LONG SHADOW OF EMILE CAILLIET

FRENCH CONNECTIONS

Part of understanding Emile Cailliet is recognizing not only his family but his French roots. Once a Frenchman, always a Frenchman. It was not only his thick accent which marked him as French, but also his loyalty and interest in his native land. We do know that being French defined him throughout his life even though he became a naturalized American citizen and lived in America for forty-five years.

His correspondence during the 1930s and 40s is quite revealing vis-à-vis his French connections. Especially during World War II, he wrote many letters to friends and family in France as well as to his own son, André, who was fighting for the French beginning in 1939. André accompanied his father on a visit to France and volunteered for the French army.[29] He was captured and spent four years in a German prison camp[30] and was liberated by American forces in 1944. One can imagine how anxious Emile was for the welfare of his son, while waiting several months after his release to see him.[31]

Cailliet was drawn into the French world during World War II not only because of his own son André, but also because many of his close friends' sons perished. He received a number of letters from French friends living in America worried about their loved ones during the war. His friend Waldo Dunn wrote, "I can only imagine how difficult it would be to have a son fighting in France while living in the U.S." In another letter from Dunn to Cailliet, he captures how other parents were experiencing anxiety for their soldier sons.

> Last Monday evening as the three of us were sitting in our living room chatting with Dorothy Drake, Sybil Mitchell Fielded and Marlene Wilde, the door opened without warning and a man in uniform entered. For a moment we were so astonished that we scarcely realized what had happened. It was our son Capt. Arthur Yale Dunn! Having been sent to the Pacific Area on a military mission he had a few hours to run over from Los Angeles to see us. He

---

29. It is not confirmed whether André volunteered during this trip with his father but it seems likely.

30. The prison camp was Stalag IX-A, also known as the Ziegenhain facility now in the city of Trutzhain, Germany

31. In an entry in Cailliet's diary he writes, December 17, 1945, "André arrives 5:41 p.m." Emile Cailliet Collection, Special Collections, Princeton Theological Seminary Library.

arrived at 9 in the evening and was off for LA at 10:27 a.m.! You will know how glad and thrilled we were to see him. Ever since, I have been wishing that you and your good wife might have the pleasure of André's walking in upon you in the same way. I have a sub-conscious feeling that André is going to pull through. What a joy it will be when he returns! How the tables have turned since this time in 1940! There is heavy work ahead, but everything now counts for us. Our strength is increasing hourly, courage is mounting everywhere. The stars in their courses are fighting against the powers of darkness. Fear is knocking at the doors of Mussolini, Hitler and Laval. [Pierre Laval was head of the Vichy Regime following France's armistice with Germany in 1940.] Prison bars are rattling, and the ghosts of the unjustly slain are rising to plague the monsters of iniquity. We are on the way to ultimate victory. France shall once more purge herself of the unfit and take her proud place among the champions of freedom. It is a privilege, even though an agony, to live through such times![32]

One should mention, as well, Cailliet's connection with the French government, which asked for his involvement in various ways. Cailliet served as Executive Vice-President of the Fighting French at their National Headquarters.[33] There are numerous letters exchanged with the staff of France Forever, Inc. (France Quand Même), which was cooperating with the provisional government of the French Republic.[34] A letter from Jacques Ferber thanked Cailliet for his valuable contributions to the French cause and a letter from La République Française's Comité de Rédaction in New York City requested that he collaborate on a project in February 1945.[35] One letter states: "Congratulations on the very excellent work of Free France in Philadelphia. I am very heartily with you in the matter of the recognition of DeGaulle."[36]

Cailliet's concerns for the war and for France translated to his academic life as well. He served as a member of the National Committee on

---

32. Waldo Dunn to Emile Cailliet, Claremont, California, May 23, 1943, Emile Cailliet Collection, Special Collections, Princeton Theological Seminary Library.

33. Emile Cailliet Curriculum Vitae, handwritten, Emile Cailliet Collection, Special Collections, Princeton Theological Seminary Library.

34. Letter from France Quand Même Philadelphia office, August 29, 1945, Emile Cailliet Collection, Special Collections, Princeton Theological Seminary Library.

35. Cailliet notes that he answered March 3 but the letter is not in the file

36. Letter from William Lingelbach (University of Pennsylvania), June 12, 1944, Emile Cailliet Collection, Special Collections, Princeton Theological Seminary Library.

Post-War Problems for the University of Pennsylvania[37] and in addition, his appointment diary notes from 1945 reveal a number of French exams that he conducted and lectures on the "Religious Situation in France." Furthermore, Cailliet wrote many articles that expressed these interests. In a letter dated May 29, 1945, Mirkine-Guetzé Vitch, from the École Libre des Hautes Études, thanks Cailliet for his article in *Cahiers Latins* entitled "Les Cahiers de l'Histoire de la Révolution Française," and asks him to recommend other French scholars in the United States.[38] In January of that same year, Nathan Pusey of Lawrence College in Wisconsin thanked him for writing the pamphlet "The French Situation."[39]

One Princeton seminary student recalls Cailliet's interest in World War II: "I remember after Pearl Harbor was attacked that I listened with my family on the big Stromberg-Carlson radio in our den. I was almost six. Cailliet related to us his going out to his car and turning on the radio to sit with his small dog to ponder another war. He did not say he got down on his knees to beg God to turn Imperial Japan around. It took MacArthur's kindness and patience in the aftermath to do that." He continues: "Cailliet, like other Princeton Theological Seminary faculty at that time, felt it important to share details of his own life vis-à-vis historic events. Mackay had his own experiences with the Spanish, and he drew together an outstanding faculty with their own times in Europe, the near and Far East and Latin America."[40]

In addition to these war-related ties to France and French culture, Cailliet helped French doctoral students, was a National Fellow of the French Academy of Science, assisted in a production of a French play at Scripps College and gave frequent speeches about France addressing religion and even classical music.[41] Cailliet delivered a lecture on November 23, 1944, on the topic of Claude Debussy's classical piece "Prélude à

---

37. Emile Cailliet Curriculum Vitae, 1952 Emile Cailliet Collection, Special Collections, Princeton Theological Seminary Library, Box 8, File 152.

38. Letter from Mirkine-Guetzé, May 29, 1945, Emile Cailliet Collection, Special Collections, Princeton Theological Seminary Library.

39. Letter from Nathan Pusey, January 31, 1945, Emile Cailliet Collection, Special Collections, Princeton Theological Seminary Library.

40. BB, letter to Evans and Bartollas, May 12, 2009.

41. Talk by Emile Cailliet on "Religion in France," Consulat de France, Los Angeles, January 21, 1939. Haverford College, March 1945. Emile Cailliet Collection, Special Collections, Princeton Theological Seminary Library, Box 8, File 157.

l'après-midi d'un faune" at André Ferrier's Théâtre Français d'Art. In addition, he had also been in correspondence with Leopold Stokowski (also conductor of the Philadelphia Orchestra) about a possible film on this piece with Universal Studios.[42]

WORLD WAR I—MILITARY SERVICE: 1914-1917

World War I presented a call to patriotism for many a Frenchman and Cailliet was no exception. He interrupted his education to volunteer for the military. The sequence of these events is important to sort out, as they were crucial to meeting his wife and converting to Christianity. Cailliet was a civilian at the time of the first Battle of the Marne (September 5–12, 1914) and sought refuge in the Marne region at the Château de Réveillon of Madeleine Lemaire. Madame Lemaire was a great artist whose salon was overflowing with artists anxious to perform and entertain her illustrious guests.[43] Cailliet and the other civilians were taken from the Château by the German Army to be executed by a firing squad when Madame Lemaire intervened, pleading that they were mere civilians and by military law should not be shot. They were spared.[44]

Emile Cailliet in his military uniform during WWI service (1914–1917) as a part of the 44th Infantry Regiment, Fifth Battalion of Sharpshooters.

There was some confusion about Cailliet's experiences during the war as his students have several additional insights from his conversations and lectures about his war experience; not all of these stories can be corroborated from multiple sources. It is uncertain whether or not these recollections are different aspects of Cailliet's accounts or the students'

---

42. Emile Cailliet Collection, Special Collections, Princeton Theological Seminary Library, Box 8, File 157.

43. Reed, *Reminiscences Musical and Other*, 85–90.

44. Emile Cailliet to Vera Cailliet, "Memo from Memsie to Choquie," 1961, Emile Cailliet Collection, Special Collections, Princeton Theological Seminary Library.

memories from their classes with him. One of their favorites was how he was standing alone before a German firing squad and received a last minute reprieve. There are different versions of this event: some students state that the German soldiers were ready to shoot Cailliet when a peasant woman of the village offered them a bottle of wine if they would spare him, and they preferred the wine, so Cailliet was spared.[45] Another story was that they shot everyone who was lined up in front of the firing squad but stopped when they came to Cailliet.[46] "I still remember his personal story about how he was standing before a Nazi firing squad and received a last minute reprieve."[47] However, based on Cailliet's own account in his memoirs to Vera, the so-called peasant woman is probably none other than Mme. Lemaire, a far cry from a peasant woman.

Having seen the raping of his country, he enlisted in the fall of 1914 and was subsequently wounded and rescued by an American ambulance. Cailliet wrote elsewhere of this war experience: "When World War I broke out I volunteered in [the] 44th Infantry Regiment, and again in the much exposed Fifth Battalion of Sharpshooters, first marching regiment. Severely wounded in action, I was rescued from German barbed wire entanglements under cross machine gun fire by an American field ambulance. I was nursed for nine months in American Field Hospital of Juilly (Ambulance B)."[48] We are fortunate to have his war diary written in French, which helps to illuminate his experiences. It is dated Lyon, January 9, 1915, Depot at Aix-en-Provence.

> We aren't leaving today but tomorrow morning. During the day we received brand new uniforms. I received a particularly fine overcoat. They also gave us some cartridges, some extra . . . canvas, and tent stakes in case we go into battle. What would they do to us there? Tonight I met two of those who leave with me, Mssrs. Dellue and Buatois. We will have a nice dinner together in the villa. They are two charming young men. Their first is a founder . . . student of the Perigueux training college. The second returned from England where he had lived for three years. He

---

45. Recollections from J. Robert Hewett and Richard Oman, Princeton Seminary alumni.

46. Recollections from Roger D. Sidener, and Abigail Rian Evans from a September 1958 lecture, Christian philosophy class, Princeton Theological Seminary.

47. RDS, note to Bartollas.

48. Emile Cailliet Curriculum Vitae, 1950, Emile Cailliet Collection, Special Collections, Princeton Theological Seminary Library.

speaks English fluently. What joy! I could learn to speak with him and when I see my Vera again, it will make her happy, I know if I speak English well.

There are several pages in the diary but now we will turn to the last days of his entries. On February 19 he writes:

Lieutenant Dupont came and talked for an hour with me. The bullets whirring, whirring around me without ceasing. "Be careful, Cailliet," the lieutenant said to me. "Watch carefully because the Germans (Boches) seem very active tonight." Then he left me after an affectionate "Good evening." I kept watching. It rained, it rained the whole time. And always too in my ears: Zî . . . Zî, Zî, Zî . . . Zî . . . and the whole time in my ears the song of death . . . February 20- midnight. The sergeant came by, spoke to me for a moment, [and] then left after having said to me, "Terrible time tonight! The bullets are falling nearby. Be careful! Good night."

Feb. 20 1:00 a.m. I'm very tired and cold. I am soaking wet. At my feet, my comrade sleeps heavily. I go to a slit in the wall to see if everything is calm . . . I look . . . Nothing! There is nothing in front of me except our barbed wire and the bodies of soldiers who fell in the last attack and who we couldn't pull back. I leave the crêneau (loophole in the lookout). Just at the moment that I get back, tic! A live round in my left arm. . .something hot washes over me and I hear the sound of blood falling on the ground. . .I am wounded! Blood gushes out. I am growing weaker. I call, "Vermeil . . . Help . . . !" and I fall. Someone carries me across the trenches and lays me out on the ground. I open my eyes. The lieutenant is there, "Well, my poor Cailliet!" he will not be my lieutenant. The lieutenant cut the sleeve of my coat and made a bandage. The blood kept gushing out . . . The lieutenant made me drink some brandy. They couldn't carry me at night through the narrow trenches. I had to wait till daylight, sleeping at the bottom of the trench. They left me alone! (They had to, of course) . . . and I suffer . . . I want to be strong, courageous, but in the end I had lost so much blood and I feared that I was growing even weaker . . . Fear took over and suffering. I cry out, I call, "Ve! Ve! Come, oh Ve I'm not well." . . .

(Last two pages) Feb. 25- this morning I received a letter from Ve (Vera) Dear Ve. She says the time seems so long that we have been separated again. What proof of love she has shown me again. Thank you Ve . . . I write these lines near the window where she will soon come and sit facing me. It is a beautiful spring day. The air is sweet, the birds sing deliciously. A . . . peace descends on everything and it is on this beautiful spring day that will bring me my fiancée on which I end my journal. I will soon give it to Vera and in it she will read these sincerely held secrets. That she will see the immensity of my love for her.[49]

Many write of their foxhole conversations during wars but this was not the story of Emile Cailliet. In fact, the dramatic events of serving in the French army only became known to his students through Cailliet's asides in lectures and conversations and his few sparse written accounts. His terse sentences about this experience leave much to be desired. "To say that this naturalistically inspired education proved of little help through front-line experiences as a lad of twenty in World War I would amount to quite an understatement. When your own buddy—at the time speaking to you of his mother—dies standing in front of you, a bullet in his chest, what use is the sophistry of naturalism? Was there a meaning to it all? One night a bullet got me, too. [An] American field ambulance crew saved my life and later the use of a badly shattered arm was restored. After a nine-month stay at the hospital, I was discharged and resumed graduate work."[50] He was in the American Field Hospital at Juilly from March to November 1915 and released from the French military on March 23, 1917.

An additional story about Cailliet's military experience was connected to the ceasefire practices on Christmas Eve during World War I. "The Christmas truce was a series of widespread unofficial ceasefires that took place along the Western Front around Christmas of 1914, during the First World War. Through the week leading up to Christmas, parties of German and British soldiers began to exchange seasonal greetings and songs between their trenches; on occasion, the tension was reduced to the point that individuals would walk across to talk to their opposite numbers bearing gifts. On Christmas Eve and Christmas Day, many soldiers from both sides—as well as, to a lesser degree, from French units—independently ventured into no man's land, where they mingled, exchanging

---

49. The English translation of selections of Cailliet's war diary was done by Mary Tiebout. In balance it appears as if the diary entries are close to the time of the actual experiences of Cailliet in the trenches of World War I during January and February, 1915.

50. Cailliet, "Emile Cailliet: The Book That Understands Me," 21–22.

food and souvenirs. As well as joint burial ceremonies, several meetings ended in carol-singing."[51]

A personalized account of this phenomenon is that Otto Piper,[52] a German, and Emile Cailliet, a Frenchman, knew each other and fought on opposite sides during the First World War. One of his students wrote, "Of course Otto Piper was German, as I am. And Prof. Cailliet was French. Both Piper and Cailliet were also of that generation that they could have, like my father, fought in the First World War. Well, I was told by Piper that he and Professor Cailliet not only fought on opposite sides in that for Europeans most catastrophic of wars . . . More than that: They knew each other. Perhaps you know that World War I was famous for its trench warfare (trench coats became a major new fashion item). And that trench warfare was marked by frequent and sometimes longer cease-fires. Cailliet and Piper were supposed to have known each other and exchanged cigarettes during one or more of those lulls in fighting."[53]

In terms of their friendship at Princeton Theological Seminary, according to one source, "They were mutually courteous and respectful of each other. Each admired the other morally and intellectually. But each was typically withdrawn, quiet, and not given to chit-chat. They loved talking as a twosome, whenever they managed to talk. They shared a conviction about the world's desperate need for Christ. Each had a sense of urgency in getting the Gospel to a warring, destructive world. Each chose

---

51. Dunn, *The War the Infantry Knew 1914–1919*.

52. Otto Piper (born November 29, 1891 in Lichte, Thuringia, Germany and died February 13, 1982), received his doctorate in theology from Göttingen in 1920 and taught there as a university lecturer and assistant professor. Piper succeeded Karl Barth in the chair of Systematic Theology at Münster in 1930. In 1933 he delivered a course of lectures on the State and the Church, as a result of which he was dismissed from his chair and no longer allowed to hold a post in Germany. He was eventually invited by the Quaker College of Woodbrooke, Selly Oaks, Birmingham, England, to teach there for a year and in 1934 became a guest lecturer at the University College of Swansea in Wales. From 1935 he became a special lecturer in Systematic Theology and Philosophy of Religion at the University College of North Wales in Bangor. In 1937 John Mackay invited him to Princeton Theological Seminary as guest professor of Systematic Theology. He stayed on to teach as Professor of New Testament and in 1941 was named the Helen P. Manson Professor of New Testament Literature and Exegesis, a post he held until his retirement in 1962. (Black, "Remembering Otto Piper," 310–27.)

53. RA, letter to Bartollas, July 7, 2009.

never to discuss their war experiences since they had been enemies in their youth."[54]

MARRIAGE AND FAMILY LIFE: 1915 TO PRESENT

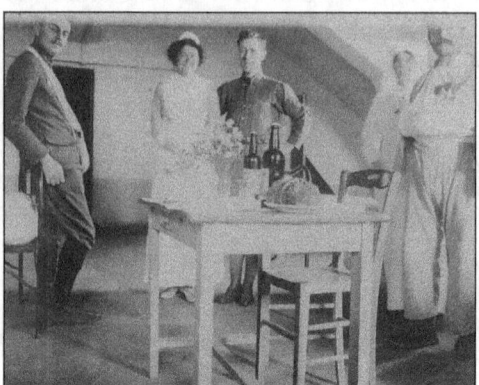

Photo of Emile Cailliet (far left) taken in 1915 after being wounded in action, near the time of his marriage to Vera Brabazon.

Cailliet's involvement with the World Wars and his family life in many ways were intertwined. After graduating in 1913 from the University of Paris, he continued studies in Danzig where he met a fellow student, seventeen-year-old Vera Ethel Brabazon[55] of Irish-Scotch extraction from Ballymore. She was a scholar in her own right, having passed exams as a junior candidate at the University of Cambridge in 1897 and the University of Oxford in 1900. Vera's father was Irish and her mother Scottish.[56] "The meeting occurred on Christmas Eve 1913. She was a well-educated young woman, staying with a German family to study German and teach English. Emile realized that a war was brewing and advised her to return to Paris for safety. He went back to Nancy and volunteered when war broke out."[57] Later she visited him in the American hospital in France. He wrote of their meeting: "During my stay at the American hospital, I had married a Scotch-Irish girl whom I had met in Germany on Christmas Eve the year before the war had broken out. She was, and always remained a deeply evangelical person. She attended both the low church of England Sunday school and the Presbyterian Sunday school.[58] I am ashamed to confess that she must have been hurt to the very core of her being as I made it clear that religion

54. Mackenzie, interview with Bartollas, spring 2010.
55. Vera Brabazon Cailliet (June 1, 1896 or 1885–March 9, 1969)
56. Cailliet, *Journey into Light*, 15.
57. Hewitt, "Story of Emile Cailliet," 819-820.
58. Cailliet, *Journey into Light*, 15.

would be taboo in our home. Little did I realize at the time that a militant attitude often betrays an inner turmoil."[59]

Emile writes of their courtship, her initial reluctance and his winning her heart and their growing and deep love for one another.[60] Cailliet and Vera married on March 25, 1915, in Paris. Vera paints a vivid account of their wedding day that was published in her school newspaper, *The Froebel Gazette* (Her school was located in Bedford, England): "I was married in March, 1915, at the little village 'Mairie of Juilly,' Seine et Marne. The bridegroom was 'Tirailleur Algérien,' wounded, and under hospital treatment, with his left arm disabled from a German bullet. Present at the little ceremony were a French lieutenant who had his cheek disfigured, another officer who had a crushed foot, a native Arab with his right hand disabled, an English hospital nurse, the village schoolmistress, and the mayor . . . It was the ordinary French civil marriage, simple and impressive. After this we went to a hotel all together, and our guests drank to our health and happiness in champagne. Though there were unfortunately no members of our families present, we felt none the less great emotion at the joining of our lives together. Finally our guests left us to enjoy our twenty-four hour leave together. The next day I returned to Paris and my husband to the American Hospital at Juilly."[61]

Both from letters exchanged between them and recollections of family, friends, and students, it is clear the Vera was the center of his life, always by his side, proud of his intellect and a true helpmate.[62] She was a typical European wife of that era, quiet, sweet, obedient and jealously caring for him and his reputation.[63] Mrs. Cailliet was a central part of his professional and personal life. In one letter to Mrs. Cailliet, a friend writes and thanks her for being welcomed into their home at the end of the war in Europe: "You have welcomed me into your family circle that has filled my heart with serenity, new courage and a sense of security that is so precious to one when life is lived at a hectic pace and home is 3000

---

59. Emile Cailliet Collection, Special Collections, Princeton Theological Seminary Library.

60. Emile Cailliet to Vera Cailliet, "Memo from Memsie to Choquie," 1961, Emile Cailliet Collection, Special Collections, Princeton Theological Seminary Library.

61. Cailliet (Vera), *Froebel Gazette*, 28.

62. Cailliet, *Journey into Light*, 11–25.

63. Assorted letters in Emile Cailliet Collection, Special Collections, Princeton Theological Seminary,

miles away." She goes on to say: "M. Cailliet is the only man outside of my father, who has by his wisdom and insight made me realize the desirable certainty of the miraculous workings of the Divine in everyday experience."[64] A former student of Emile Cailliet wrote, "Mrs. Cailliet invited the women (girls) in our class to tea in their home and that was a grand but simple occasion and I enjoyed being in their home. Dr. Cailliet was not present however. But in some ways this allowed her to be more the focus of our visit."[65]

Cailliet talked a great deal about his family to those he knew well. Another letter to him mentions how difficult and painful the illness of his wife over past years must have been and "yet there has been so much joy and tenderness between you."[66] One telegram of sympathy to Emile Cailliet on her death expressed the pain of Vera's illness, "who spent long years under the cross of disintegrating faculties." His teaching assistant and friend, Richard Oman, instructor at Princeton Seminary in the 1950s, described Cailliet's marriage as a love relationship.[67] One very touching insight into his deep love for his wife was in his words to Oman who was to preach at the Presbyterian Church in Cape May in September 1972, where the Cailliets were members. His wife had recently died and Cailliet wrote to Oman that he would be at the service and "my wife will be listening from the cemetery next door."[68]

Their Children

Emile and Vera had four children: Hélène, André, Suzanne, and Doris. Cailliet's students did not know much about his personal life, as he was reserved about this part of himself, but his close friends knew how important the children were to him. They were all academically inclined and excelled in their various professions. There are glimpses in various letters about his relationship with his children and their importance to him. An interesting letter that he wrote to Paul Bodine, Salvation Army manager

---

64. Letter from Washington DC, May 11, 1945, Emile Cailliet Collection, Special Collections, Princeton Theological Seminary Library.

65. BKH, interview with Evans and Bartollas.

66. Emile Cailliet Collection, Special Collections, Princeton Theological Seminary Library, Box 9.

67. Cailliet, *Journey into Light*, 11–25.

68. Emile Cailliet to Richard Oman, Emile Cailliet Collection, Special Collections, Princeton Theological Seminary Library.

(later Brigadier) in discussing Bodine's son, reveals his views on child rearing. "Do not force him into any pattern. Watch him. Encourage him. Never rebuke him. And above all, love him. Each time I myself became impatient with one of my children I lived to regret it . . . do not attempt either to try or have your child realize a pattern of your own for his happiness . . . He may be your child, but his life is his and God's appointed."[69]

Several of Cailliet's children followed in his academic footsteps. Daughter Hélène C. Adcock[70] taught at Peppperdine University in California and attended Scripps College, Claremont College and the University of Southern California. She received her master's degree from Claremont.[71] His second daughter Suzanne C. Gardon was born May 10, 1922. She became a nurse, graduating from the Yale School of Nursing in 1946, and served on the faculty there from 1950 until 1951.[72] She married Robert Gardon and remained involved in philanthropy. She eventually settled in Poughkeepsie, New York and later, Seattle, Washington. Cailliet's third daughter and youngest child, Doris Brunzie,[73] was also an academic. Waldo Dunn, a friend and colleague from Claremont, California, wrote about his own daughter receiving the Crombie prize for the best senior thesis at Scripps College. In the letter, he added, "I was reminded of Doris's achievement two years ago, and shall always be glad to associate the success of the two girls. We may well be happy in having such daughters."

His son, André[74] as mentioned previously, served in the French army during World War II and was captured. After he was freed he worked as a United States army translator. As one of Cailliet's friends wrote, "J'ai souvent pensé—à votre fils André—Je suppose qu'avec la fin de la guerre vous devez avoir de ses nouvelles. J'espère sincèrement qu'il se trouve en bon état." (I have often thought about your son André.

---

69. Emile Cailliet Collection, Special Collections, Princeton Theological Seminary Library, Box 9, File 214.

70. Hélène Cailliet Adcock (July 7, 1916 in France- June 14, 2001).

71. Ancestry.com, "Hélène Adcock," accessed March 2011.

72. "Yale School of Nursing: A Brief History," accessed March 12, 2011, http://info.med.yale.edu/library/nursing/historical/shorthist/NursHist.htm.

73. Doris Cailliet Brunzie (December 19, 1923–).

74. André Cailliet (June 16, 1919–June 8, 2006).

I suppose that with the end of the war you should have news of him. I sincerely hope that he is well.)[75]

André married Lois Walker in December 1959. They raised three children, Alan, Meg, and Eric,[76] and were divorced in 1962. He then married Edna Davis in March 1969. He received a bachelor's in business administration from Claremont in 1951 and pursued a career in public service which included working as a probation officer on the staff of an adoption agency. He was very active in the Whidbey Presbyterian Church in Oak Harbor, WA, where his funeral services were eventually held.[77]

Perhaps the most reliable window into Cailliet's family life is his daughter Doris's recollections: "It was our concern for André's safety that took the whole Cailliet family to a steady association with the Claremont Church, its minister and the minister's wife. When I was sent away to college, I too heard from André by letter and Dr. Haver, the College President, as a family friend, and Mrs. Haver too invited me (and my two roommates—Ellen Nell and Louise Moore) to dinner in their home. It was most consoling to be looked after in that way; don't forget André had saved me from drowning in South Laguna [the family had a summer cottage there: André and Doris were teenagers].[78] Doris continues: "My most vivid memory of Emile Cailliet, my Papa? Well, the walks we took together near 31 Alexander St., Princeton. It was a regular routine. Papa and I did our walking by the golf course, practically adjacent to our Princeton home. . . . Also my memory of Papa's work because of my typing his manuscripts, which became his books, from *Life of the Mind*, on."[79]

His family life should also include mention of his dog nicknamed by his students "yippee Cailliet."[80] The students, in fact, sent the dog a get well card when he had to go to the veterinarian and the dog wrote back a thank you letter (See chapter 3).[81]

---

75. Howard Stoven to Emile Cailliet, June 5, 1945, Emile Cailliet Collection, Special Collections, Princeton Theological Seminary Library.

76. It appears from research that at least two of these children came from a previous marriage of Lois.

77. Ancestry.com, "André Cailliet Obituary," accessed March 2011.

78. Brunzie, interview with Evans and Bartollas.

79. Brunzie, interview with Evans and Bartollas.

80. Oman, comment to Evans and Bartollas.

81. Cailliet wrote in 1955: "I have seen my seventeen-year-old dog laugh more than once in his younger days." Cailliet, *Dawn of Personality*, 35.

EDUCATION: 1913–1937

Cailliet was European, educated with the usual array of classical languages and subjects as well as in-depth training in his areas of interest. Because of his service in the military and his work in Madagascar, his formal education was extended over twenty-four years. He began his education, earning his BA at the College of Chalons at the University of Paris, France in 1913. He continued his studies in Leipzig, Germany from 1913–1914, which were interrupted by his enlisting in the French army at the outbreak of World War I. Then he resumed them at the University of Nancy for his Masters of Arts in 1923. "He returned to graduate studies, first at the University of Nancy, then at Montpelier, with the resolve of finding out whether the universe was like a tale told by an idiot, full of sound and fury, signifying nothing. He first turned to literature and made a personal selection of great texts expressing the various moods of man in his quest for truth."[82]

Next he received his doctorate in anthropology from the University of Montpellier in connection with research he had done on the island of Madagascar in 1926. Subsequently he pursued studies at the University of Strasbourg. Not only was Professor Cailliet awarded his ThD *summa cum laude* in 1937, but also by unanimous vote the faculty took the unusual step of having his thesis published in their official series "Etudes d'Histoire et de Philosophie religieuses de l'Université de Strasbourg."[83] In addition, he had a higher degree in Malagasy dialects and commendations from the President of France for research in Ethnology.[84] He received a *Licence lettres-philosophie*, a dual degree that affirmed that he was well-equipped to be conversant in the fields of anthropology, science, religion, philosophy, theology, existentialism, and education. He was a brilliant student and later scholar with a zeal for learning and appreciation for a variety of sub-disciplines.

He received numerous honors including being elected to Phi Beta Kappa and being listed in Who's Who in America, volume four of the sixth edition of the *Directory of American Scholars* 1974 and volume four

---

82. Hewitt, "Story of Emile Cailliet," 819–20.

83. Emile Cailliet Curriculum Vitae, 1938, Emile Cailliet Collection, Special Collections, Princeton Theological Seminary Library.

84. Emile Cailliet Curriculum Vitae, Emile Cailliet Collection, Special Collections, Princeton Theological Seminary Library.

of *Men of Achievement* 1977 edition. He was a member of the American Philosophical Association and a national fellow in the French Academy of Sciences. His most prestigious award may have been the medal he received from the French Government for "distinguished service in the field of letters." (See section on the Madagascar years)

Since Cailliet taught in a theological seminary for twelve years, it is interesting that he never attended a theological seminary per se, but did study theology and religion at the University of Strasbourg. Based on his teaching, speaking and writing, this fact was never apparent as he moved with ease in the world of theology.

His education did not end with his formal studies but was a lifelong pursuit. There is no doubt that his own education influenced the way he taught and related to his students. He assumed a foundational knowledge for entering Princeton seminarians that he quickly learned was not there. As well, his high expectations of his students reflected the rigor in his own studies so he constantly challenged them to do their best.

THE MADAGASCAR YEARS: 1923-1926

Emile Cailliet's approach to education was more than simply academic; field-based research was key, as seen by his approach to studying symbolism and magic. In 1923, he moved with his family to Madagascar. Three years later, his wife and children had to return to France on the "*Explorateur Grandidier*" because of daughter Hélène's typhoid; they lived in Berck-Plage, near Calais.[85] It appears that Cailliet went to work as an official representative of the French Governor General[86] with the London Missionary Society as the director of the Schools of Ambatonakanga and Kilasamandry of Amparibe, which were in Antananarivo. These schools were founded by James Cameron of the London Missionary Society.[87] Cailliet left the school after several years to return to his family in France before taking up his post at the University of Pennsylvania. An extract

85. Emile Cailliet to Vera Cailliet, "Memo from Memsie to Choquie," 1961, Emile Cailliet Collection, Special Collections, Princeton Theological Seminary Library.

86. Letter from Provost Josiah H. Penniman (University of Pennsylvania), 1928, Emile Cailliet Collection, Special Collections, Princeton Theological Seminary Library, Box 8, File 159.

87. "James Cameron," *Dictionary of African Christian Biography*, accessed March 10, 2011, http://www.dacb.org/stories/madagascar/cameron-james.html.

from a report of the London Missionary Society indicates that "The unexpected resignation of M. Cailliet was a serious blow to the Boys' High School and the general work of education. During his short term of less than four years' service he did excellent work, and proved himself to be a first class educationist."[88]

While in Tamnariva (now Antananarivo), he worked on his first doctoral thesis, "Essai sur la Psycholigie du Nova" for a PhD from the University of Montpellier and under the auspices of the School of Ethnology of Paris (1923–1926).[89] Cailliet's life as an anthropologist and his work in symbolism, religion, and magic seems a far cry from his theological works but in some ways, they were related. He was inspired by the theories of Lévy-Bruhl of Sorbonne University on the so-called "primitive" or "mystic" mentality he researched in Africa. During a three and one-half year inquiry into primitive thought and symbolist expression, he learned dialects of the Malagasy language in order to share first-hand documentation in his field work. His work in Madagascar represented one of his greatest scholarly achievements. Dr. Cailliet also worked out the religious implication of his research. Later in his academic career, he submitted to the theology faculty of the University of Strasbourg a thesis entitled *Mysticisme et Mentalité Mystique*.

THE AMERICAN YEARS

University of Pennsylvania 1926–1931; 1941–1945

Since this book is not strictly a biography, the reader can tell by now that we have chosen a number of vignettes to highlight the life of Cailliet, the man. However, for us, the primary focus is on his years in the United States. Cailliet became an American citizen in 1937 and taught in a number of different academic institutions throughout the country.

Cailliet's academic career in the United States involved many changes. He began teaching at the University of Pennsylvania as his brother Lucien recommended him to J. P. W. Crawford at the University. He made very little money but by living frugally was able to send money to his

---

88. Notes from the London Missionary Society.

89. Emile Cailliet Curriculum Vitae, 1952, Emile Cailliet Collection, Special Collections, Princeton Theological Seminary Library, Box 8, File 152.

family in France.⁹⁰ The provost Josiah H. Penniman, of the University of Pennsylvania, wrote a letter to the immigration services which stated that under the immigration Act of 1924 section 4(d), Cailliet, as a professor, should be admitted to the United States as a non-quota immigrant. He then requested any assistance they could provide to facilitate the entrance of Cailliet, his wife and children to the U.S. Cailliet served on the faculty of the University of Pennsylvania as an instructor from 1927–1928 and then was promoted to Assistant Professor of French Literature for a three-year term from 1928–1931.⁹¹ He returned to the Graduate School of Arts and Sciences at the University of Pennsylvania from 1941–1945 as a professor and permanent chair of the French Literature and Civilization department. While there he had numerous meetings in the greater Philadelphia area. He later traveled to Chicago, Portland and Claremont, California to give various lectures and also to Princeton Theological Seminary to teach at the Institute of Theology.

Scripps College 1931–1941

Vera and Emile Cailliet and dog, crossing the Atlantic en route to the United States on the *Ile de France*, 1930.

In 1931, Cailliet left the University of Pennsylvania and was appointed as a full professor and chairman of the Department of Modern Languages and Literatures and Coordinator of the Junior Humanities Program at Scripps College as well as professor of French Literature and Civilization at the Claremont Graduate School in California. At last his family could join him in the United States, as Scripps paid for their first class fare on a French ship.⁹² He spent ten years there (1931–1941)

---

90. Emile Cailliet to Vera Cailliet, "Memo from Memsie to Choquie," 1961, Emile Cailliet Collection, Special Collections, Princeton Theological Seminary Library.

91. Letter from Provost Josiah H. Penniman (University of Pennsylvania), 1928, Emile Cailliet Collection, Special Collections, Princeton Theological Seminary Library, Box 8, File 159.

92. Emile Cailliet to Vera Cailliet, "Memo from Memsie to Choquie," 1961, Emile

and was obviously loved by the faculty and students. This was reflected by an op-ed piece in the school magazine *The Scripture* of December 8, 1938, with a wonderful cartoon rendition of him. The accompanying article from a student perspective mentioned his superb teaching and concluded, "Indeed it is because of his sincerity and his open-minded and wholehearted attitude toward life that we all love him and call him 'papa.'"

In subsequent years he continued to receive letters about his being missed and how wonderful he had been as a teacher.[93] He did return to lecture several times at the invitation of the Scripps president and there is a very warm correspondence between him and Cailliet in 1945 about his upcoming lecture.[94]

Emile Cailliet attending a dinner at Scripps College (1931–1941), Claremont, CA.

Did he leave because of some precarious economic crisis at the college or did he simply want to return to the University of Pennsylvania? This is hard to determine from the material available. We do know that a letter from Waldo Dunn written May 23, 1943, speaks of the loss of students and instructors and the conditions of the Department of English so perhaps these events contributed to Cailliet's decision.[95]

Wesleyan University 1945–1947

From Scripps, Cailliet returned to the University of Pennsylvania, as mentioned earlier, and then went to Wesleyan University in Middletown, Connecticut as professor of French Literature and Philosophy. The reason for this move, that Cailliet desired to teach within a Christian-related institution, is revealed in a letter: "I do want to send you, however,

Cailliet Collection, Special Collections, Princeton Theological Seminary Library.

93. Emile Cailliet Collection, Special Collections, Princeton Theological Seminary Library, Box 2.

94. Emile Cailliet Collection, Special Collections, Princeton Theological Seminary Library, Box 8, File 144.

95. Emile Cailliet Collection, Special Collections, Princeton Theological Seminary Library.

this brief word in order to give you my cordial congratulations. Your departure from Philadelphia will be a great loss for the University of Pennsylvania where I know that you have brilliantly succeeded. But I do understand, as you said in your letter, that you have preferred a milieu in which you feel in complete sympathy with regard to the great spiritual values and where you will be able in your work to engage in depth not just intellectually but also in your soul (spirit). It is a noble conception of our task as educators in which I am in brotherly sympathy with you."[96] Cailliet was highly regarded at Wesleyan and in 1946 was given an honorary MA degree by the college.

The Princeton Theological Seminary Years

Cailliet's final post was as the Stuart Professor of Christian Philosophy at Princeton Theological Seminary from 1947–1959. In a letter to President Victor L. Butterfield of Wesleyan University, he indicates his six month struggle over whether to leave Wesleyan and accept the Princeton Seminary position. Butterfield wrote a number of letters imploring him to stay because of his unique and important contribution and what a deep vacuum his leaving would create. Of course, he indicated that he would respect wherever Cailliet felt called.[97] Cailliet's decision was obviously influenced by the seminary's re-naming the chair to Christian philosophy as well as changing the rules so that laymen could become part of the faculty.[98] In addition, he and the president, Mackay, were good friends. It was clear that Cailliet was motivated by a strong sense of destiny to bring the insights of philosophy to a theological institution and its students.

This position came by a direct invitation from John Mackay, who served as president of Princeton Theological Seminary from 1936–1959. Cailliet describes the invitation in a letter to James McCord (Princeton Theological Seminary president 1959–1983), that he and Mackay had discussed the invitation to the Stuart chair on December 31, 1946 at the

---

96. Bannu (Department of Religion at University of California at Berkeley) to Emile Cailliet, June 30, 1945, Emile Cailliet Collection, Special Collections, Princeton Theological Seminary Library. Translated by Louise Winfield from the original French.

97. Emile Cailliet Collection, Special Collections, Princeton Theological Seminary Library, Box 2, File 43.

98. Emile Cailliet to Victor Butterfield, May 29, 1947, Emile Cailliet Collection, Special Collections, Princeton Theological Seminary Library, Box 9.

Savarin Restaurant at Penn Station in New York City.[99] It is important to note that prior to coming to Princeton Theological Seminary, Cailliet and Mackay had carried a cordial correspondence beginning in 1942 and that Cailliet had already spoken at the Institute of Theology, the seminary convocation and other venues, and was serving on the editorial board of *Theology Today*, the Princeton Seminary Journal. It was obvious from this correspondence that they were kindred spirits and shared the same theological vision.[100] It took a special action by the Princeton Theological Seminary Board of Trustees to issue an invitation to Cailliet. The resolution is included in the formal letter from John Mackay: "Resolved: That in the judgment of the Board of Trustees of the Theological Seminary of the Presbyterian Church at Princeton it is desirable to amend Article IV, Section 2 of the Plan of the Seminary to read as follows:

> Second 2.
> No person shall be inducted into the office of President other than an ordained minister of the Presbyterian Church in the U.S.A. And no person shall be inducted as Professor who is not a member of the Presbyterian Church in the U.S.A.
> Further Resolved that the Secretary of the Board of Trustees be and he is hereby authorized and directed to present a request for such amendment to the General Assembly, and to make such arrangements as may be necessary to secure the adoption thereof by the Assembly.
> Both actions were taken unanimously and with enthusiasm."[101]

President Mackay's letter continues: "Since we were together two things of great importance have happened. First: The University has expressed very real interest in having you give a course each semester, in the event that you came to the Seminary. I have discussed the matter with Professor George Thomas, the head of the Department of Religion, and with Dr. Robert Scoon, the head of the Department of Philosophy, and, also, with the President of the University." His letter continues: "Second: The Curriculum Committee recommends that the President of the Seminary

---

99. Emile Cailliet to James McCord, October 16, 1959, Emile Cailliet Collection, Special Collections, Princeton Theological Seminary Library.

100. Emile Cailliet Collection, Special Collections, Princeton Theological Seminary Library, Box 3, File 56.

101. John Mackay to Emile Cailliet, February 12, 1947, Emile Cailliet Collection, Special Collections, Princeton Theological Seminary Library.

be authorized to confer with Dr. Emile Cailliet to see whether he will accept appointment to a Chair of Christian Philosophy, if the Plan is amended to permit others than ministers to become professors; and to invite him to serve in such a Chair as Guest Professor for the year beginning September, 1947, at a salary of $6,000.00 a year, a residence, and participation in the pension plan."[102]

Mackay goes on to say, "It would have done your heart good to see how deep and real was the desire of all the members, very especially of those who know you personally and have read your books, that you should become a member of our Faculty . . . This morning in a further conversation with Dr. Scoon he authorized me to assure you that in view of his interest and my conversation with the President of the University, some arrangement would, in due course, be worked out whereby you could serve the University as well as the Seminary."[103]

In referring to his post at Princeton Theological Seminary, Cailliet had this to say: "As you may know, I am not an ordained man. The reason I was called to the Princeton Seminary campus was essentially that they seemed to need some insights into the secular world as observed from the wider college and university campuses in our day. I have spent most of my career on such secular campuses, especially at the University of Pennsylvania."[104] Cailliet's daughter is clear as to how he felt about the opporunity to teach in a seminary. "Dr. Cailliet decided to teach at a theological seminary because although a Frenchman and well-educated, he was qualified to teach French at first, he really had been yearning to reach out to young people and lead them toward service to their fellow human beings . . . Perhaps he might have had some qualms at the thought of his being a layman, a follower of the leadership of others, at first. But that didn't last. After all, Dr. Mackay himself was recommending him for the task! For several years by then, Cailliet had taken part in summer seminar which assembled church leaders and led them to greater service in reach-

---

102. John Mackay to Emile Cailliet, February 12, 1947, Emile Cailliet Collection, Special Collections, Princeton Theological Seminary Library.

103. John Mackay to Emile Cailliet, February 12, 1947, Emile Cailliet Collection, Special Collections, Princeton Theological Seminary Library.

104. Emile Cailliet to Rudolph Herden (Editor-in-chief, Lutheran Church, Missouri Synod, in Chicago), Emile Cailliet Collection, Special Collections, Princeton Theological Seminary Library.

ing out to lay people, asking them to serve just where they were! That is, to accept what might have been limitations and then to reach out."[105]

Cailliet himself came from a place of deep faith and wished to help shape the future Christian Church leaders. "My call in life is to try to bridge the gap that is still yawning between the Church and the lay-world which is her mission field. It was in this connection that the Bobbs-Merrill Field Company recently published *The Dawn of Personality* which was meant as a means of penetration into that difficult field represented by college-educated people. I wrote it under a great sense of commitment, and I hope that you can use it in your Commission on College and University work."[106]

Cailliet did a good deal of speaking and preaching during his years at Princeton Seminary including engagements at Dwight Chapel at Yale University, Trinity Episcopal Church in Princeton, commencement addresses at many colleges and schools including Biblical Seminary, New York City, Pikeville College, Kentucky, Wilson College, Chambersburg, Pennsylvania, "and The Stony Brook School, Long Island, NY. He also preached at numerous churches in the greater Princeton and Philadelphia areas. His sermons were Christ-centered, erudite and either devotional or scholarly in style.[107]

It would be true to say that in some ways his Princeton years were a mixed experience. He experienced some slights by the seminary and chose never to return once he retired in 1959. It is clear that Cailliet came with high hopes for what he surely regarded as his last post but was disappointed in the direction of the seminary, embracing a Barthian anti-philosophy stance. According to one of his teaching assistants, he came to Princeton Theological Seminary to revive knowledge of Augustinian theology, which for him stemmed from his research into Pascal. He believed that Calvin and Augustine were essential in saving a warring world. He was disappointed that instead of a conservative, Calvinistic direction with

---

105. Brunzie, interview with Evans and Bartollas.

106. Emile Cailliet to Rudolph Herden (Editor-in-chief, Lutheran Church, Missouri Synod, in Chicago), Emile Cailliet Collection, Special Collections, Princeton Theological Seminary Library.

107. Emile Cailliet Collection, Special Collections, Princeton Theological Seminary Library, Box 5, File 85. His speech at Biblical Seminary was published in Edwin H. Rian (Editor) *Christianity and World Revolution*: Harper and Row: New York, 1963.

the appointment of Paul Lehman, the seminary seemed to be moving in a different direction.[108]

However, he threw himself totally into the life of the seminary and was one of the charter members of the Princeton Theological Seminary journal, *Theology Today*. In a tribute by Frank Gaebelein, the Journal editor has this to say of Cailliet: "We publish this tribute by a personal friend in recognition of a scholar of versatile talent and restless spirit. Ever moving beyond, toward new vistas of truth. His own Christian commitment gave his life an unusual quality of grace and composure."[109]

Cailliet had a major impact on the students at Princeton Seminary. Even after more than fifty years, many students testify to his profound influence on their lives both in terms of their Christian faith and later vocations. As the reader will find in this book's chapter "The Teacher," some of his students found him to be unapproachable, while others were charmed by his French accent and viewed him as kind and caring. Despite disparate perspectives on his personality, he was chiefly viewed as an insightful believer and scholar. In describing his relationship to his students, most of them would not describe it as a friendship, but rather a mentoring relationship.

There are a number of letters from former students asking Cailliet a variety of questions. One such letter asked whether retarded children are created equal, a question asked to the pastor by one of his parishioners.[110] (We do not have Cailliet's response but we can certainly summarize from what we know of Cailliet that he believed in the equality of all people.) Cailliet took time with young scholars as both a friend and a mentor. In the chapter, "The Teacher," we cite many letters from two decades of seminary students attesting to how his teaching influenced them.[111] In addition, he had an impact as a person. One student thanked him for a brief mediation that he gave: "Dr. C. I am so glad for our school that you have joined us this year. Your contribution is not only academic but personal—because of your faith. I look forward to your course in Pascal."[112]

---

108. Mackenzie, interview with Bartollas, spring 2010.

109. Gaebelein, "Friendship an Election of God," 57.

110. Hank Vigevano, (Absecon Presbyterian Church, Absecon, NJ), January 19, 1953, Emile Cailliet Collection, Special Collections, Princeton Theological Seminary Library.

111. Letter from Julian Alexander, May 25, 1951, Emile Cailliet Collection, Special Collections, Princeton Theological Seminary Library, Box 1.

112. Letter from Betty Bonneville, November 19, 1947, Emile Cailliet Collection,

One of his students, author Abigail Rian Evans, kept her exam paper from Cailliet's 1958 philosophy course. The graded paper had personal remarks from him as to the high quality of the paper which was a real encouragement as she was one of five women students in the entire seminary and many challenged her right to be studying for ordained ministry. In addition, as missionaries in Brazil, she and Robert Evans received a kind letter from Cailliet in January, 1960, with many loving words, concluding, "It has been a blessing to get to know you and love you. Write us a line whenever you find time. We'll always be happy to follow you in thought and prayer."[113]

There were also non-Princeton Theological Seminary students who felt his influence. One such student at Bryn Mawr from 1946–1950 was writing a thesis on Pascal and asked Cailliet for any assistance he might give her in her research. He took an active role in helping and wrote a wonderful letter in 1949 giving substantive assistance on her Pascal research.[114] Her father, Frank Gaebelein,[115] thanked Cailliet, "Thank you for your great kindness, to Gretchen . . . The fact that a man of your achievement would take time so promptly to write her and to send such full information has meant much to her."[116] One of his TAs, also a student, writes: "We met each Monday morning to discuss his latest book on Christian culture. I did much of the research on it. I still see him sitting behind his desk, looking at me, counseling me, sharing his views on culture. I have taught courses on 'the clash of Cultures' and have found that his material was of timeless value."[117]

Special Collections, Princeton Theological Seminary Library, Box 1.

113. Emile Cailliet to Abigail and Robert Evans, personal correspondence, January 3, 1960.

114. Gretchen Gaebelein Hull, interview with Evans, March 26, 2010.

115. Frank Gaebelein recounts his own debt to Cailliet in opening up the depth of Pascal's Pensées (See Gaebelein, "Friendship an Election of God—A Brief Memoir of Emile Cailliet," 57.)

116. Frank Gaebelein to Emile Cailliet, March 11, 1949, Emile Cailliet Collection, Special Collections, Princeton Theological Seminary Library.

117. Mackenzie, interview with Bartollas, spring 2010.

HIS FRIENDSHIPS

Conventional wisdom suggests that you can always know a person by his or her friends. Cailliet's friendships were wide-ranging, both in the United States and abroad. His correspondence, most of it handwritten in French and English, includes a diverse group of individuals, though a majority were academic and Christian leaders. His letters also reveal his deep ties to his native France.

Cailliet wrote to and received letters from businessmen, playwrights and government officials. One of the challenges in relying on his correspondence is that the bulk of it consists of letters received by Cailliet rather than those written by him. Among these letters is one from J. Edgar Hoover, director of the FBI, to Cailliet in November 1960 thanking him for his article, "The Ultimate Reference of American History."[118] Although Cailliet was a true scholar and immersed in the academic world, he also was concerned about other events and people outside of his sphere. His correspondence reveals the range of his interests and of people who sought his advice, such as a letter dated March 1958 from a man who was confined for two years in a psychiatric institute and believed that his mental illness was connected with sin.

In an interesting letter to the Ford Motor Company, Cailliet made a suggestion about their cars. In response, he received a letter with the following words: "Thanks to Emile Cailliet for the constructive criticism of our current models. It is letters such as yours that enable us to improve our products and will be relayed to our Products Department for future planning."[119]

An unexpected interest of Cailliet's was in modern plays. He wrote reviews of Broadway plays for *Eternity Magazine* including one for Archibald McLeish's "JB," for which Caillet received two tickets for the January 17, 1959 production, and a review of Eugene O'Neill's "Long Day's Journey into Night." This review, entitled "Darkness over Broadway," begins, "Now I know what Hell is like. I have just been there for three hours and forty-five minutes, which is the length of the performance of Eugene

---

118. Upon further research it is likely that Cailliet wrote to Hoover because Hoover had received recognition from Young Life for his contributions to American Society and of course, Cailliet was very involved in Young Life, which is a worldwide, non-profit, parachurch ministry primarily aimed at youth.

119. Ford Motor Company, Office of Seasonal Sales, April 1958, Emile Cailliet Collection, Special Collections, Princeton Theological Seminary Library.

O'Neill's posthumous drama 'Long Day's Journey into Night.'" Cailliet felt as if he were entering Dante's inferno. The play enjoyed much popularity and was marked by a strong strain of fatalism where the characters grind inevitably toward their tragic destiny, bereft of any belief in God. Cailliet worried about its appeal to a nation intent on abandoning God. He concludes with these words: "'Long Day's Journey into Night' should have taught us by now that the surest way to Hell is that refusal to believe in Hell." In response to this he received the following letter: "I am profoundly thankful for your article, 'Darkness over Broadway,' and for the point of view from which it was written. I appreciated the theological, biblical perspective into which your analysis of Eugene O'Neill's 'Long Day's Journey into Night' was cast. Across distance and denominational lines, we appear to speak the same language."[120]

Much can be gleaned about Cailliet from his correspondence through the years. One interesting letter to Harry E. Fosdick, pastor of Riverside Church, New York City from 1926–1946,[121] reveals his generosity of spirit. While the letter is mostly about theological figures such as Oscar Cullman, Cailliet asks for Fosdick's forgiveness: "The first aim of this letter is to apologize to you for having opposed your views both in some of my writings and from the lecture platform in the days when I kept close to the Biblicism of Pascal. I did so in good faith while at all times paying high tribute to your well-known intellectual honesty. I now know I was wrong in my criticism and only feel sorry that I have delayed so long acknowledging it to you personally." He goes on to encourage Fosdick to have Harper and Brothers reissue *The Man of Nazareth* which gives a needed understanding of the real Jesus.

There are a number of other letters which reflect the breadth of his interests and munificence. In March, 1961, Cailliet wrote a tribute to Donald Barnhouse, pastor of Tenth Presbyterian Church in downtown Philadelphia, describing Barnhouse as a true Christian gentleman through whom the love of Christ flowed. Cailliet had many invitations to speak or write letters of reference. In 1960, Stuart Merriam asked Cailliet for a letter of reference to Broadway Church in New York City, where he was applying to be the pastor.[122] Walter Lowrie, noted theologian and

---

120. Cailliet, "Darkness Over Broadway," 12.

121. Emile Cailliet to Henry E. Fosdick, October 16, 1956, Emile Cailliet Collection, Special Collections, Princeton Theological Seminary Library.

122. An interesting side note—Abigail Evans served as associate pastor at that church

interpreter of the Danish philosopher Søren Kierkegaard, asked Cailliet in a letter on April 1, 1949 to represent Princeton Theological Seminary at a special ceremony where the Danish ambassador was to appoint Lowrie as the first Honorary Member of the Kierkegaard Society of Denmark.[123]

In terms of his Princeton years, one is, of course, interested in knowing how Emile Cailliet regarded his Princeton Theological Seminary colleagues. According to Richard Oman, he viewed them "with respect and collegiality."[124] His daughter, writes, "Dr. Cailliet was *impressed*! He had a high regard for his faculty colleagues at Princeton."[125] Some thought he did not have many close friends at Princeton but that he did keep in touch with friends from the University of Pennsylvania.[126] Most of his correspondence with his colleagues seemed mainly to focus on seminary business.

Many faculty members valued his opinions, as Lefferts Loetscher wrote, "Fellowship with you in the work of the seminary is a great pleasure. Your contributions to faculty discussions are always thought provoking and in fine spirit."[127] Elmer Homrighausen, dean and professor of Christian Education at Princeton Seminary wrote requesting him to speak at a student retreat on "Being a Christian Leader Today" and closes with these words: "I cannot tell you how good it is to have you in Princeton. I know you must be happy here. Already several students have remarked to me how much they appreciate what you teach and what you are. God bless you!"[128] It is clear that Cailliet was welcomed with open arms by the faculty.

Cailliet showed concern for faculty on a personal level as Hugh Kerr wrote in a letter how much Cailliet consoled him on the illness of his father.[129] Cailliet also gave an old oil painting of Calvin to Edward Dowey

in the 1970s.

123. There is no record as to whether he attended.
124. Oman, interview with Evans, 2010.
125. Brunzie, interview with Evans and Bartollas.
126. Mackenzie and Stine, separate interviews with Bartollas and Evans, spring 2010.
127. Lefferts A. Loetscher to Emile Cailliet, May 28, 1955, Emile Cailliet Collection, Special Collections, Princeton Theological Seminary Library.
128. Elmer Homrighausen to Emile Cailliet, October 3, 1947, Emile Cailliet Collection, Special Collections, Princeton Theological Seminary Library, Box 1.
129. Letter from Hugh Kerr, March 1950, Emile Cailliet Collection, Special Collections, Princeton Theological Seminary Library, Box 1.

in January 1959; this is certainly the act of a friend. In a letter to John Hick in Ithaca, NY, April 15, 1959, he wrote, "The sense of congeniality was immediate on our part. There was also in my case a feeling of alleviation reminiscent of that experienced on the front line during the War when a relieving unit appeared on the scene.... [I] read one of your books and found it admirable."[130] (This letter was written in January 1961 on occasion of Cailliet's retirement with Hick succeeding him; Hick was sorry that Cailliet was not invited to his inaugural.)

Cailliet threw himself with great enthusiasm into Seminary life. He was active in the Faculty Club which had its first meeting on November 2, 1948, where they discussed over dinner "Confronting a Revived Fundamentalism," especially in relation to the questions of the verbal inerrancy of the Bible.[131]

However, Cailliet was a man of strong opinions so there were sometimes lively exchanges with faculty colleagues and administration on curricular matters. For example, Howard Kuist, then professor of Old Testament, reported that Cailliet said to Mackay, "The Fall meeting was not a retreat—because we did not meet God." One reported incident was that Kuist's class ran late and Cailliet marched in the room to indicate the room was his now.[132] There is no doubt that much like the students, his faculty colleagues found him a formidable person. One story illustrates this assessment regarding McCord's invitation to give the Princeton Theological Seminary Stone Lectures in the Spring of 1958. The custom was that at each lecture, the speaker was introduced by a different faculty member. Cailliet, when introducing McCord, said he had jitters about introducing the new president and McCord said the jitters were all his.[133]

It is clear that Cailliet did have some close friends at Princeton including Richard (Dick) Oman, Seminary instructor and Cailliet's teaching assistant. That Cailliet regarded him as a son is clearly seen by their correspondence through the years. Oman first met Cailliet in September 1950 when he was Cailliet's student in a Princeton Seminary course on Christian Philosophy. This encounter began a friendship/mentor rela-

---

130. Emile Cailliet to John Hick and John Hick to Emile Cailliet, January 1961, Emile Cailliet Collection, Special Collections, Princeton Theological Seminary Library.

131. Emile Cailliet Collection, Special Collections, Princeton Theological Seminary Library, Box 1, File 26.

132. DS, interview with Evans.

133. DS, interview with Evans.

tionship which lasted until Cailliet died in 1981. Their friendship began in the classroom but led to meals in Cailliets home, walking together discussing philosophy, and finally, visits to Cailliet's retirement home in Cape May. They also continued a correspondence on many subjects through the years and Cailliet attended his wedding on July 25, 1959, in Pennsylvania.

Many people wonder if Cailliet and Einstein (1879–1955) were friends because their time in Princeton overlapped. Einstein was in Princeton from 1933–1955 and died in the Princeton Medical Center. "The two families were neighbors. Dr. Cailliet often referred to Dr. Einstein in his books. As to how often they met, I cannot say."[134] However, one student recounts their walking together. "I remember his distinctive walk: head up, hands clasped behind his back, and how this contrasted with Dr. Albert Einstein: head down, when they strolled the campus together."[135] As well, Cailliet recounted the story about Princeton seminarians Christmas caroling on the porch of Einstein's house. President John Mackay called to apologize to Einstein since he was Jewish. Einstein replied it was a wonderful occasion and he joined them by playing the violin on the porch of his house. Another person said that Cailliet knew Einstein and in fact he was invited to join them in one of their meetings, but he thinks they only met a few times. In the vast correspondence with other friends and colleagues there are no letters exchanged between them; of course that is not to say they do not exist simply because they were not in the Princeton Theological Seminary archives. "He knew Einstein both by reputation and some personal contact. Einstein was just down the street from us, retired there I believe. No, they scarcely met. Sorry!"[136]

Of course, since Einstein and many of the Princeton Theological Seminary faculty were literally living in each other's backyards, there was a natural interchange among them. Professor of Homiletics Andrew Blackwood's, son James did shopping for Einstein; he especially brought him his favorite tennis shoes and drove him to various places. History professor Norman Hope and Einstein were seen walking down the street together and Dean Elmer Homrighausen's children talked to Einstein.[137]

---

134. Oman, interview with Evans.
135. SAH, email to Bartollas, June 17, 2009.
136. Brunzie, letter to Evans and Bartollas.
137. Eileen Moffett, interview with Evans.

These were common events but reflected the natural interchange between Einstein and seminary faculty.

It is clear that one of Cailliet's greatest friendships may have been with Frank Gaebelein, founder in 1922, and headmaster of the Stony Brook School in New York.[138] They had fought in World War I, loved and played music together, climbed mountains,[139] enjoyed fishing,[140] and shared an erudition that evangelical scholars brought to their Christian faith during these decades. Cailliet made numerous trips to speak at the Stony Brook School. Gaebelein said of his preaching there, "His sermons were listened to by both boys and faculty with rapt attention."[141]

These two friends, Cailliet and Gaebelein, exchanged numerous letters through the years on matters of faith, theology, and mutual projects such as the founding of the Evangelical Theological Society. In two letters, Gaebelein thanks Cailliet for suggesting names for a small group of evangelicals to be invited to discuss faith and culture.[142] In a subsequent letter Gaebelein referred to the importance of working out the wording of

---

138. Frank E. Gaebelein (March 31, 1899–January 20, 1983), Headmaster, Emeritus, of the Stony Brook School, former co-editor of *Christianity Today*, and General Editor of *The Expositor's Bible Commentary*.

139. Cailliet did not write directly about his mountain climbing expertise, although it is reflected in some of his writings on other subjects. In a piece he wrote about his journey through the Cévennes Mountains in the summer of 1923 with his sick son André ("I Met the Huguenots," Emile Cailliet Collection, Special Collections, Princeton Theological Seminary Library), he refers to a Huguenot village and describes hiking to reach a doctor in a distant village that "could only be reached through goats' trails across the mountain." In a Lenten address titled "This I Believe" (see Appendix) given on March 12, 1940, Cailliet concludes with these words: "My life may be likened unto one of my hiking days, when I start slowly climbing up through the fog. I know that the sun shines up there somewhere, but a companion who had never seen it would find this hard to believe. And yet, here and there, patches of white now growing dimmer and smaller, [and] then brighter and larger, to me are unmistakable signs that sooner or later we shall emerge in a glory of luminous blue."

140. Loose notes on Cailliet's life, Emile Cailliet Collection, Special Collections, Princeton Theological Seminary Library. Box 9, File 194.

141. Gaebelein, "Friendship an Election of God—A Brief Memoir of Emile Cailliet," 57.

142. Frank Gaebelein to Emile Cailliet, December 1948 and January 1949, Emile Cailliet Collection, Special Collections, Princeton Theological Seminary Library.

a document to launch the Evangelical Theological Society;[143] Cailliet did join that society in 1950.[144]

Cailliet, according to Gaebelein called friendship an election of God.[145] They obviously visited each others' homes. "It was, I assure you, a privilege for Mrs. G. and me to entertain you in our home. To meet a true scholar who combines with his learning the deep devotion to Christ which characterizes you is a refreshing experience and is in these days all too rare." He goes on to write that the difference in the liberal and evangelical perspective on truth is answered by Pascal in *Pensées*.[146] His informal memoir of Cailliet for *Theology Today* must have been nearly the last thing Gaebelein wrote and something he looked forward to seeing published.[147] Of Emile Cailliet and Frank Gaebelein we may apply the words relating to Saul and Jonathan that they were "lovely and pleasant in their lives, and in their death they were not divided (11 Sam. 1:23)."[148]

Cailliet also corresponded with a number of clergy who sought his advice on many different subjects. Of particular interest was his concern about racism in America during the 1950s. Princeton Theological Seminary's faculty and students took a strong stance opposing racism. Professor Dowey marched in Selma and a 1953 MDiv seminary graduate, James Reeb, was martyred in Selma when he responded to Dr. Martin Luther King, Jr.'s urgent call to clergy to join him there in March of 1965. The Blizzard chair in Church and Society was established during the 1950s, a clear indication of societal concerns.[149] Dick Oman wrote to Cailliet about a race problem when he was a pastor in Oxford, PA. Cailliet exchanged many letters in the 1950s with pastors about this subject. One such letter to Cailliet begins: "I seek your ear, your mind, and your heart, and from that perhaps the will of God." The letter, from Richard Taylor,

---

143. Frank Gaebelein to Emile Cailliet, April 1949, Emile Cailliet Collection, Special Collections, Princeton Theological Seminary Library.

144. Emile Cailliet Collection, Special Collections, Princeton Theological Seminary Library. Box 2, File 29.

145. Gaebelein, "Friendship an Election of God—A Brief Memoir of Emile Cailliet," 57.

146. Frank Gaebelein to Emile Cailliet, February 13, 1948, Emile Cailliet Collection, Special Collections, Princeton Theological Seminary Library.

147. Gretchen Gaebelein Hull, interview with Evans, March 26, 2010.

148. Gaebelein, "Friendship an Election of God," 55.

149. See *Princeton Theological Seminary Bulletin*, 1950–1970.

goes on to discuss how the Presbyterian Church in Orange, Virginia was divided over the issue of segregation with some members attempting to prove that it is biblically based. "For several years I have spoken as strongly as I could against the sin of segregation. I have done it as scripturally, and as free of emotion, as possible. I have tried to be objective. Please don't get the idea it is all I have spoken about . . ." Taylor continues: "Now the purpose of this letter is to say that this effort is beginning to be threatened by what may be a first class split in this church . . . I am aware of the danger of letting an issue like this make a kind of cheap martyr out of oneself. Being on the side of ultimate right offers temptation to let it carry one either up the ladder of success or down to a kind of cheap and glorious defeat. Neither of which seems true to Christ, and the idea that one is embroiled in such an issue frightens me. Being sincere is not enough. Being right is the only thing that counts. The only motivation must be His love. The only reward His smile." Taylor asks if he might be better off moving north and poses to Cailliet the question, "What does Christ say? What is right?"[150] Unfortunately we do not have Cailliet's response but one can surmise that Taylor anticipated a sympathetic ear and wise counsel from him as is indicated in a follow-up letter: "This note is to thank you even in the hurried fashion for your very helpful letter. It had the kind of wisdom that gave light and certitude together. Thank you and I hope the Lord will lead me to Princeton even if only for an hour."[151] In summary, it is clear that Cailliet's sojourn in America was fulfilling in many ways and drew him into the political, societal, and theological issues of the day.

HIS PERSONALITY

Much of what we know of Emile Cailliet's personality comes across in his students' impressions and correspondence and a few words from friends and family. As with any forceful personality, people had very different views of Emile Cailliet. This was correlated to some degree with how well they knew him. His critics described him as arrogant and rigorous,

---

150. Letter from Richard F. Taylor (minister, Orange Presbyterian Church, Orange, VA), January 15, 1957, Emile Cailliet Collection, Special Collections, Princeton Theological Seminary Library.

151. Richard F. Taylor (minister, Orange Presbyterian Church, Orange, VA), January 29, 1957, Emile Cailliet Collection, Special Collections, Princeton Theological Seminary Library.

whereas others found him to be thoughtful and helpful to his students. All agree that he had a razor-sharp intellect with a thirst for the truth. He had a photographic memory, rarely used notes, and quoted large portions of books, as reflected especially in his lectures.[152] He was very well-organized and always finished his lecture precisely as the bell was ringing to end the hour.[153] One student wrote, "He was a very good teacher who had high expectations and a love for his subject. His appearance was rather severe and a bit intimidating in his seriousness. His beautiful accent was enhanced with his enthusiasm. Dr. Cailliet was a lover of great literature and connected it with the Christian Faith in a meaningful way and I have carried that love with me too."[154]

Some colleagues and students at the Seminary described him as "aloof, shy, old world French" and as a man who always sought to be a Christian in all he did.[155] One student wrote: "He seemed, to this Southern boy, an austere, remote figure—but I did hear from those closer to him that he could be very engaging and supportive as a good friend."[156] Oman says: "[Cailliet was] somewhat austere at first; [but] warm and open as you got know him."[157] Another student shares: "As a second career Seminary student I held all of my professors in great awe, as I was being introduced to areas of study that were entirely new to me. I had majored in economics at Princeton University. Because of his accent, demeanor, and somewhat austere countenance, Dr. Cailliet was somewhat intimidating."[158] Doris Brunzie wrote: "As his daughter, one who admired, loved, and esteemed him tremendously, I would describe his 'personality' as open, reachable, but also as a bit forbidding to those who had not gotten to really know him."[159]

Frank Gaebelein, his friend for forty years, wrote in 1983 for *Theology Today* about their first exchange of letters after Gaebelein wrote to Cailliet about the impact of his book, *Pascal-Genius in the Light of Scripture*. Cailliet's response began, "It is essential that those who are the Lord's

---

152. Oman, interview with Evans.
153. JA, interview with Evans.
154. BH, letter to Evans and Bartollas.
155. Mackenzie, interview with Bartollas, spring 2010.
156. JC, handwritten note on letter to Bartollas.
157. Oman, interview with Evans.
158. JA, email to Bartollas, August 2010.
159. Brunzie, letter to Evans and Bartollas.

should know one another so as to be better co-laborers in his service."[160] Cailliet obviously hungered for deep Christian friendships and saw those as the heart of meaningful life.

Many students experienced Cailliet's openness and Christian friendship. "Cailliet had a great position or approach and was such an enlightened prophet on scripture, politics, and the world. His approach was not narrow or exclusive. He realized the ability to craft good questions. My take of what he was saying that he represented an approach to life. It was not intellectual or abstract, but it was an earthy approach, like the Hebrew. The Christian is in the world, but he is not captured by the world."[161] Cailliet seemed to especially identify with "whom others might not hold in high regard. "My initial impression of Dr. Cailliet was very positive; I classify him as a respectable, saintly scholar. I always evaluated him as an excellent professor who treated students without any discrimination. Since I am Puerto Rican, a minority that was treated 'as trash' in the US, I was able to detect who was treating me as a human being and people who were trying to put 'my self esteem down,' including people at Princeton. . . . Dr. Cailliet treated me with justice and he graded my courses fairly. Unfortunately, I was able to take only one elective course about the French philosopher Blaise Pascal later on."[162]

Sometimes Cailliet's forceful personality, in combination with his high expectations of others, could overwhelm and put off colleagues, students and friends.

> After I was accepted into the ThD program at Princeton Seminary in 1955, I was required to take a series of prelims. One of them was in Christian Philosophy. I should say that I was a philosophy major in college. As a graduate student at Harvard in History and Philosophy of Religion I took two courses in philosophy. And in my undergraduate program at Union Seminary in New York I wrote my MDiv—then BD—thesis with the philosopher, Richard Kroner. I also had courses with Reinhold Niebuhr and Paul Tillich. However, my grade from Dr. Cailliet for the prelim exam was a failure, but I was allowed to retake the exam. In preparing for the retake I read published material by Dr. Cailliet in order to grasp his point of view. I was successful in the second attempt. Afterward, Dr. Cailliet's assistant, whose name I don't remember,

160. Gaebelein, "Friendship an Election of God," 55.
161. Riviere, phone interview with Bartollas, September 2009.
162. PCL, letter to Bartollas, May 13, 2009.

came to see me. He had read my exam and he wanted to say that it was his opinion that, while I understood Dr. Cailliet's Christian Philosophy, I didn't believe it. I did not respond.[163]

Cailliet not only had high expectations in the classroom but in other areas of life as well. An example of this is an exchange of letters between Cailliet and David Jones, who was the organist and choir director of the Princeton Seminary chapel. Jones apologized to Cailliet for the absence of a choir at chapel when Cailliet preached, as Cailliet had wanted them to sing "King Jesus Is a-Listening" and he was very upset that this did not happen.[164] Cailliet wrote a very unhappy letter to a pastor who arrived late to perform his son's wedding. The pastor apologized profusely.

Cailliet did have strong feelings on a number of subjects and some found him abrupt. For example, because of the new editorial board of *Theology Today* in April 1961, Cailliet wanted his book review withheld. Others report his abruptness. "My only contact with Dr. Cailliet outside the classroom was the night a group of us junior students and our wives were invited for a semi-compulsory evening in his home. At one point in the evening, Mrs. Cailliet asked if there were anything more she could get for any of us; and Dr. Cailliet immediately replied, as if there were a script, 'No, they were just leaving.'"[165]

However, there are also many glimpses of the compassionate side of his nature. His letters of concern to a wide group of people help us understand this side of his personality. He wrote a letter to Francis Joseph Cardinal Spellman, of New York, about the unjust trial and conviction of Cardinal Mindszenty in February 1949. He also wrote to Leonard Evans worried about his health, because he had not heard from him in quite some time. There was even a former student who was later confined to a mental institution who wrote to Cailliet for help. Cailliet noted that he answered the student's letter ten days later though his letter is not available in the Seminary archives. He also gave thoughtful gifts to unknown people such as Genji Yasui, a Japanese scholar, interested in learning as much as possible about Pascal. "I have just received your valuable [important] book: *Pascal—Genius in the Light*

---

163. HHC, email to Bartollas, May 28, 2009.

164. David Jones to Emile Cailliet, November 16, 1959, Emile Cailliet Collection, Special Collections, Princeton Theological Seminary Library.

165. BB, letter to Bartollas, May 12, 2009.

of Scripture, with my profound thanks. Prof. Morris Bishop advised me to read this book of yours in the letter that he gave me last year. Also he told me that you [are] 'one of the greatest Pascal scholars of our time' and that he asked you to send me your work. But in fact for me it was completely unexpected that you would so quickly give me your book. What a surprise and what joy for me who am nothing but a humble unknown person from the Far East. My poor vocabulary is not sufficient to express to you my thanks and my joy."[166]

Of course, Cailliet felt connected to France and its people and culture; his early years there did much to shape who he was. One student wrote: "He was a Frenchman in the true ego-sense of the word. His book, *Journey Into Light*, reveals personality insights that are truly French in character. He spoke with authority in such a way that was truly French. He would openly speak of his convictions with an air that he doubted that anyone out there would challenge him; yet when someone would dare challenge him, he would treat the issue humorously, he was hard on himself; he would meticulously meditate on a task until he had finally put it in order. Then he would reveal the task with authority.[167]

THE FINAL YEARS 1959–1981

One always hopes in reviewing another person's life that their last years are filled with a sense of accomplishment and fulfillment, a degree of peace, a modicum of good health, and an enjoyment of leisure. It seems on the whole this was not to be the case for Emile Cailliet. He left Princeton with some ill feelings towards the seminary over questions of sabbatical and salary about which he felt he was not fairly treated.[168] James McCord, who became president of Princeton Theological Seminary in the fall of 1959, kindly drove Cailliet to Cape May, New Jersey to ease his transition to retirement. He also answered some of Cailliet's financial concerns vis-à-vis the seminary. An interesting footnote to Cailliet and Princeton is that one of his students, Daniel Theron, commissioned a portrait of

---

166. Genji Yasui to Emile Cailliet, Nakagyo-ku, Kyoto-shi, Japan, February 7, 1949. Emile Cailliet Collection, Special Collections, Princeton Theological Seminary Library.

167. Brossoie, letter to Bartollas, June 16, 2009.

168. James McCord to Emile Cailliet, October 16, 1959, Emile Cailliet Collection, Special Collections, Princeton Theological Seminary Library.

him to be painted by E. M. Fabian, which was presented in May 1998, with Calliet's daughter Doris present, and now hangs in Stuart Hall at Princeton Theological Seminary.

Photo of Portrait

Doris Brunzie, Cailliet's daughter and youngest child, on left with artist Eileen Fabian in front of portrait of Emile Cailliet, now hanging in Stuart Hall, Princeton Theological Seminary.

After Calliet retired from Princeton Theological Seminary in 1959, he did continue to lecture and give speeches around the country. It even seems that he was seeking some involvement with the Salvation Army as evidenced by a letter he received from Brigadier Paul Bodine[169] of the Seattle, Washington Salvation Army office. "Your reference to your willingness to serve with The Salvation Army is certainly appreciated and I am going to write our New York Headquarters for a contact through that office. I do not know what activity in that locality where you are located might be. I am 3,000 miles from that side of America and I am not so sure that we have any particular work. At any rate, I think some Salvation Army representative should look you up and welcome you and get to know you. As for your inquiry about Advisory Boards—I would say that The Salvation Army still has them and in many communities, they are very active and render The Army a tremendous service."[170]

Cailliet and his wife, Vera, retired to Cape May, NJ where they had bought a vacation home several years earlier. Their home, "Fairfield," was

---

169. Bodine was a longtime friend; he wrote Cailliet in Philadelphia from Portland, Oregon in March 1943 and refers to living near Hélène and helping out with a new baby on the way. He was interested in serving as a chaplain in the U.S. Army but apparently the Salvation Army did not necessarily look favorably upon this. In Cailliet's response he encourages Bodine to stay in the Salvation Army where he is needed and thanks him for his concern and care of Hélène and family.

170. Paul E. Bodine to Emile Cailliet (Brigadier of The Salvation Army, Seattle, WA), Emile Cailliet Collection, Special Collections, Princeton Theological Seminary Library, April 11, 1960.

on Bayshore Road. Their daughter has some insights as to why they decided to retire to New Jersey:

> The decision to retire in Cape May? Well, it's a long story. He had been very much attached to a seaside area—particularly at first to South Laguna, where a rental arrangement was made several summers in a row in the 1930s. Then, when retirement neared, it seemed wise to settle, and where better than by the shore. We spent several of our vacations at a Cape May boarding house run by Mrs. Shaffer for birders. Cailliet was not a birder, but enjoyed the remote solitude in that tidal area before buying his Cape May home. The area chosen was in farmland, but close to the sea, a lot with a dear little house built on it. The cottage had two or three entrances—one into the kitchen, another at a porch fronting the house, the third built as an entrance to the study, to a room with a long shelf full of books! We loved it and promptly adopted it. There was gardening to be done, to be sure, a lot of weeds, but worth it in the end! So the cottage became ours, Rural Delivery, across the street from a farm. Shopping was done in Cape May. There was a butcher named "Fire Ball," there, a general store, as well as a gas provider, and a bookstore an essential to this family. There was even a bus stop if one needed public transportation to any of the shore stations. We loved the area! And so it was he retired with Vera near Cape May.[171]

Cailliet became active in the community as well as being elected as an elder at the Cape May Church, but when his wife became sick he scarcely attended. A minister who knew Cailliet recalls, "From 1961–65, I pastored the PCUSA congregation in Cold Spring, Cape May, NJ where Dr. and Mrs. Cailliet lived in retirement. He attended whenever he could, but his wife was not well and he was occupied with her care. I did call in their home but he wasn't eager to have visitors."[172]

Cailliet's beloved wife Vera developed dementia and died twelve years before he did. In his diary from 1972 while he still lived in Cape May, there are a number of entries concerning his ill health, including gall bladder surgery on January 4th and complaints of weakness, stomach and intestinal problems. His daughters called him frequently and were obviously concerned about his health. There are a number of entries about

---

171. Brunzie, letter to Evans and Bartollas.
172. GJ, email to Bartollas.

Rhys Price, Cailliet's faithful friend in Cape May[173] and about taking walks which were obviously of great interest to him.[174]

It is no happenstance that his last book was titled, *Alone at High Noon*. Following his retirement from active teaching in 1959, Cailliet spent a considerable amount of time thinking and reflecting on one of the most pressing issues of life—loneliness. As he expressed in his volume, *Alone at High Noon*,[175] there is a large difference between feeling alone and being solitary. Aloneness can become painful, and like a disease, it threatens to invade and destroy the self. Cailliet's answer is to capture a sense of the Presence of God and to recover a purpose in life. He believed that with this mindset we would be able to experience the solitary life with enjoyment and fulfillment.

In his final years of ill health Cailliet went to be with his daughter in California. He later suffered from dementia and in fact did not recognize Richard Oman when he came to visit him in a nursing home in Santa Monica, California.[176] He died in a nursing home there in 1981 after having lived with his daughter Hélène during the last years of his life. His memorial service was held at the Cold Spring United Presbyterian Church on August 16, 1981. There was a memorial minute recognizing him from the Clerk of the Session. The family asked for donations to the church instead of flowers as a memorial to Emile Cailliet. The service was conducted by David Crawford of Princeton Seminary and the Reverend Fred Bischoff, pastor of the church. He was buried in the church cemetery next to his wife.[177] Richard Oman also attended but we do not know who else from his seminary years was there.[178] Cailliet's daughter Doris wrote in a note on June 18, 1981 that the service was attended by old family friends, neighbors, and former students.

His family received letters of sympathy from college and seminary presidents and from many friends and colleagues saying what a great loss

---

173 Letter from Nancy Price at Cailliet's death, Emile Cailliet Collection, Special Collections, Princeton Theological Seminary Library, Box 8, File 153.

174 Emile Cailliet Collection, Special Collections, Princeton Theological Seminary Library. Box 8, File 142.

175. Grand Rapids: Zondervan, 1971

176. Oman, interview with Evans, December 2, 2009.

177 Emile Cailliet Collection, Special Collections, Princeton Theological Seminary Library, Box 9.

178. Oman, email to Evans.

his death was to the scholarly and theological world. A former student wrote to the family, describing how he had used Cailliet's book *Journey into Light* in his adult discussion group in a California church in 1972. His class had sent thank you notes, to which Cailliet replied on being released from the hospital. He quotes one of Cailliet's prayers: "And so bear me on as I learn to sing in the darkness of this world the song of thy redeeming love—until on thy kind arms I fall."[179]

Emile Cailliet's last reported words as he lay dying were . . . "I'm a Christian: I am not a churchman!"[180]

---

179 Paul M. McKowen (Reverend, Irvington Presbyterian Church of Fremont, CA), August 6, 1984, Emile Cailliet Collection, Special Collections, Princeton Theological Seminary Library. McKowen is quoting "My Prayer" from *Christianity Today*, March 30, 1973.

180. Hélène C. Adcock (daughter), Emile Cailliet Collection, Special Collections, Princeton Theological Seminary Library. Box 8, File 147.

2

The Believer

A Christian Centurion

When he entered Capernaum, a centurion came to him, appealing to him and saying, "Lord, my servant is lying at home paralyzed and in terrible distress. And he said to him, "I will come and cure him." The centurion answered, "Lord, I am not worthy to have you come under my roof, but only speak the word, and my servant will be healed. For I am a man under authority, with soldiers under me, and I say to one, 'Go,' and he goes, and to another, 'Come' and he comes, and to my servant, 'Do this,' and the servant does it." When Jesus heard him, he was amazed and said to those who followed him, "Truly I tell you, in no one in Israel have I found such faith." (Matthew 8:8–10)

WHEN RICHARD OMAN, EMILE Cailliet's former teaching assistant, and later himself a seminary professor, wrote a memorial piece for Emile Cailliet he titled it "Emile Cailliet: Christian Centurion." It was an image of faith which Cailliet himself often used in his talks and books. "The Centurion type of Christian," he wrote, "has only one concern—to do the Lord's will in joy and simplicity of heart. His life is no longer a miserable sequence of broken vows and vain resolutions. It is no longer perpetual effort and struggle or longing for some extraordinary vision. It is a life of love and power because it is a redeemed and fully surrendered life, a life in line with the will of God."[1]

Many will recognize the allusion to the centurion praised by Jesus in the Gospel of Matthew for his faith, but far fewer North Americans recognize a second source of this image and its importance for Cailliet—the novel *Le Voyage du Centurion* by Ernest Psichari, a young lieutenant in the French army and the grandson of Ernest Renan, who gave his life on August 22, 1914, in the opening salvos of World War I, defending his beloved France at the battle of Rossignol in Belgium.[2] His commanding officer, writing to the family after the battle, could say of him, "Duty, as he conceived and accomplished it on that day, was duty at its most enthusiastic and heroic."[3] Listen to Cailliet as he briefly tells the story of Psichari to his class on "The Christian Pattern of Life" in the winter of 1953:

> You know that the lives of Christ began to appear in the 19th century, with the intention of presenting Christ as a man, a great man to be sure, but a mere man. The first life, as you know was that of Strauss. In the second half of the 19th century there appeared a beautiful literary masterpiece, Renan's *Life of Jesus*. This work was probably more responsible for the spread of modernism than any other similar work. Later in life Renan turned to skepticism, which you may see by reading his philosophical discourses . . . Renan had a daughter who married a Greek by the name of Psichari. They had a son . . . The experience of the young Psichari was certainly varied. He danced on the knee of Renan, went to college, graduated and desired to major in philosophy. So he went to the University of Paris to study the type of philosophy I studied.
>
> You remember I called this earlier the "shooting gallery" kind of study: put up the thought of a man and then knock it down. This kind of study is productive of skepticism. One day at the age of twenty young Psichari felt that his life was empty and completely lacking motive. He desired some sort of discipline for his life and so he volunteered for the army. He wanted a bugle to rouse him out of bed in the morning and to send him to bed in the evening.

---

1. Cailliet, *Journey into Light*, 98.
2. Psichari, *Le Voyage du Centurion*. There have been a number of recent studies of Psichari, including: Frédérique Neau-Dufour, *Ernest Psichari: L'ordre et l'errance*, (Paris: Les Editions du Cerf, 2001) and Hughes Moutouh, *Ernest Psichari: L'aventure et la grâce*, (Monaco: éditions du Rocher, 2007).
3. Weber, "Psichari and God," 31.

Yet he was not satisfied. So in disgust, he volunteered for the colonial army. Here he was decorated for valor and later became an officer. Under his charge were Arabs, men of the Moslem faith. He was a solitary man. One night while pacing up and down, the Arabs who were sitting around a fire were discussing religion. (And Arabs are truly a religious people, this I know for I served with them also.) As he continued pacing he could not help but overhear their conversation, and lo and behold, they were talking of Jesus. He drew nearer, keenly interested in what they were saying. They did not say anything bad about him, but they did not say enough. This he began to feel as he listened, so he entered the conversation, saying that Jesus was more than they were saying he was. And he preached to them Jesus. Then he caught himself and realized what he was actually doing. Later in that night, in the solitude of that night, he gave his heart to the Lord. He wrote [his close friend Jacques] Maritain about this, and also about a matter of conscience to him, whether he should continue smoking his pipe as a Christian or not. He strongly desired to enter the ministry and he turned out to be a wonderful Christian . . . Later, in the midst of heroic action, he was killed with a bullet in his forehead. [4]

Le Voyage du Centurion was published posthumously in 1916, and it struck a chord with many young men of Cailliet's generation. The family Psichari was born into had high moral standards, but no strong religious convictions. "There was no hostility to Christianity, but a feeling that one could and should get the best out of it, and then go beyond it, indeed rise above it."[5] Friendship with Charles Péguy and Jacques Maritain, who themselves had moved along a path from skepticism to faith was certainly instrumental in Psichari's own move to faith. He dedicated his first novel, *L'Appel des Armes,* which explored the distinctive character of the soldier, to Péguy. *Le Voyage du Centurion*, though in the form of a novel, traces Psichari's own pilgrimage of the mind and spirit, his deep inner longing for faith and certitude, in parallel with the outward journey of a military campaign, the camps and the fighting, and the long hours of silence and solitude in the Mauritanian desert. When Psichari returned to France after his African service he became a lay Dominican and was looking

---

4. Typescript of student notes on "The Christian Pattern of Life," Winter 1953, 45–47, Emile Cailliet Collection, Special Collections, Princeton Theological Seminary Library, Box 3, File 53-A.

5. Weber, "Psichari and God," 19.

forward to studying for the priesthood when the outbreak of the First World War called him back to the front lines and, shortly, to his death.

It is not hard to see the inner identification Cailliet had made with Psichari, a man who deeply loved his culture and his country, who had faced the horrors and inner questioning born of serving on the front lines of battle, and who had wrestled through honest doubts to come to a deep and living faith. Psichari's example may have even played a role in Cailliet's own later decision to spend a significant amount of time in a part of France's African colonial empire. We do well to keep in mind Psichari's image of the centurion/soldier who comes to faith, along with the figure in Matthew's gospel, when examining the life of faith and prayer of Emile Cailliet under the rubric "Christian Centurion."

CAILLIET AND THE BIBLE

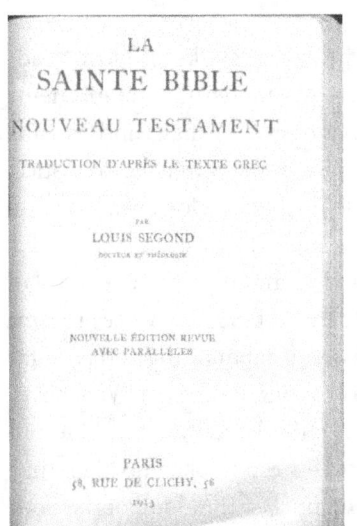

Photograph of Emile Cailliet's first Bible, *La Sainte Bible*, received from Vera Cailliet on December 17, 1917.

Perhaps one of the most personally revealing pieces in the Cailliet Collection at Princeton Seminary is his French Bible. He writes on the title page that the Bible was given to him by his wife, Vera, on December 17, 1917. It is heavily marked in red and blue pencil, with additional notes added here and there. It opens most easily to the closing chapters of the Gospel of John, the gospel of eternal life, where the binding has been broken from frequent use. Cailliet once wrote that for him, the gospel was "essentially a message of eternal life... The trail of Light we follow through the whole Bible leads up to the Glory of that Gospel of eternal life." He goes on to recount that Paul refers to eternal life forty times and that the Johannine writings "speak ninety times of eternal life or of being alive... Christian experience through the ages, but more especially in its fullest manifestations, has been both that of an encounter with the living Christ and a tremendous awareness of being alive in him, through him, and with him. This is the glory of Easter."⁶

The story has already been told of his beginning his reading of the Bible with the Beatitudes, the Sermon on the Mount and the gospels. Not surprisingly, another favorite section of the Scripture for him was the Psalms. When WFIL-TV, Channel 6, in Philadelphia, announced in 1955 a series of programs for seventeen consecutive Friday mornings on "The Greatest Book in the World," to be presented by the faculty of Princeton Theological Seminary, it was the Book of Psalms on which Cailliet chose to speak and the title he gave his talk was "The Bible and Personal Religion: A Study in the Psalms."⁷ In his own Bible he had marked the 23rd Psalm as the favorite Psalm of his wife, Vera. He carefully highlighted Psalm 119; a notation in the margins reads, "Psaume de Pascal" (Psalm of Pascal). Psalm 139 is underlined almost in its entirety and bears the notation, "Je pénétrer de chaque mot du psaume 139 jusqu'au verset 19" (I entered each word of Psalm 139 until verse 19); his underlining picks up again at verses 23 and 24.

Other sections of scripture which bear the marks of close reading in his Bible are favorite passages such as the Ten Commandments in Deuteronomy, the Suffering Servant passages of Isaiah, and Micah's famous lines concerning the fundamental requirement that we do justice, love kindness and walk humbly with God (Micah 6:8). However, there are also firm markings and multiple notations near the passages in Exodus that describe the setting apart of the priesthood and that of the renewal of the covenant after the incident of the Golden Calf. Several verses toward the very close of the Book of Exodus receive special marking and annotation, including the final words of that book about a journey: "Whenever the cloud was taken up from the tabernacle, the Israelites would set out on each stage of their journey, but if the cloud was not taken up, then they did not set out until the day that it was taken up. For the cloud of the Lord was on the tabernacle by day, and the fire was in the cloud by night, before the eyes of all the house of Israel at each stage of the journey" (Exodus 30:36–38). Notes in red pencil along the bottom of that page read: "Quelle magnifique éducation dans un esprit d'obéissance!!! . . . et quel splendide

---

6. Carbon copy of questionnaire, 1953, Emile Cailliet Collection, Special Collections, Princeton Theological Seminary Library, Box 9, File 216.

7. Typescript of "The Bible and Personal Religion," Emile Cailliet Collection, Special Collections, Princeton Theological Seminary Library, Box 2, File 49-B.

résultat: ALORS . . ." and along the side is the note, "Voila comme il faut vivre!" (What a magnificent education in the spirit of obedience and what a splendid result . . . This reveals how one must live!) Cailliet's special interest in the theme of eternal life is also manifest by especially heavy marking in both red and blue pencil of the passages on the resurrection in the closing chapter of the Book of Daniel.

In the New Testament there seems to be no page that is not marked, sometimes quite heavily. Only a few highlights can be pointed out here. Naturally, the Beatitudes and the Sermon on the Mount receive strong attention. He also made some particularly heavy marking in passages on eschatological times, such as the parable of the wise and foolish bridesmaids and the insistence on the necessity for watchfulness of Matthew 24 and 25. In the institution of the Lord's Supper in Matthew 26, an emphasis on the forgiveness of sin for *many* is stressed by an unusual double underlining of the word "plusieurs." Cailliet also heavily highlighted the Great Commission in Matthew 28, where Jesus tells his disciples to go and make disciples of all nations, teaching them "to obey everything that I have commanded you" and promising an eternal presence to the end of the age.

In Mark, the Parable of the Sower (Mark 4) is noted as "très importante" (very important) and the command to "watch and pray" in Mark 14 is doubly underlined and accompanied by a side note, "le mot d'ordre"—the watchword. A note on Luke 6 draws attention to how the choice of the disciples was made "après une nuit de prière!!!" (after a night of prayer!!!) In several places there are dates written that were apparently significant for Cailliet. For instance, near the passage "No one who puts a hand to the plow and looks back is fit for the Kingdom of God," (Luke 9:62) Cailliet has written the date "Aug. 15, 1943 sqq." The Lucan passage urging fearless confession (Luke 12:8–10) receives a comment in English: "Do not hide your flag." Other Lucan passages with especially heavy marking are the Parable of the Prodigal Son, the passages on the coming of the Kingdom of God in Luke 17:20–37 with the note "à étudier mot à mot" (to study word for word) and the discussion of eternal life in Luke 20:27.

The extended prayer of Jesus near the close of John's gospel receives very close attention and underlining, particularly chapter fifteen which speaks of abiding in Jesus, the True Vine, and the sixteenth verse of this chapter, "You did not choose me, but I chose you. And I appointed you to go and bear fruit, fruit that will last." Next to this verse Cailliet has written, in English, "This *is* the source of true peace of mind." Strong notations in the margins were also made near the close of John's gospel, where the Risen Jesus asks Peter if he loves him and then commands Peter to feed his sheep.

The story of the early church in the Book of Acts and the various New Testament epistles are also well marked, and when we come to the Apocalypse we find particular attention paid to the letter to the Laodiceans, who were neither hot nor cold in their faith, but lukewarm, and to the final chapters, which speak of the Book of Life, the Tree of Life and the Water of Life. On the next to last page of his Bible Cailliet has drawn attention to Revelation 20:3 and written in large letters at the top of the page "Le Livre de VIE!" (The book of LIFE!) and at the close of the book he writes:

> La Bible se ferme sur une gracieuse invitation de Dieu
> — sur un avertissement
> —et sur une prière et une bénédiction!
> (The Bible closes itself on a gracious invitation from God—on an advertisement—and on a prayer and a benediction!)

Regular reading of and meditation on scripture was clearly an important part of Cailliet's life and personal spiritual discipline. Perhaps one of the most moving accounts of the way he found God speaking to him through the scriptures is to be read in a notebook in which he jotted down some of his more personal religious experiences during the third decade of the last century. At the time feeling very unwell, in pain, and preparing to go to the hospital for an operation, he began reading from the thirteenth chapter of Jeremiah. Several times he was tempted to finish his reading, but a voice kept telling him to read on, to read just one more chapter, and then one more. Verse after verse began to speak directly to him and bring forth self-examination and prayer. Finally coming to the closing section of the fifteenth chapter of Jeremiah, where Jeremiah speaks of his own unceasing pain and an incurable wound, a situation which seemed to echo Cailliet's current situation so closely, he reads the opening sections of verse 19: "Therefore thus says the Lord: 'If you return, I will restore you, and you shall stand before me. If you utter what is precious and not what is worthless, you shall be as my mouth . . .'" The words probed the depth of his soul and spoke directly to his heart, urging him to reconsecrate himself and his life to the Living God. And the result was an experience which he compares to that of Pascal when Pascal wrote his *Memorial*. Finally, he writes, after so much pain and struggle, "Je m'en dormis dans la béatitude." (I fell asleep in a state of bliss.)[8]

One final note from Cailliet's Bible may be mentioned in this section, pointing to the great importance Cailliet gave to the reading and study of scripture as central to his own religious life. Near the Johannine account of the Last Supper, at the bottom of the page, and just one page beyond where his Bible naturally opens, he wrote in English: "*Resolved*: never to allow any book to usurp the central place of the Bible in my life."

A FAITH IN SEARCH OF UNDERSTANDING

It was in the course of reading Scripture that Emile Cailliet was found by the Living God and he would never give up on the centrality of the witness of the Bible for the Christian believer. "It is not safe for a Christian to lose himself in a multiplicity of religious books unless he is firmly grounded in *The* Book." He wrote:

> I remember in my younger days having stood for hours in front of the well-stocked shelves of my library in a state of mind and spirit bordering on paralysis. Where was I to turn next in my quest for truth? . . . At times I have seen seminarians in such a plight. However poor, they would wait at the theological bookstore for the most recently publicized book in their field. Surely the last theologian who had spoken would help them out of the wilderness in which they had lost their bearings! So they waited for his weather report to know what they could believe, perchance proclaim in their next sermon, or say in their pulpit prayer. The main trouble was that having lost their first love for the Book, they found themselves caught in the snare of substitutes.

Nevertheless, he would go on, "it is high time to realize the Bible is not a grave, it is a cradle."[9]

Emile Cailliet had had a great grandfather who had been a teacher in the days of Napoleon and a famous bibliophile. His private library had

---

8. "Memo Book," 32–39, Emile Cailliet Collection, Special Collections, Princeton Theological Seminary Library, Box 8, File 154.

9. Cailliet, "Books and the Book," 3.

included numerous first editions of great classics, all of which had been handed down through the family and had come to Emile. He had been nourished on the best books of western civilization and he knew their value.[10] In a course he offered at Princeton Seminary on "Great Books in the Light of Christianity" he told students that "this course is offered in the belief that as a Christian student you should be well-read. The best and most beautiful that has been written in world literature is not too good for you. You should read a great deal of it and read to good purpose ... Should truth and faith be divorced in the education of your mind, a sense of frustration would immediately result." He encouraged his students not only to read, but to think, to discriminate, "to weigh carefully, then choose ... That is why reading sometimes means hard work; but that is also why the life of the mind can be so noble."[11] He likened the life of the mind to an "inner conversation" which cannot be avoided by anyone who is honest with themselves.[12]

Remembering his own struggle to faith, Cailliet always respected a person who had honest doubts but who was sincerely seeking for the meaning and truth of life. "Only a superficial and uncharitable view can lead one to feel that skeptics are villains willfully turning from the light so as to remain free to gratify their own selfish motives."[13] Having come to faith in the Living God, it was his deep desire to come to a better understanding of it. He plunged himself into the explorations of religion that were being discussed and written about at that time in France. August Comte had suggested that the religious mind was a backward mind and proposed three successive stages in human development—the theological mind, the metaphysical or abstract mind, and the scientific or positive mind. Lucien Lévy-Bruhl had tried to show that the so-called "primitive" mind was not just a backward form of thinking, but actually an alternative way of approaching reality, different and distinct from western scientific thinking, but with its own inner consistency and logic. Cailliet was attracted to this positive approach of Lévy-Bruhl and used the methods of

---

10. Handwritten draft of note addressed to Julius Birge, Emile Cailliet Collection, Special Collections, Princeton Theological Seminary Library, Box 1, File 25.

11. Syllabus of "Great Books in the Light of Christianity," Emile Cailliet Collection, Special Collections, Princeton Theological Seminary Library, Box 3, File 50.

12. See chapter two of Emile Cailliet, *Life of the Mind*.

13. Typescript, Emile Cailliet Collection, Special Collections, Princeton Theological Seminary Library, Box 7, File 130.

Lévy-Bruhl in his study of the beliefs of the natives of Madagascar, which provided the material for his first doctoral thesis and later in his explorations of the meaning of symbols. He became interested in the writings of Emile Durkheim and Rudolf Otto, both of whom were exploring the notion of "the sacred," though from very different directions. He read the work of Marcel Mauss on magic, and Roger Bastide's probing into the problems of religious mysticism. On the philosophical side, he read Etienne Gilson and was intrigued by his claims for a "mystical function" in humans, which might be seen as a parallel to the "logical function" so emphasized by western forms of education. He read the writings of Evelyn Underhill on the history of Christian mysticism and William James on the varieties of religious experience. He explored critically the stimulating writings of Henri Bergson, who presented a philosophical reaction against the scientific positivism of the nineteenth century, and the process thought of Alfred North Whitehead and Charles Hartshorne. He read in the Christian personalism of Jacques Maritain and Emmanuel Mounier, and the Christian existentialism of Gabriel Marcel.

While on the staff of the University of Pennsylvania, his further research led to publications on some of the "abnormal" aspects of religious life as experienced in the occult and on the role of magic in nineteenth century European literature. In his second period at the University of Pennsylvania he produced a major study, published in French, on the traditions of ideology and rationalism in French writers of the eighteenth century. It came out in the midst of the Second World War and was dedicated to his son André, who had been born in France and had been one of the first American volunteers to join the French army at the outset of the war. At that very time, André was being held captive in a German prisoner of war camp.

Cailliet's years of living in Claremont also helped develop his thinking. There he enjoyed a close friendship with the American personalist philosopher Hartley Burr Alexander, who had argued that all metaphysical concepts should be grounded in human experience if they were to have any intelligibility, but that because of the limited and changing nature of human experience, such concepts must always be provisional.[14] He

---

14. Cailliet spent many hours on long walks and in discussions with Hartley Burr Alexander about his life and beliefs. He completed a partial draft of a life of Hartley Burr Alexander in French, "Dr. Hartley Burr Alexander," which is housed in Box 8, File 158 of the Emile Cailliet Collection at Princeton Theological Seminary Library. This draft

became acquainted with other American personalist philosophers, Albert C. Knudsen and Ralph Tyler Flewelling, and contributed an article on symbolism to their journal, *The Personalist*.[15] Alexander in particular, he later wrote, had helped him to move beyond the approach to religion he had learned under Lévy-Bruhl. Alexander was a great admirer of Blaise Pascal. "His is the most prophetic genius of modern times—penetrating in its comprehensions, withering in its judgements, and lighted with the graces of angels," Alexander once wrote.[16] Alexander encouraged Cailliet's interest in the life and thought of Pascal.

During his time at Scripps, Cailliet was able to enjoy a sabbatical leave enabling him to study with the theological faculty in Strasbourg. This allowed him an opportunity to read more fully in the traditions of French Protestant thought. One of the professors there was Fernand Ménégoz who had written critically on the problem of prayer in Schleiermacher and also a book exploring the differences between historical certitude and the certitude of faith.[17] Fernand Ménégoz was the nephew of Eugène Ménégoz, one of the grand old figures of French Protestantism who had led the way to a renewal of that tradition along with Auguste Sabatier. The thought of Auguste Sabatier and Eugène Ménégoz is usually referred to under the title of "Symbolo-Fideism" or often just "Fideism" in short. Eugène Ménégoz and Paul Sabatier, who began their writing careers in the late nineteenth century, shared a deep interest in "reconciling the demands of the moral and religious consciousness with the equally imperious and rightful demands of modern scientific conscience."[18]

According to Eugène Ménégoz, "the basis of symbolism is the psychological observation that the essence of things escapes us, and that we know only their manifestations in the forms of images, figures and

---

was eventually translated and completed by Hartley Burr Alexander's son, Hubert G. Alexander. It was privately published in a limited edition: *Hartley Burr Alexander: A Biography*, (Decorah, Iowa: Anundsen Publishing Company, 1992). For a brief introduction to the life and thought of Hartley Burr Alexander see Thomas M. Alexander, "The Life and Work of Hartley Burr Alexander," *Pluralist* 3 (Spring 2008) 1–10 and subsequent articles in that issue.

15. Cailliet, "Inquiry into Symbolism," 157–67.

16. Alexander, *Truth and Faith: An Interpretation of Christianity*.

17. Fernand Ménégoz, *Gebetsproblem im Anschluss an Schleiermachers Predigten und Glaubenslehre* (Leipzig: Hinrichs, 1911) and *La Certitude de la foi et la certitude historique, étude sur la problème du fondement de la vie religieuse* (Basel: Fincke, 1906).

18. Horton, "Theology of Eugène Ménégoz," 175.

symbols."[19] As we cannot know God as God is in Godself, we rely on more or less anthropomorphic representations which we form in our thought, such as "Father" or "Lord" or "Master" or even by representations of some attribute of God, like "Rock" or "Fire." He wrote, "These symbols are without doubt the expression of a living reality, but the conformation of our brain is such that it cannot grasp that reality naked; our mind can apprehend it only when it presents itself in the garment of a more or less sensuous representation." Ménégoz felt that the whole idea of salvation could be summed up in the theme of "eternal life." It is what human beings basically desire—"we are created for life, not for death, for happiness and not for suffering." He made a distinction between "faith" and "beliefs." "By faith is meant the movement of the self towards God—a movement which implies forsaking sin, repentance. The man who repents and gives his heart to God is saved, whatever his beliefs may be." Faith is "an activity of the self in its unity, and therefore must comprise all the elements of the soul's faculties—thought, feeling, and will. But the essential factor in salvation is the inward movement toward God, not intellectual adherence to some doctrinal tenet." Doctrines are important for their pedagogical value and poor doctrine can easily lead one astray, but "the faith which saves is something different from intellectual assent . . . it is *union with God*, ensuing upon an initial act of self-surrender, which springs from the will."[20] This approach to salvation by faith, independently of beliefs, makes it possible to find a middle path between a form of Christianity which tends to substitute belief for faith, whereby a person comes to rely for salvation "upon an intellectual acceptance of the inspiration of the Bible *in abstracto*, instead of responding vitally, from the heart, to the message which the Bible brings," and a liberalism which ends up being a simple moralism or legalism. People find a too facile liberalism shallow because "it has nothing to nourish them with; it can speak to them only of duties, not of pardon and salvation."[21]

> Ah! How great is the joy of him who has arrived at the certainty that no error of thought can condemn him, and that God, in order to receive him into his favor, asks of him but one thing: his heart . . . With peace of soul, he has found liberty of thought. He is deliv-

---

19. All quotations in this section taken from: Ménégoz, "Symbolo-Fideism," 151–52.
20. Horton, "Theology of Eugène Ménégoz," 175.
21. Ibid., 181.

ered from the yoke of legalism and orthodoxy. He enjoys the precious liberty of the children of God. And now he can, with a calm and confident mind, without painful apprehensions, and without danger for his inner peace, turn to the study of the traditional doctrines of Christianity and those numerous critical questions which preoccupy the modern world. Whether he finds the truth or fails to find it, the salvation of his soul is assured.[22]

For Eugène Ménégoz it is not that faith is independent of beliefs, for a saving faith does have intellectual elements, but the limited intelligence of human beings is not fit to reach absolute knowledge of the truth. "*All of us are in error, in one way or another, for we see through a glass darkly; but in spite of our errors we are saved by faith, and may be certain of our salvation.*"[23] What is available to us is not intellectual certitude but religious certitude. And in this respect even those who might deny the existence of a personal God intellectually may in their hearts "believe in the God their reason denies."[24]

If one looks at Cailliet's post-Strasbourg writings, one finds that he has a deep affinity for this approach to Christian faith and life. On the opposite side of the title page of his Bible he has pasted the account of a witness Eugène Ménégoz gave to his faith on the occasion of his eightieth birthday. It is the original French version of the extended quotation we have just given, together with an affirmation by Ménégoz that this passage essentially sums up the faith which has sustained him over so many years. The notes in Cailliet's Strasbourg-era files also make it clear that it is on this sabbatical that he begins to gather the material for his future work on the life and thought of Pascal, the work for which he became perhaps best known in the English-speaking scholarly world. He had previously announced a seminar on "French Fiction" as his offering to his advanced students when he came back from his sabbatical, however on his return, he decides instead to announce a seminar on "Pascal." After making this change, he begins to have some doubts that American undergraduates would sign up for what may appear at first glance to be a rather abstract set of readings, and is tempted to perhaps change the topic once again to a seminar on "Molière." However, he decides to stick with Pascal and is

---

22. French original from Eugène Ménégoz, *Réflexions sur l'évangile du salut*. English translation ibid., 181–82.

23. Horton, "Theology of Eugène Ménégoz," 186.

24. Ibid.,186.

gratified when a dozen students actually elect to take the course. It is in the life and thought of Pascal that Cailliet finally finds the most important framework for his own mature reflection on Christian faith and its meaning. "I found in the encyclopedic and deep genius of Pascal," he wrote, "an inviting principle of integration."[25]

PRAYER AS "ACTED RATHER THAN UTTERED"

The silence and solitude of the desert experienced by Maxence, the hero of Psichari's *Le Voyage du Centurion*, play an important role in the book. Near the beginning he learns what is in store for him: "Henceforth, a life of true solitude and silence begins for Maxence. Here on this plot of some thirty square yards, with no longer even the hubbub of departures and arrivals to disturb him, he learns what solitude really is, as it exists deep in the bosom of silent Nature. For the Rule of Africa is silence. As the monk in the cloister keeps silence, so does the white-cowled desert. And the young Frenchman too conforms unhesitatingly to the strict observance of the Rule. Piously he listens as, one by one, the hours drop down into the all-encompassing Eternity. He dies to the world that has deceived him."[26] And later there is an extended paean to Silence: "Silence is a little corner of Heaven that comes floating down to men . . . Silence is a wide African plain over which a biting wind is blowing. It is the Indian Ocean by night, with the stars above it . . . Silence first closes the lips, and then penetrates to the very soul, finding its way to those inaccessible regions where God reposes within us . . ."[27]

The theme of Emile Cailliet's final book is also solitude—*Alone at High Noon: Reflections on the Solitary Life*. In writing to his publisher regarding it he says, "The author has retired in his country home where he lives alone with his dog. [Vera had died some time before.] Friends impressed by his happy frame of mind have suggested that since he has solved for himself the problems of the solitary life, he should help others do so." The book is meant to be "a study of life and its inherent solitude . . .

---

25. Typescript of "Research Project on the Emergence and Nature of Personality," March 5, 1954, 2, Emile Cailliet Collection, Special Collections, Princeton Theological Seminary Library, Box 1, File 25.

26. Psichari, *Soldier's Pilgrimage*, 28–29.

27. Ibid., 154–55.

from childhood to old age, until the very spectre of death is confronted in a context of cosmic solitude."[28] It moves from elected solitude such as that praised by the author of the *Imitation of Christ* or written about by Henry David Thoreau in *Walden*, through the experience of loneliness and aloneness in contemporary life, and ends with a chapter on "Transfigured Solitariness." In this last chapter, the Parable of the Prodigal Son is presented as an "epic of solitude." The Prodigal Son goes through several phases of self-centeredness and attempts at self-sufficiency until he finally realizes his errors, remembers his Father's loving care for him, and turns once again to his waiting Father. "And so, there is ushered in, on the part of the son, a life of love and utter dependence upon the father in whose presence he will henceforth live all the days of his life . . . What we now have is an initiation into the practice of the presence of God." True prayer, writes Cailliet, is "acted rather than merely uttered." Authentic solitary life is a life of living prayer, "a life lived every moment in love for God and in utter dependence upon Him."[29]

While this final book is Cailliet's most extended reflection on the topic of solitude, it is a topic which had long been with him. In the mid-1930s Cailliet had written a little book published in French and dedicated to his children with the title *Le Service Social: Orientations Philosophiques*. It is somewhat in the genre of André Maurois' *Open Letter to a Young Man*, R. M. Rilke's *Letters to a Young Poet*, or Romano Guardini's *Briefe über Selbstbildung* in seeking to offer some personal advice to young people based on what the authors have learned from their own experience. A central chapter is a plea for the value of silence. "Silence! How good it is to take refuge in silence! Touch with events has fatigued us; it has disturbed our poise and left us wavering, indecisive. Only by ourselves may we get our bearings, readjust our forces, return to normal tone; we must, in a word, *recapture* our *self* . . . Of solitude Ravignon has well said that it is the fatherland of the strong, and of silence that it shapes their prayer. Thereby he indicates the profound difference that lies between the passivity of mere mutism and that withdrawal into meditation which is itself eminently active. The latter is the privilege of the human person . . .

---

28. Carbon dated June 21, 1970, Emile Cailliet Collection, Special Collections, Princeton Theological Seminary Library, Box 5, File 106.

29. Cailliet, *Alone at High Noon*, 92.

Silence—preparation of the inner person for the assaults of life! Silence—vigil of arms in the heart of the brave!"[30]

On his bookplate, inserted into many of his books, Cailliet includes a motto from Pascal, "We should keep silence as much as feasible and let our conversation be only with God, whom we know to be the truth . . ." It is in the silence and solitude of Mount Sinai that Moses received the Ten Commandments. It is to the silence and solitude of the desert that Christ is taken after his baptism and faces his temptations. And Cailliet feels that it is in silence and solitude before God that we can best come to understand what is being asked of us in our own lives. "Look prayerfully at your past life, read afresh the circumstances which brought you to the point at which the problem of guidance is now needed. God will not blueprint all your future, but He will lead step by step and you do well to view all these successive steps in the light of His past working in your life."[31]

Another key theme in discussing prayer, for Cailliet, is the relationship between prayer and certitude. Perhaps the most concentrated presentation of this aspect of Cailliet's understanding of prayer is to be found in a talk he gave for a Day of Prayer at Princeton Seminary in the fall of 1955, later reprinted in the *Princeton Seminary Bulletin*.[32] The whole of this address repays careful study, as it reveals some of the basic understanding of Cailliet as to the relationship between Christianity and culture, which is spelled out in more detail in his other books. It also touches on the particular standpoint of the Christian scholar. Here we will look primarily at the opening section of the talk and its examination of the theme of prayer and certitude. "It is not only that prayer is conditioned by certitude, but certitude naturally issues in prayer," he writes. He admits there are varieties of understandings of prayer, such as prayer as "an expression of duty," or prayer as "a scheduled exercise in faith," but the kind of prayer of which he is speaking he calls the "prayer of the believing heart." He chooses as his text Hebrews 11:6. "He that cometh to God must believe that he is, and *that* he is a rewarder of them that diligently seek him."

---

30. Cailliet, *Le Service Social*, 59–61.

31. "Christian Pattern of Life," 31, Emile Cailliet Collection, Special Collections, Princeton Theological Seminary Library, Box 3, File 53-A.

32. All quotations in this section are taken from Emile Cailliet, "Prayer and Certitude," 13–19.

Cailliet finds in this text three basic propositions. The first is the affirmation of the "reality of God," and not just any god, but specifically the God testified to in the Scriptures. He wishes to make clear that God understood primarily as the term of a metaphysical argument or in the context of some sort of esoteric mysticism or generalized religious experience is inadequate. "I remember on occasion," he writes, "when a learned preacher opened his prayer with a far-reaching apostrophe aimed at some cosmic nowhere. My neighbor on the bench, a godly pastor of souls . . . could not help but exhort the preacher in a murmur: "Call him 'Father' and ask him for something!"

The second proposition he finds in the text is that God is "a rewarder." He hastens to add that this should not be understood in some mercenary sense, encouraging us to pray for what we can get out of it. Rather, he takes this phrase as an indicator that the God testified to in the Scriptures is a God who cares. "Indeed the reason our God is eminently the God of prayer is that he is the personal God who cares—a rewarder." However, the verse in Hebrews, he points out, does not end here, but adds a third proposition: God is a rewarder "of them that diligently seek him." Although Cailliet often speaks of God as the 'great Seeker' and admits that the heart of the biblical witness is to a God who is seeking after us ("We would not be seeking God had he not already found us"), he also acknowledges that the human being is "neither a robot nor a clod of earth." Therefore it is also proper to speak of our responsibility to seek after God. "To seek diligently is to seek with a steady, earnest, preserving attention, as one who highly esteems the object of his quest." This definition, he says, "is not far from characterizing prayer itself." But since a genuine quest for God in prayer cannot be isolated from the rest of our activities, this quest becomes "as it were, the line of force" of our entire life and conversation.

Cailliet now goes on specifically to present what he means by the close link between prayer and certitude, and how a deterioration in the latter inevitably leads to problems in the former, or, as Cailliet puts it, "when the life of prayer is on the wane, the implication is that our certitude has deteriorated." The key point he makes is a distinction between "certitude" and "assent." Calling on Newman and his *Essay in Aid of a Grammar of Assent*, and in a move reminiscent of the thought of Ménégoz, Cailliet sees the giving or withholding of "assent" as pertaining essentially to the realm of scholarship and of the fluctuations of human knowledge. A few seminary courses or some new theological text or piece of Biblical scholarship, for instance, may shake up our former ideas and understandings of God and the Christian faith. The question then becomes whether we allow fluctuations of human knowledge, the outcome of the practice of free inquiry and free discussion, to begin to destroy our very soul. What we assent to may and does change as we are exposed to new ideas and new information. This is the very nature of honest scholarly work. "Certitude" on the other hand, refers to "a God-given faith which is the prior fact." It is a fundamental reality, the "very anchor of our life," the "Axiom of all axioms." The true life of prayer, says Cailliet, "is in the last analysis a way of being." It is allowing "our whole reborn personality" to "emerge in the power of God's life and light" as we are increasingly guided and carried along by a renewed Christian certitude.

The plan of the Day of Prayer at the seminary left time for further questions and discussion between the seminarians and the speakers on the topic of prayer. A short mimeographed summary record of the questions and answers explored in these discussions is preserved in the archives.[33] In again addressing the question "What is prayer?" Cailliet responds that true prayer cannot be separated into a *theory* of prayer and the *practical use* of prayer. "Christian truth is of one piece, like the seamless robe of our Lord ... The heart of such Christian truth is prayer. In a way, the best history of our faith would be a history of prayer." Since prayer, for Cailliet, is in very essence the practice of our relationship to God, our prayer is "the truth that we do."

In fielding a question on "the greatest obstacle we face when we pray," Cailliet pointed not in the first instance to such issues as personal distractions or lack of time, but to a more pervading cultural milieu. Our greatest obstacle, he felt, was "the wasteland of this modern age" in which we all participate. In this cultural climate we are allowing ourselves to be "slowly asphyxiated" by our cultural neglect of the reality of God. He reminded the seminarians that restoring a true life of prayer in the midst of such a cultural climate is not easy. However, as we seek to live our lives honestly before God, and as the unknown and unexpected in our lives brings us to our knees again and again, we learn ever more fully to "move in the truth." "Our life is our prayer, our prayer is our life ... What we call

---

33. The following quotes are taken from mimeographed notes on "Prayer: Its Meaning and Significance" from the Student Day of Prayer, November 16, 1955, 3, Emile Cailliet Collection, Special Collections, Princeton Theological Seminary Library, Box 3, File 53-A.

'periods of prayer' are simply more *intense* moments when we pause to look and listen."

The seminarians went on to ask Cailliet's views on other questions concerning prayer. On being asked about intercessory prayer and whether it had any purpose, Cailliet affirmed its importance in his own life practice and as recognition of the corporate nature of the body of Christ. He shared his reflections on the question of seemingly unanswered prayer, on what it might mean to "pray continually," on how one should go about praying for God's guidance, and on our own share in helping God answer the prayers that we pray. His answers come quite personally from his own life experience and his study of Scripture, and when he does not have an answer he still seeks to be as honest as he can. "Beware of those who know from beginning to end why God does this or that," he tells the students. "We must preserve a sense of mystery."

ON READING DEVOTIONALLY

At the 1947 Summer Princeton Institute of Theology, Emile Cailliet gave a series of talks on "Devotional Classics." The topics of the four lectures were the "Nature and Scope of Devotional Reading," "Browsing through Great Books," "The Watersheds of Devotional Literature," and "The Reformed Tradition of Holiness." As soon as the series was announced, people kept asking him, "What great books have you chosen?" However, Cailliet refused to begin with a list. For one thing, he told the audience, largely of working pastors, time was too short to do justice to any list. Further, he did not wish to just push off his own favorite titles on others. Rather, he felt that the question was best pursued by beginning with an understanding of what it is we should have in view as we read devotional classics. Checking his dictionary, he found that the root of the English word "devotion" was to be found in the Latin "*vovere*"—to vow. Thus, at its very center is the idea of a solemn pledge, an agreement entered into by two or more parties, or, to use a more theological word a *covenant*. "With this word," he tells his audience, "we reach to the heart of our Bible religion."[34]

---

34. Note cards for the lectures on "Devotional Classics" given at 1947 Summer Princeton Institute of Theology, 1–3, Emile Cailliet Collection, Special Collections, Princeton Theological Seminary Library, Box 2, File 49-B.

With this background he then explores the contrasting poles of Pelagianism and Augustinianism in Christian history and the tendency of various spiritual classics to gravitate to one or the other side of this divide. For instance, in the *Spiritual Exercises* of Ignatius of Loyola, which he admires for their deep understanding of the human psychological makeup and their sophisticated use of sensory imagination, he nevertheless finds a kind of "boot-strap" approach to salvation where there is too much emphasis on human striving. Such devotional literature, he feels, can easily become a sort of "cardboard rosary." On the opposite extreme he cites Martin Luther's condemnation of all exercises of self-discipline as "filthy rags."

What is needed, he tells his audience, is not a list of approved or disapproved devotional literature. This would be too simplistic and clean cut. Rather, what is needed is a method by which one may evaluate all of their reading to see how such reading can make one more and more aware of their Christian commitment.[35] It is this, he feels, that real devotional reading does for us. For the Protestant Christian, Cailliet maintains that all great literature (not just "religious literature") can serve as devotional literature if read in this light, and we can read and benefit from Sophocles, Plato and Aristotle; Dostoevsky, Tolstoy and Claudel; as well as Augustine, Dante and the *Imitation of Christ*. In making up our personal list of devotional reading we might do well, he says, to peruse some list of "100 Great Books" as well as those suggested by books with titles like *Classics of the Soul's Quest* or *Great Christian Books*.

In his lecture on "The Watersheds of Devotional Literature" Cailliet returns to the issue of the impossibility for Protestant Christians of drawing up some dividing line between "classics" in general and "devotional classics." "Great literature [is] often truer to the Bible and closer to Biblical realism than many a 'devotional' book so called." The "devotional value" of a given book, he points out, lies in its interpretation, and thus much depends on the reader of the text, not just the text itself. This said, and admitting the imperfection of his scheme, he then goes on to lay out three main "watersheds" of devotional literature (certainly not comprehensive nor the only divisions one could make). The first, a very broad one, he calls the "pagan" watershed. He related this to a sort of vague sense of "spirituality" which he saw as becoming increasingly visible among the

35. Ibid., 8.

"intellectual elite" and in institutions of higher learning (even some fifty or sixty years ago). This broad category ranges from Plato and the ancient Greeks, to the European Romanticism of authors like Novalis and Wordsworth, to James Joyce, Rilke and D. H. Lawrence. He does not look down on such literature, for he feels it can open the way for many persons to search more deeply, just as Augustine's reading of the Neoplatonists was an important stage in Augustine's own spiritual search.

A second "watershed" is what he calls the "Roman Catholic Watershed." Cailliet feels the greatest works in this tradition are those that pre-date the Reformation and that Protestant Christians, in a sense, share with Roman Catholics as a part of their heritage. Augustine's *Confessions*, Dante's *Divine Comedy*, Tauler's *Sermons*, the *Theologia Germanica*, and the *Imitation of Christ* are all examples. The *Imitation*, he feels is especially valuable ("I read it once a year"), though he also admits that he reads the book not only for the inspiration it can provide, but with a critical eye as well, and is not altogether happy with certain passages and tendencies he finds in it.

The last lecture in the series is given over to "The Reformed Tradition of Holiness." By "Reformed" he means "Protestant" in general, and he begins his talk with an informal "Introduction" in which he shares how much the devotional writings of the Salvation Army have meant to him over the years. Of this literature he singles out in particular the writings of Samuel L. Brengle on holiness. He had received a copy of a biography of Brengle when speaking before a group of Salvation Army cadets in San Francisco many years before and was inspired by the way Brengle had actually lived out his faith (another obedient Christian Centurion?).

Having completed this introduction, he moves on to his main point, that for Protestant Christians the Bible itself is the great book of devotional literature and sometimes, he felt, too often neglected by those who read devotional literature regularly. Devotional treatises composed by saintly Christians in the past or biographies written about them sometimes seem to present an almost impossible level of holiness, he points out. "Therefore we get the wrong impression that saints of other days were made of nobler clay than other mortals and we groan in our spirits." The Bible presents us with more wholesome and honest records. "David was simply a sinner saved by grace . . . Peter denied his Lord . . . Paul was held in contempt for his poor speech . . . If God used them mightily so he can use us mightily." This, he feels, is "the best devotional use of the Bible . . . Let us not look for rapture or some romantic or mystical pleasure seeking adventure in the higher realm. Let us get our bearing in a God-controlled world."³⁶

Cailliet then turns to the second major part of his talk on the "Reformed Watershed," an exploration of John Bunyan's *Pilgrim's Progress*, which he notes "starts from the Book." He had read it through many times, and continued to find great insight in it with each reading. "What impresses me more and more about *Pilgrim's Progress* is that the frailties, struggles, failures, [and] defeats of the Pilgrim are recorded *after* the burden has fallen at the Cross. The fact is this always comes to me as a fresh revelation. And even as the mature and seasoned Pilgrim crosses the River in full view of Zion he falters. By that time he has attained unto human holiness, but to the end he must be reminded of his entire dependence upon the Lord of the Hill."³⁷

Cailliet also returns at this point in the lecture to the notion of "Centurion faith." His notes read: "The essential feature of Bible faith brought out in Bunyan's great classic is that of the Centurion, perfect commitment and obedience. 'Not my will but Thy will.' The mastery of self, realized by the surrender of self to the Master." There is "no mysticism, no devotion*s* [with the plural "s" actually underlined twice in his notes] in Bunyan's *Pilgrim's Progress* but a *walk* on the *way*, the narrow way cast up by the Patriarchs, Prophets, Christ, and His Apostles, and as straight as a rule can make it. That is the way we must go—and to go along that way from the City of Destruction to Jerusalem the Golden is our whole conversation and practice and 'devotional' life."³⁸

THE ACTUALIZATION OF THE REALITY OF THE COMMUNION OF SAINTS

While Cailliet placed great value on the importance of silence and solitude in the spiritual life, he did not want to be misunderstood on this point. "What I am advocating is a 'spirit of solitude,' not isolation. One can truly have the spirit of solitude on Fifth Avenue in the midst of a crowd." But besides this, Cailliet eventually finds that association with

36. For Cailliet's notes on the "pagan" and "Roman Catholic" watersheds, see ibid., 19–28.
37. Ibid., 34–35.
38. Ibid.

others on the Christian path was particularly important and what he calls "the actualization of the reality of the communion of saints."[39] He admits that "as one who had been called to Christian discipleship through the Word," it had taken him awhile to accept full membership in the church, the "Body of Christ." He had had some misgivings about the institutional church as he had seen it from the outside; he also felt that the institutional church had not "pressed the invitation in such ways as to effectively speak to my condition." Cailliet further recognized that it took time to satisfy his "impenitent French logic," and convince him that "authentic Church membership was essential" to his Christian profession. Finally, he says, "it became clear to me that there was no such thing as a Christian in isolation under God's high heaven."[40]

He felt that too often Christians restricted their idea of "church" to a building used for public worship and the programs conducted there. Where was the church that understood its mission to go into all the world and make disciples, carrying the love of God to those who needed to hear the message of the Gospel? Where was that community of "dedicated people, seeking others wherever they may be found"? His idea of what the church should be was grounded in his reading of the New Testament. "There is in the Christian tradition no known reference to a church building before the second century. The first-century gatherings of Christians were actually held in the private houses of those concerned, as may be seen in Romans 16:5, 1 Corinthians 16:19, Colossians 4:15, and Philemon 2."[41] He urged his students to think creatively about their ministry, to consider whether they might be called to some specialized ministry that would reach out beyond the standard parish program and take up a ministry that sought out persons in their own environments—perhaps an industrial mission, or a rural calling, or in the media, or as a chaplain to students in universities, colleges and schools, or in the field of missions overseas.[42]

---

39. "The Christian Pattern of Life," 47, Emile Cailliet Collection, Special Collections, Princeton Theological Seminary Library, Box 3, File 53-A.

40. Incomplete typescript, 91–92, Emile Cailliet Collection, Special Collections, Princeton Theological Seminary Library, Box 5, File 85.

41. Cailliet, *Young Life*, 12.

42. "Christian Pattern of Life," 82–97, Emile Cailliet Collection, Special Collections, Princeton Theological Seminary Library, Box 3, File 53-A.

Throughout his life he sought out those who were embodying Christian love by reaching out to those outside the established Christian community. Particularly meaningful to him was the lifestyle he saw embodied in the Salvation Army. His first acquaintance with that movement was in France:

> Where would Jesus be? The question came to my lips some thirty odd years ago in France. Two lassies had just passed by on a bicycle. They were dressed in a strange uniform, the Salvation Army uniform. I had never seen it before. So I looked on. But the two lassies had already alighted and were smilingly helping someone along the road . . . Where would Jesus be, but with them? Nothing formal about it. Galilee all over again, as through some sudden shift of scene, except that there had been no bicycles in those days . . .
>
> Later I saw their 'post'. Jesus' abode must have been something like that, insignificantly small, and yet giving the impression that it was the threshold to Heaven. Christianity is nothing more complicated than this—Heaven breaking in on earth, a luminous transparency suddenly disclosed in the most commonplace of all human situations . . .
>
> Sometime after I met the two lassies, I went to a mass-meeting of the Armée du Salut in a small city of the Huguenot country, in the Cévennes. The French Commissioner Albin Peyron was there with some of the best leaders of the Army. They had what many of the churches seemed to have lost, that unique blend of simplicity and depth which characterized the proclamation of Jesus in Galilee . . .
>
> Reader, my friend, have you lost the Christ? Then acquaint yourself with the Salvation Army post nearest you. You may find him elsewhere, I know, but you are sure to find Him there.[43]

"Wherever I have gone," he writes, "whether in Europe, in Africa, or in America, the Salvation Army has remained the Army I love . . . It was one of my greatest joys, upon arriving in the United States, to find the Army so active in this land."[44] In California he served on its Advisory Board, and at the time of his retirement from Princeton Seminary he wrote to a Salvation Army Brigadier of long acquaintance about possibly

---

43. Emile Cailliet, "Where Would Jesus Be?" Emile Cailliet Collection, Special Collections, Princeton Theological Seminary Library, Box 8, File 186.

44. Ibid., 4.

serving with the Army in some capacity or at least on some Advisory Board again.[45]

It is not with the Salvation Army, however, that Cailliet found a calling that occupied much of his time in the immediate post-retirement years, but with another group that was experimenting with ways to reach out with the Gospel to persons outside the bounds of institutional Christianity. Having always had a concern for young people and having spent all of his adult life in the field of education, Cailliet became interested in the activities of the Young Life workers as they sought to go to where young people not connected to churches were and befriend them "on the athletic field, in the corner drugstore, at the high-school play."

> My own interest in Young Life was awakened by the fact that here was a company of persons who, instead of lamenting the plight of our teen-agers, were doing something about it. It may also be that a man in his late sixties experiences increasingly that mysterious affinity between the old and the young which has found such wonderful expression in Victor Hugo's *The Art of Being a Grandfather*. Possibly, too, having as a college professor freely indulged in the writing of philosophical treatises, I have felt a certain debt to my fellow man, an obligation to do something practical when the chance offered.[46]

In speaking of his time as a professor at the University of Pennsylvania, he once told his seminary classes that the "most blessed among my experiences as a teacher have been those of personal counseling." He decided that in order to win the respect of his students as a counselor, he would try "to be the best kind of professor possible and to show this by grading the papers more personally and carefully than many of the other professors and to prepare my lectures with the greatest possible care." And then, he felt, he would have established the basis to reach out in friendship.[47] In his book *Young Life*, Cailliet sought to show the value of the kind of "personal friendship evangelism" that characterized the Young Life style at its best, to interpret the movement to a wider audience, and also help idealistic Young Life staffers become more realistic about the challenges

---

45. Paul E. Bodine to Emile Cailliet, April 11, 1960, Emile Cailliet Collection, Special Collections, Princeton Theological Seminary Library, Box 1, File 5.

46. Cailliet, *Young Life*, 4.

47. "Christian Pattern of Life," 96, Emile Cailliet Collection, Special Collections, Princeton Theological Seminary Library, Box 3, File 53-A.

of their work, with sections like "Patience and Prayer," and attention to the mistakes, difficulties and roadblocks they were likely to run up against. The church was at its living and most vital, he felt, when it sought, despite difficulty and temptation, to live out its centurion life of faith and make actual the communion of saints which it proclaimed.

"In the Book of Acts," Cailliet wrote, "there is not a single event later acknowledged to be decisive that is presented as happening in a purely incidental way. Rather, every such event, especially in the life of the Apostle Paul, is seen in a setting of obedience; that is, of determination on the part of those concerned to do the Lord's will. According to John, further guidance is dependent on sustained obedience (John 3:21). Only he who 'does the truth'—a pungent Hebrew phrase—is said to come to the light."[48] Cailliet spoke of the church as "the 'beloved community' now gathering about the Lord Jesus Christ for mutual understanding and strength, in love,"[49] and he saw groups like the Salvation Army and Young Life as vital to the health of the whole church. They were, in his mind, strong examples of what it might mean to be obedient to Christ's command to go into all the world and make disciples, seeking to reach out with the Gospel in practical ways to those outside the institutional church.

TWO PRAYERS

Emile Cailliet has left us no book of prayers, such as that produced by Lancelot Andrewes or John Baillie. For those wishing to re-acquaint themselves with Cailliet (or become acquainted with him for the first time) the short book *Journey into Light* may serve well. It tells a few of his most personal stories and serves as a record of those thoughts to which he had given the most consideration over the years, including his thoughts on living a life in the Presence of God. There are, however, among his papers a very few prayers, which he took the trouble to write out. It seems fitting to close this piece on Cailliet: The Believer with two of them. Here is the first. The reader will note the echoes of John Bunyan's *Pilgrim's Progress*, which Cailliet found so helpful as a map of the various possible states we might find ourselves on our spiritual journeys.

---

48. Cailliet, *Young Life*, 20–21.
49. Ibid., 118–19.

> Jehovah, Thou Living Lord of the Covenant, Eternal Lord of Life in whom a Pilgrim of good will beginning from within doeth authentic Truth, grant me to ascertain ever more clearly thy guidance, as evidenced through the long range pattern of days gone by. Enable me in thy grace to abide at the very core of my being where my Christ-redeemed life springs out of thee, and the secret of my identity remains hidden in thy merciful love. Grant that I may trust in thee alone, and be careful for no thing, as no man by taking thought can add one whit to his stature. O thou Lord of the Hill, vouchsafe that I may thus live in the constant awareness of thy might within me in the setting of the Delectable Country, even as the Hobgoblins, Satyrs, and Dragons of the Pit would frighten me. God of our Lord Jesus Christ, preserve me from a false humility of inferiority speaking before men, and grant that my humility be like that of Jesus, the humility of a Son, humility before thee, Almighty God in whom I live, and move, and have my being. May I shun meddling, aggressiveness, and all forms of antagonism, and absorb what happens to me—accepting it as a contribution to the long view I take of my life under thee. Grant that I may deepen rather than fret, in the realization that all the good I may do or say, is but thy utterance through my infirmity. Vouchsafe that I never indulge at the close of action in any vain brooding, whether of self-congratulation or self-despair, but merely forget the things that are behind, the moment they have come to pass, leaving them with thee to overrule or to bless. And so bear me on as I learn to sing in the darkness of this world the song of thy redeeming love—until on thy kind arms I fall. In the name of our Lord Jesus Christ. Amen.[50]

And the second closing piece returns us once again to the theme of the Christian Centurion. It is a record of the final words he spoke as part of an evening talk on "Life and Prayer" which he gave at Trinity Episcopal Church in Princeton on January 7, 1948:

> It may be said that I did not put the question the right way when I asked, "Why did you come tonight?" I should have asked "Why did *you* come tonight?" And it is *you*, and *you*, and *you* for whom I am now going to answer the question:
> "O Lord, our Living God, I came out tonight to be enrolled as thy Centurion, as the Lord's free man under thy authority. What wouldst thou have me do? As I wake up every morning give me the

---

50. Prayer, Emile Cailliet Collection, Special Collections, Princeton Theological Seminary Library, Box 5, File 85.

faculty to read thy will for my life and thy grace for obedience in love. Let my Prayer be my Life, O Living Lord. Let my Life be my Prayer."
"Lord, I give Thee All."[51]

---

51. "Life and Prayer," 7, Emile Cailliet Collection, Special Collections, Princeton Theological Seminary Library, Box 5, File 85.

3

The Teacher

The Princeton Years

THIS CHAPTER WILL CONSIDER several topics in evaluating Emile Cailliet as a teacher: his decision to teach at Princeton Seminary, initial impressions, the influence of his prayers in the classroom, his pedagogy, the scope of his teaching, courses he taught, his qualities as a teacher, his mentoring of students, connections with students, proposed curriculum revisions, and his overall impact.

DECISION TO COME TO PRINCETON

Upon being invited to join the seminary faculty, Dr. Cailliet had some reservations because he was a layman. As he put it in a letter he wrote: "As you may know, I am not an ordained man. The reason I was called to the Princeton seminary campus was essentially that they seem to need some insights into the secular world as observed from the wider college and university campuses in our day. I have spent most of my career on such secular campuses, especially at the University of Pennsylvania."[1]

One of Cailliet's daughters made it clear that his reservations were short lived. She said: "Dr. Cailliet, who was French and well-educated, decided to teach at a theological seminary because he really had been yearning to reach out to young people and lead them toward service to their fellow human beings. A longtime friend, John H. Mackay, then president

---

1. Emile Cailliet to Reverend Rudolph Herden. Emile Cailliet Collection, Special Collections, Princetlon Theological Seminary Library.

of Princeton Theological Seminary, telephoned him one day to say that a teaching opening had developed and Dr. Cailliet would be welcomed to fill his place in the very near future. And so Dr. Cailliet was ready to accept President Mackay's, offer."[2] His daughter went on to say that her father enthusiastically accepted the challenge. Having taught ministers and laymen for several years in summer seminars, he did not find it particularly difficult to teach future pastors. As she put it, "he relished the idea."[3]

INITIAL IMPRESSIONS OF STUDENTS

In Cailliet's introductory required Christian Philosophy course, in Stuart Hall at Princeton Seminary, the seats were nearly filled, and there was an intense energy present. This large, silver-haired man with a heavy brow and thick spectacles, who looked to be in his late fifties, entered the lecture hall. He walked to the front of the class and began. He had a distinctive French accent, and a rather stern demeanor. He seemed larger than life. As a student noted, "His coke bottle eyeglasses supplanted by his white hair glowed in winter morning sunlight, but we forgot all this when he began to talk."[4]

Certainly Cailliet's physical appearance reinforced his dynamic personality. "With his great shock of silver hair, his massive brow, the thick lenses of the glasses through which his penetrating eyes shone, Emile Cailliet was always a dramatic presence. As he stood in our school pulpit for the first time, after introducing his text, he looked over his audience and said, in his unmistakable French accent: 'I know why some of you are smiling; you think I sound like Charles Boyer.'"[5] Almost every student of Emile Cailliet commented on his commanding physical presence. "Seeing him in person I was reminded of the Labor Union leader, John L. Lewis, in stature and marvelous head of hair."[6] Others commented on his imposing figure, that he was "a 'bear' of a man with bushy eyebrows and an accent."[7] There was no doubt that he filled any room that he entered.

2. DB, interview with Bartollas, 2009.
3. Ibid.
4. HC, letter to Bartollas, May 12, 2009.
5. Gaebelein, "Friendship an Election of God," 57.
6. Oman, interview with Evans.
7. DG, letter to Evans and Bartollas.

The combination of Cailliet's personality and physical charisma was intimidating to students, but also inspired their respect. One former seminarian recalls: "I do remember that I was in awe of him. I never heard someone who showed such a passion in his lectures. His long white hair seemed to be in constant motion as he passionately pleaded that we earthlings would be with him to soar into the great heights and depths of Christian Philosophy. I felt he had a huge mind and a wonderful soul. His French accent only made me sit up and take more notice and try not to miss a word of anything he said."[8]

MAN OF PRAYER

Emile Cailliet always began class with prayer, and his prayers had quite an impression on his students. One pastor reported that "he taught me the seriousness of prayer. As you know, he prayed before every lecture—such simplicity, humility, thoughtfulness, and urgency." He went on: "One day I remember so well. It has been over 50 years since I sat under him, but it is still very vivid in my memory. He bowed his head and prayed, 'Lord, we love you, amen.' The next day, the same, 'Lord, we love you.' The third day he prayed, 'Lord, you know we love you.' We had no idea where he was going but on the fourth day, he prayed: 'What is that you are saying to us? What? Feed my sheep'—God help us."[9] Many of the students realized that he was making a reference to John 21 and it touched them deeply.

Another alumnus talked about the spirituality Cailiet conveyed: "I remember his prayers. Beginning each class with prayer was not an empty ritual for him. We were truly drawn into the presence of God by those prayers. And they always began, 'Our Living Lord.' There was a truly mystical dimension to this person, and we were drawn into the situation."[10] The fact that Cailliet opened class with praying to the Living Lord was noted by other students as well.

Another former student also commented on Cailliet's prayers in class: ". . . on the next day after the coordination of Pope John XXIII, I was sitting in the front row of a large lecture hall to the left of the teaching podium. Dr. Cailliet [had] often been over behind the podium when he

---

8. GH, email to Bartollas.
9. DM, letter to Bartollas, May 16, 2009.
10. TM, email to Bartollas, June 10, 2009.

prayed but for some reason I observed him and I could see his face." As he remembered: "His words went something like this: 'Our living Lord, when I saw your representative last night on TV I know how you felt when he was wearing a triple tiered crepe crown of the papacy.' At that point in the prayer, his face filled with tears gushing down his cheeks, and he bent lower and violently shook his face sending the water flying everywhere. In that instance, I knew I was in the presence of a man of God."[11]

Through his prayers, Cailliet's students saw a man of deep Christian faith. Most seminarians took his Christian Philosophy course early in their seminary career, usually the first quarter, and found it to be a comfort, beyond its rigor. His prayers, no doubt, opened students to responses that might not have been possible had they not perceived him as a man of belief.

PEDAGOGY

Cailliet was an outstanding teacher, as cited in one way or another by the vast majority of his former students. Authors Evans and Bartollas sent a number of interview questions to Cailliet's students from 1950 to 1957 and received more than sixty responses. Many of his students still have vivid recollections from their experiences with him from over fifty years ago. One former student emailed, "Not a month goes by that I don't think of Cailliet. [I] can't escape his influence."[12]

Dr. Cailliet was a very complex human being, which was reflected in his teaching and his demeanor. In many respects, he could be extremely sensitive. He knew what it felt like to be hurt; one person revealed that years before he came to Princeton, a college student had rebuked him and that the event had deeply affected him, and he carried that hurt for a long time. This experience, as well as others, made him more sensitive. Accordingly, he could show incredible kindness. He gave one student a book for her reading pleasure. He went out of his way on countless occasions to do such acts of kindness. He encouraged students who were having trouble with his courses to come see him and even invited students to his home.

---

11. TB, letter to Bartollas, July 30, 2009.
12. BB, email to Bartollas, May 14, 2009.

On the other hand, he could be formidable and humorless.[13] He did not tolerate tardiness and did not welcome interactions with students, apart from time allocated for questions about course material. He seemed set apart, as if he were preaching from a high pulpit found in a European church. He blew in like the wind, lectured without notes, was always finished just as the bell rang, and left without conversation. He was the professor and, in the minds of some, his students were just lowly seminarians sitting at the feet of a great man. It was this side of Cailliet that was intimidating. As a disciplinarian and a no-nonsense type of professor, it is not surprising that some even feared him. One student shared that he left Princeton Seminary after one year because of Cailliet. Another told of his intolerance for being late to class:

> This is a memory from class that I can still picture as vividly as if it happened yesterday. One day one of the students (I don't recall who it was) was late to class, and came in after Dr. Cailliet had already begun. He stopped his lecture—I think maybe even in mid-sentence—and glared at the student all the way while the student came around the side aisle of the lecture hall and found a seat. Then he said, in the French accent you would know well, and I still remember, but can't describe in writing, "This will not happen again." And it didn't. I think many of the students were terrified of him.[14]

Dr. Cailliet's relationship with his students was no doubt affected by the fact that he was schooled in the European tradition of maintaining a gulf between students and professors. He cared deeply for his students, but generational and national differences often confused him. He did not understand that students wanted two-way conversations, so he did not invite their thoughts.

Remembering Cailliet as a professor through the eyes of his students reflects the wide range of his pedagogy. Some experienced immediate rapport and understood the richness of his thought. For them, Cailliet's classes and lectures were a delight, and represented the most stimulating and fulfilling educational experience of their lives. Others learned through fear because they did not want to fail the class, disappoint him, or misunderstand his insights and interpretations; these students were largely aware that Cailliet's classes would eventually lead to new insights.

13. TG, interview with Evans.
14. GH, email to Bartollas, May 23, 2009.

Others were intimidated and taken aback by this Frenchman, who seemed larger than life, and it affected their performance in the course.

One thing that became clear through interviews and research is that the students who knew Cailliet best, who worked closely as a teaching fellow or junior colleague, had a greater appreciation for his basic kindheartedness and erudition. All agree that his style was that of a consummate European scholar who had command of a vast array of material.

Cailliet was very helpful in illuminating the deep truths of the Christian faith in new ways as he was thoroughly versed in philosophy, yet had a deep, personal Christian faith which emphasized the place of special revelation. He greatly impacted most of his students. Especially noteworthy is that not only pastors remember him, but also those students who went on to become movie producers, scientists, sociologists, and businessmen. Several attributed Cailliet's influence in their becoming professors of philosophy. One student wrote:

> I was a first-year student at the seminary in 1953–54 when I had Dr. Cailliet's course of philosophy and Christianity. It was an extremely interesting course and helped to reinforce my growing interest in philosophy and, especially at that time, the relations of Western philosophy to Christianity. I was greatly impressed with the fact that Dr. Cailliet had two earned doctorates! I later became a professor of philosophy at Colorado State University where I taught for thirty-six years. Dr. Cailliet's class was no doubt an important factor in this later choice of careers.[15]

Another student, later a professor himself, noted: "He was very well-organized in his lectures ... I had been a philosophy major in college, and thought that he made balanced and quite credible presentations of major thinkers."[16]

Cailliet had a strong influence on many people destined for the parish. There were no practical theological courses in "pastoral care" at the time, apart from one on the Cure of Souls by John Bonnell, and Cailliet seems to have anticipated this need and dealt with it in a responsible manner. In contrast, he also wrote for those with serious intellectual difficulties with Christianity and was able to connect with students who came from more evangelical backgrounds, who had struggled with the

---

15. DS, email to Bartollas, December 4, 2009.
16. AS, email to Bartollas, June 10, 2009.

intellectual examination of the Bible and theology. Cailliet was able to communicate with those from all sides of the theological divide.

Finally, Cailliet was unquestionably a taskmaster in the classroom. Before Princeton he had taught at the University of Pennsylvania, Wesleyan University in Connecticut, and Scripps College in California, and, as a result, he felt he was familiar with American students and education in this nation. He made it very clear that he was in total control in the classroom and did not expect or accept challenges to his authority. He had very high expectations from his students, which came through in his lectures, lengthy reading assignments, and the examinations he gave in his classes. To do well in Dr. Cailliet's courses, it was necessary to have a real mastery of the material.

SCOPE OF TEACHING

Before coming to Princeton, Dr. Cailliet had taught courses during the Seminary's continuing education summer series, the Princeton Institute of Theology. During his twelve years at Princeton, he continued teaching a number of summers in the series. In a letter Dr. Cailliet received on July 30, 1957, shortly after the class was over, one participant wrote:

> Sitting in on your classes on Pascal this year at the Institute was certainly one of the highest privileges my life has afforded. I did, indeed, find [that] the naked soul of Pascal brushed my own naked soul, and the experience was deeply spiritual and unforgettable. I pray that it will be the will of God that someday his presence will shine through me with some of the magnetic humility, relatedness, and dedication that mark your very being. Thank you, Dr. Cailliet, for your courage to be as of God, and for the immeasurable witnessing power of that courage.[17]

Cailliet also gave visiting lectures at other colleges and universities, as well as churches and schools, during his Princeton years. One individual wrote in a letter that he had heard Cailliet speak when he was a student at the Stony Brook School (New York) when he was fifteen years of age. This individual, who later graduated from Princeton Seminary, concluded that Cailliet was "a genuine saint and affected the lives of everyone." He

---

17. Letter from TB, July 30, 1957.

added: "Princeton Seminary needed him; Princeton University would have shown him far greater appreciation."[18]

During his time at Princeton, Dr. Cailliet taught six different courses, two each semester. Introduction to Christian Philosophy, a required course for juniors (first year students), was taught usually during their first quarter. His course, Great Books in the Light of Christianity, was a required course for MRE (Master of Religious Education) candidates during their second year and was an elective course for BD (Bachelor of Divinity) students. Cailliet's other four courses were all electives: The Philosophy of Science, The Making of the Modern Religious Mind, The Christian Pattern of Life, and Pascal. The catalogue's description of these courses can be found in the Appendix.

Dr. Cailliet did not use lecture notes but, fortunately, there are what appears to be nearly verbatim copies of most of his lectures prepared by students in the archives. Reading these notes leaves one with several impressions. First, it is clear, from his opening prayer and then throughout the address, that Cailliet designed these lectures for men and women going into the Gospel ministry or those who would be working in Christian Education. The lectures are pastoral and directed toward those who have a high calling in the ministry. Second, Cailliet was a scholar of the first rank. For those who have spent a career in teaching in universities or seminaries, as the authors have, we marvel at the countless demonstrations of this scholarship. Third, it is evident that beyond the challenging basis of Cailliet's ideas, he continually reminded his listeners that the church needed erudite and intellectual minds. Finally, the rigor of his teaching was directed to MRE candidates—who had a three year program at the time—as much as to BD students.

Also, before Cailliet came to Princeton in 1947, John Mackay, president of Princeton Seminary, wrote to him: "The University [Princeton University] has expressed very real interest in having you give a course each semester, in the event that you came to the Seminary. I have discussed the matter with Professor George Thomas, the head of the Department of Religion, and with Dr. Robert Scoon, the head of the Department of Philosophy, and, also, with the President of the University."[19] For some

---

18. Letter from BB, July 15, 2009.
19. Mackay to Emile Cailliet, February 12, 1947. Emile Cailliet Collection, Special Collections, Princeton Theological Seminary Library.

reason this never took place.[20] However, Cailliet did give several lectures at the University during his twelve years at Princeton Seminary.[21]

Faculty of Princeton Theological Seminary, 1958; Cailliet stands front row, third from right.

COURSES TAUGHT AT PRINCETON

Emile Cailliet was an artist in the classroom. His lectures were well researched, with up-to-date reviews of the literature, crafted in what he felt would be persuasive to his audience, and always geared toward men and women preparing for the gospel ministry or Christian education in local churches. Cailliet was an imposing figure in the classroom, as he memorized his lectures and concluded just as the bell rang, but it was the content of these lectures that would have a life-long impact on his hearers. In re-reading his lecture notes, one realizes how fortunate we were to be his students, receiving his knowledge, his insights, and his commitment to the Christian faith.

Christian Philosophy

A large portion of the material in Cailliet's 1953 book, *Christian Approach to Culture*,[22] was contained in the lectures for his Christian Philosophy class. Cailliet's review of Greek philosophy was masterful, especially his material on Socrates and the comparison between Heraclitus and

---

20. Letter from the Princeton University Library, February 21, 2011. Emile Cailliet Collection, Special Collections, Princeton Theological Seminary Library.

21. Ibid.

22. Cailliet, *Christian Approach to Culture*.

Parmenides. His later materials on Thomas Aquinas, William of Ockham, Descartes, Kant (he often referred to the long shadow of Kant from which the authors applied to Cailliet in the book title), and, of course, Pascal, were outstanding.

Christian Pattern of Life

This course had profound and life-long impact on its students. Cailliet saw it as a type of "retreat." Beginning with an extensive devotional biography, Cailliet expected students to read widely and to examine their own life situations. He said in the syllabus of the course:

> It will be up to you to discover it in the material of the course, through readings, discussion and prayerful appraisal what speaks to your condition. Keeping faith with our aim last defined, you will be expected to work out a term paper in which the general pattern outlined in this course will become a *personal* pattern. The title of this paper will be accordingly: *The Pattern of My Own Christian Life and Ministry*. This "blue-print" will naturally take into consideration the professional aspects of your call *as far as you can see them at this point*.[23]

In the first lecture, Cailliet advised that this term paper was not so much a personal confession as much as an objective evaluation. He felt that students needed to know where they stood intellectually, spiritually, physically, and professionally. He added that it was of the highest importance to know where they were going.[24]

The Making of the Modern Religious Mind

Cailliet begins this course by saying: "whenever we are about to do anything, we should always pause to ask ourselves—Why should I do this?"[25] He then suggested that the justification of the course is that it is "mostly devoted to an inquiry into the validity of Christian metaphysics."[26]

---

23. Quoted from the syllabus for the course. Emile Cailliet Collection, Special Collections, Princeton Theological Seminary Library.

24. Statement made during a lecture and contained in the notes of his lectures. Emile Cailliet Collection, Special Collections, Princeton Theological Seminary Library.

25. Quoted from a lecture and contained in the notes of this lecture. Emile Cailliet Collection, Special Collections, Princeton Theological Seminary Library.

26. Ibid.

This course—demonstrating Cailliet's wide breadth of knowledge—included lectures titled Christian Metaphysics, Modern Ideologies in the Making, The Long Shadow of Kant, If Modern Liberalism is Not Christianity, then What Is It?, A Critique of Dialectical Existentialism, and The Pilgrims' Apprehension of Reality.[27]

Cultural Anthropology

This course was invaluable for those going into the mission field. Cailliet—who had done field work in Madagascar and had a PhD in anthropology—brought much to the classroom. One of the central questions he raised was: Does the ancient man think as we do? He examined the structure of the primitive mind—prelogical, mystical, and laws of participation. He also reviewed the major fields of anthropology.

Philosophy of Science

One of the values of this course, according to Cailliet, was that it was important for the man of God to be in conversation with the man of science. His general perspective in the course was to move from Aristotle, to the Newtonian paradigm or classical physics, to Einstein and to Planck, Schrödinger, and other Quantum thinkers. What is really impressive is that Cailliet, long before it was realized by most academics, acknowledged the bankruptcy of the Newtonian paradigm and had moved beyond Einstein to what is known today as the Quantum view of the world.

QUALITY OF TEACHING

Ultimately, a teacher is evaluated by the value and quality of his or her instruction, and it was in this matter that Cailliet received the most favorable comments. Dr. Cailliet's course in Christian philosophy was for many students the most interesting course and the best course they had at Princeton. He began the first class by saying, "The philosophy of Western society has represented the extension of Parmenides, a philosophy of being. In this course, we will be focusing on Heraclitus, a philosopher who advocated change and becoming. We will examine what Western history

27. Ibid.

and philosophy might have been if we would have followed Heraclitus rather than Parmenides."[28]

Professor Cailliet continued throughout the quarter redesigning what Western society would have been if we would have believed in a world of perpetual change and becoming. It was easy to remain spellbound throughout the course and to be intrigued by his process view that everything was in a state of emergence. The students would discuss the content of lectures for hours after class. The more they thought about it, the more it seemed that his viewpoint was valid and real.

Now, the way in which Cailliet electrified classes at Princeton during the first quarter course in Christian Philosophy is what took place repeatedly in other teaching contexts as well. Whether it was a university or seminary class, a congregation on a Sunday morning, the students at a college lecture series, a group of Young Life workers, or some other group, Cailliet's commanding presence and presentation excited his audiences. Certainly, a major part of this response was the novel nature of his ideas.

Letters poured in from students, wishing to express their remembrances of Cailliet. One former student indicated that "he seemed like a prophet that was way ahead of his time, but he was showing me the path."[29] He went on to say that one of his significant classes with Dr. Cailliet was when his teacher said that the greatest struggle in the ministry would be between the Hebrew and the Greek. "That insight," the interviewee said, "was a keynote experience with me."[30] He loved Hebrew and after his seminary education went on to become a professor at Columbia Seminary. Part of what he appreciated was that Cailliet's "position or approach was such that he was an enlightened prophet on scripture, politics, and the world. His approach was not narrow or exclusive. He had the ability to craft good questions."[31]

Several noted how much they appreciated what they had learned of Christian philosophy from Cailliet. As one student expressed it, "I found Dr. Cailliet to have an amazing depth of the history of philosophy and to present this information with amazing clarity for the complexity of the subject."[32] Another noted, "Without a doubt I feel that his teaching

---

28. Bartollas and Evans' notes from this lecture, September 1958.
29. MR, interviewed in September 15, 2009.
30. Ibid.
31. Ibid.
32. Letter from WJ, June 1, 2009.

prepared us to face the various philosophies and world views that were and continue to be abroad in our world with a Christian Philosophy."[33] He went on to say, "So, in a way it was a course in apologetics, and yet coming from Dr. Cailliet, it was not only apologetics in terms of intellectual arguments, but apologetics in terms of an overall witness of the Christian in a non-Christian world."[34]

Another student further contributed: "I found him more of the European old-school than most of the professors I had . . . "[I] always envisioned him at an elevated lectern. Nevertheless, he was an important teacher for me in that he communicated and embodied a Christian dialogue with philosophy that was not defined by dogma." He explained: "Dr. Cailliet spoke with an almost brotherly fondness of noted philosophers who had gone before."[35]

Cailliet's course in philosophy illuminated and stimulated the minds of his students. One former student tells what understanding of philosophy he took from Cailliet's course: "1) Everyone has a philosophy of some kind guiding their thought and it is much better to try to know what yours is than to let it remain unconscious. 2) Even theology is thought out within some philosophical context (hopefully a broad one). 3) When trying to understand the broadest issues of life and meaning, a good place to begin is with philosophy. It gives the most comprehensive perspective."[36] One day this same student asked: "Was Socrates a Christian?" The questioner went on to say: "Perhaps it was only the light reflecting off his glasses as he looked over them, but I recall his eyes almost glimmering as he replied, 'I don't know that he was a Christian, but I look forward to meeting him in heaven.' Calvin might have winced, but for me and others it was an answer that was liberating. Where there is truth and insight, there is God and we need not be embarrassed at acknowledging that."[37] Another wrote: "I was so moved in Professor Cailliet's lecture about Socrates during that fall, that I wrote a short poem which I gave to him and he gratefully acknowledged.

---

33. Emailed from DS, May 14, 2009.
34. Ibid.
35. Letter from BJ June 18, 2009.
36. Letter from WJ, June 1, 2009.
37. Ibid.

After reading Plato's *Apology*
Addressed to Socrates

Then did thy noble words meet waste
When Men of Athens came to jeer?
Was all washed free with hemlock's taste,
When Men of Athens gave no ear?
Rest gently now, most honored one,
Who glimpsed beyond your time
The fight you fought had but begun;
What you discerned was half divine.
Another did come after you,
Whose cause was like to yours.
Whosoever belies in Me,
Though he died, endures.
Thy words not waste, but as the stars
That guide men through their night;
Then set before the dawn appears
To bring the Brightest Light.[38]
[October 4, 1957]

Of Cailliet's class on "The Christian Pattern of Life," one student wrote: "His course . . . was a key factor in my spiritual growth. The writing of the paper for that class brought my past journey into view and furnished a pathway for future evaluation.[39] A second wrote to Dr. Cailliet and said: "Before closing, I would like to let you know how very helpful this course [The Christian Pattern of Life] has been to me in opening up to me the field of devotional literature, and bringing me closer to Christ. I appreciate very much the thought and prayer you have put into making these early morning sessions a vital experience in the lives of all your students."[40] Perhaps, a retired pastor aptly summarized the quality of his teaching when he said:

> For all his reading and synthesizing (and isolating) of philosophical currents, Cailliet taught from the places he knew: his experiences, his encounters, his vast reading that jibed with his experience. He wasn't a mystic, but sitting before him was a mystical experience in that he enabled me to make sense of Thomistic heavy-handedness

---

38. Letter from SBG, June 30, 2009.
39. Letter from BJ, May 14, 2009.
40. Letter sent to Dr. Cailliet from BA, May 25, 1951. Emile Cailliet Collection, Special Collections, Princeton Theological Seminary Library.

and Aristotelian considerations. He could get rhapsodic about Blaise Pascal. He spoke of Pascal's inventions and innovations. I had read Pascal as an undergraduate, but I learned Pascal from Cailliet. He was an old school teacher, you sat at his feet. Only years later did one come to value much of what he said—if you could remember it.[41]

MENTORING STUDENTS

A graduate student, who went on to receive a ThD, wrote: "He left an indelible mark upon my life. We met at least twice a week and discussed just about everything under the sun."[42] Cailliet, as several reported, went out of his way to help students. One former student reported that he had two required courses scheduled at the same time. As a result, he went to Dr. Cailliet who agreed that he would read his book, the course's main text, come to review sessions, and meet with him if he ever deemed necessary. He would be expected to take exams when they were given and to take them with other students. He added, "Professor Cailliet was very understanding of my dilemma. I followed the proscribed regimen and received an A for the course."[43] Another reported how he had had done poorly in the first exam. Dr. Cailliet invited him to come to his office to help him, which he put off for some time. When Cailliet would meet him on campus, he would question why he had not gone to see him. Finally, he complied and noted:

> He remembered every bad answer that I had [written]. I had studied the material and had become much more knowledgeable of the course. We became friendly and he was a great help in my struggle to learn rapidly a whole new area of thinking theologically. I went to his house a number of times. Once I had a great talk with Mrs. Cailliet where I asked about the brilliance of her husband. She explained that he had a total recall mind. He could scan page after page at a very rapid pace and his photographic mind could read and study during his sleep time, recalling everything.[44]

41. Letter from BB, May 12, 2009.
42. Letter from CM, October 27, 2009.
43. Letter from WD, May 19, 2009.
44. Email from DR, December 3, 2009.

CONNECTION WITH STUDENTS

Professor Cailliet connected with his students in several ways. First, he invited them to his home. One student told of how he would go over to Dr. Cailliet's house in the evening on a regular basis. Another former student remarked: "Dr. Cailliet was one of the few professors who regularly invited students into his home. He and his wife were most gracious hosts, and I recall having a very pleasant evening in their living room on Alexander Street."[45]

Second, students felt that Dr. Cailliet took a personal interest in them. A student who later spent his career teaching at Princeton Seminary added, "I was impressed by his knowledge of his students and their backgrounds. He must have spent hours studying our files. That alone showed how much he cared about us as individuals."[46]

Third, some students were impressed that Cailliet read each examination and term paper himself. One expressed it this way, "He was profoundly related to each student in his classes and took the teaching profession as a pastoral one."[47]

Fourth, former students told stories of personal contact with Cailliet outside the classroom. One student told how he, an amateur photographer, wanted to take a portrait of Dr. Cailliet, and he agreed to "sit" for the portrait—which the retired pastor still has. Another retired pastor tells that his eating club, Calvin-Warfield, was located next to the Cailliet's residence, and so they felt they had a special relationship with him. They had given his beloved dog a special name, Yippie-Yi-Yo-Ki-Yay, which was taken from the refrain of the 1940 Oklahoma cowboy song. When Yippie was hospitalized at the Lawrence Hospital for Animals, the eating club sent a greeting card. In response, Dr. Cailliet posted a note of thanks on our bulletin board, which expressed his warmth and humor.

> Greeting Card to Yippie
> Lawrence Hospital for Animals
> Province Line Road, Princeton, N.J.
>
> To the two-legged pals barking next door at 'chow' time.
>
> Dear two-legged neighbors:

---

45. Email from DA, August 3, 2009.
46. Ibid.
47. Ibid.

My tail has been wagging ever since your amulet found its way to my cage and reminded me of your smell. Yet that image of a dog you sent me did not smell as does a real dog. Let my bark warn you to beware of idols.

It is hard for me to understand the ways of my master. It has always been so. For instance, he would go and shut himself up in a big kennel and bark at you all instead of going out with me in the open, even on a bright day. A moon ago he made me up into that little rolling cage of his—an Austin he calls it—and brought me to this new master who pricks me with a big needle ever so often. Two-legged creatures have funny ways of having fun!

Yet I trust my master who orders for the best whatever comes to pass for me. I am a good Presbyterian dog. I merely bark to tell when I smell danger ahead, the way you bark on Sunday because you probably smell danger ahead for people too.

Yours in a common trust in the Master of all masters—and please tell the cook to keep a bone for me when I smell my way back to you.

With a big lick and a noisy bark,
As ever, Dip, alias Yippy

Dictated from my cage on the fifth moon, fifteenth constellation of the Dog.[48]

PROPOSED CURRICULUM REVISIONS

Dr. Cailliet strongly felt that the curriculum at Princeton Seminary needed revision. He suggested that the curriculum be organized around a new Biblical humanities program. Dr. Cailliet proposed that the Seminary create this program, which would constitute a course taught over a three year period for three hours a week. He suggested that the readings could come largely from the English Bible and from classics of the period.

IMPACT OF HIS TEACHING

The evaluations of Cailliet as a teacher were overwhelmingly laudatory. Perhaps, what would have been the feeling of many was summarized by

---

48. Email from GM, December 9, 2009.

one who said, "He met the true definition of 'scholar and gentleman.'"[49] Another student remarked: "It is good to have letters such as yours to remind me how very fortunate we were to have professors like Dr. Cailliet—and indeed there were giants on the faculty there in my time."[50] A third commented, "Dr. Cailliet was my favorite teacher during my years at Princeton Seminary."[51]

Another former student indicated that his impact was "from the quality of his faith, life, and service. They gave me security to be more open and listen to more voices."[52] Another responded, "I was particularly enthralled with Professor Cailliet. He had a kind of quiet majestic presence about him, and a wonderful French accent. I was so interested in the course that I still have his textbook, *The Christian Approach to Culture*, on my bookshelf."[53]

Dozens of students commented on his character, erudition, skill as a professor, and tolerance. "In my opinion, Dr. Emile Cailliet added heart and spirit to Princeton Theological Seminary when I was a student."[54] The evaluation of still another: "I cannot speak for others, but his impact on me stemmed mainly from the sense of unity that he brought to faith and previous studies in philosophy. He provided a thread of continuity between my undergraduate education and my theological formation."[55] A Puerto Rican student considered him an excellent professor who treated students without any discrimination. I was used to being treated "as trash" in the United States, but "I can sincerely state that Dr. Cailliet treated me with justice, and he graded my exams fairly."[56]

The content of Cailliet's lectures left an extraordinary impression on his students. One student shares his insights on Cailliet's overall impact:

> I think his impact on so many students had several grounds: the breadth of his knowledge and understanding of philosophy; his, by then, many years of trying to help students get a useful understanding of philosophy that would give them a context for their

49. Letter from MR, May 19, 2009.
50. Letter from GM, June 29, 2009.
51. Email from GA, December 9, 2009.
52. Email December from TJ, 10, 2009.
53. Letter from MR, June 30, 2009.
54. Ibid.
55. Letter from GA, June 18, 2009.
56. Letter from GH, May 13, 2009.

life and thinking; the ways he had developed (or reworked from others) ways to make philosophy a useful tool for his students in understanding their world, such as grouping historical trends; and (I assume that was his own since I have never heard of it from others) his pointing out the "ontological deviation" which I have always used as one of my tests in my own philosophical thinking. His "sausage machine" for understanding Kant was another helpful creative expression that I still remember.[57]

A telling and positive evaluation of Emile Cailliet as a teacher is found in the following statement: "I first met Dr. Cailliet in September 1958 when I began studies at PTS. From day one to the end of the year, I regarded him as the consummate professor, erudite beyond description entertaining by accident, with a presence that commanded respect and an old world demeanor that made him doubly authentic."[58] He went on to say that he had recently graduated from the College of William and Mary, where he had majored in philosophy and classical language. He saw in "Dr. Cailliet a kind of 'father' figure that I had relished in one of my classics professors. Both men were just 'larger than life.'"[59]

Other former students had this to say: "You can easily imagine what Dr. Cailliet did for me, a fellow Frenchman, a scholar highly conversant with a wide range of scientific knowledge, and a man who deeply loved his Lord." He goes on, "Obviously, without his knowing it, he set me free from fundamentalism to a new life in faith."[60]

"Dr. Cailliet looked his part. His hair seemed to stand up in a pattern of his own, as if a charge of electricity had just passed through him. His trousers and his jackets never seemed to be meant for each other. He was never seen in the Princeton uniform of tweeds and button-downs. He walked with a kind of trundling gait, his hands often clasped behind him, his head tilted up to the heavens. He was accused of walking into parked cars. Ah yes, every inch a professor, easy to make fun of and snicker about."[61] He adds, in his statement that was written shortly after Cailliet's death: "[He wasn't] all that easy to get along with. His opinions, his ideas, were precious to him, won at the expense of 'many hours alone within

---

57. Letter from GH, June 5, 2009.
58. Letter from TB, June 16, 2009.
59. Ibid.
60. Letter from TNB, June 16, 2009.
61. Jones, "Keeping the Faith," 1.

four walls,' as he put it, yet to hear him in class, to have an hour with him in private consultation, was like striking fire, the sparks flying off his mind in this direction in that direction and that. I wish I had pressed him more for such hours."[62]

Extending from Cailliet's impact on former students to impact on the Princeton faculty and community, a retired pastor made this contribution: "During the year after Dr. Cailliet retired, I was in the presence of a faculty member at Princeton Theological Seminary who commented on the impact Dr. Cailliet had on the PTS community. This faculty member said, 'Of all the professors I have ever known, Dr. Cailliet was the only one who was conversant on an authoritarian level with all of the academic disciplines taught at the school ... Every one of my colleagues could mention the latest developments, new authors, discoveries in their fields, but Dr. Cailliet had already became conversant with these breakthroughs and their impact.'"[63]

Despite the high praise given by many, not everyone liked him. Cailliet's grading policies met some criticism. One dissatisfied student told how her class had heard he was an easy grader, and she felt he made up for it in her class. She said that she did not do well, and she was not alone. She added, "I was left with a poor attitude toward philosophy."[64] Other students felt that Cailliet was closed to students' interpretation. One student a year or two ahead of another told him, "'Just remember, whatever Dr. Cailliet asks, write as much as you can remember him saying in the course. Your own ideas aren't really so important.' That may have been cynical and a gross over-simplification, but as a technique, it worked."[65] There were other responses that challenged this or that about his teaching style. One questioned: "I remember that after our first test in the introductory class Dr. Cailliet announced to all of us that the highest grade had been earned by an engineer, a graduate of the U.S. Military Academy at West Point. I'm still wondering about and questioning the motivation behind that gesture."[66]

62. Ibid.
63. Letter from BR, in May 2009.
64. Letter from TJ, June 18, 2009.
65. Ibid.
66. Letter from GA, May 12, 2009.

CONCLUSION

Emile Cailliet was an effective teacher for most of his students for the following reasons. First, he was in total command of his subject matter. There was no question in students' minds that he had mastered the materials he was teaching. Second, he had a passion and enthusiasm for what he taught. His passion and enthusiasm, as interviews in this chapter reflected, was contagious. Third, he was a man of faith, and this gave him more credibility with theological students. Fourth, he had high expectations, and this motivated most of his students. Some students, however, were intimidated by his standards and approach. Fifth, most students felt that they were having a first-rate learning experience, and some students evaluated Cailliet's classes as the best educational experience of their careers. Finally, students felt that what they were learning in his classroom had application to their ministries. This is, of course, is one of the highest compliments a student can make of a teacher.

Thus, beyond the occasional criticism, most of us who sat in his classroom believed that Emile Cailliet was one who had mastered the art of teaching and who had enormous impact on the lives of his students. He might have sometimes referred to Einstein as "the great one," but we held him as "the great one." So many of us believed that he was more than great, he was truly a Man of God. We were blessed to have been his students.

4

Christian Scholar
Evangelical Intellectual

For much of his teaching career, at the University of Pennsylvania, as well as at Scripps and Wesleyan, Cailliet was viewed by others in the academic world primarily as a scholar, especially of French literature and the humanities. Yet for Cailliet himself, the challenge was how to see himself as a *Christian* scholar. As he once put the question, "How can one at the same time be a Pilgrim [as in John Bunyan's classic] and a scholar in this modern age of ours?"[1] To this question he returns repeatedly in a number of his writings and speeches, not only in his various presentations of Pascal as the ideal model of how to be a Christian scholar or a Christian philosopher, but also in books like *The Life of the Mind*, *The Beginning of Wisdom*, and especially *The Christian Approach to Culture*, and in carefully worked out lectures like "The Path Out of This Wilderness,"[2] "Outlines of a Christian Positivism,"[3] "A Scholar of Good Will Gets a Hearing,"[4] and "The Human Quest for Truth."[5] One of his final treatments of this topic is to be found in the second part of *Journey into Light*. "Like the scientist," he writes, "yet in a different setting, the Christian scholar has to cope with mystery. His first step in this capacity is to realize that set in its proper context mystery does not imply utter darkness. It may rather be likened

---

1. Cailliet, "Christian Scholar," 35–36.
2. Cailliet, "Path Out of This Wilderness," 17–26.
3. Cailliet, "Outlines of a Christian Positivism," 28–37.
4. Cailliet, "Scholar of Good Will Gets a Hearing," 29–32.
5. Cailliet, "Human Quest for Truth" lecture, 12–15.

to a luminous focus which grows ever clearer and brighter as one dwells on it with ardor and fervor—two words, incidentally, which suggest a fire burning. Mystery is an invitation to pilgrimage, and such a pilgrimage any Christian life is bound to be."[6]

The true Christian scholar, Cailliet maintains, is the opposite of Kierkegaard's "Professor," a modern day Judas Iscariot who no longer sells his master for a paltry thirty pieces of silver, but "is a highly cultured man, calm and endowed with a shrewd understanding of life and profit." Rather than a quick lump-sum payment, "the Professor" is willing to take up religious writing and teaching as a profession, betraying his Lord by coming up with rather questionable but crowd-pleasing conjectures that lead to popularity in return for a regular income, suitable for supporting a wife and family over "a long and enjoyable life." Cailliet feels sorry for seminarians and ministers who come under the sway of such Christian teachers. "They may well preach polished sermons . . . it has become only too obvious that their heart is no longer in what they say."[7] When the fundamental bedrock of our own living faith is undermined, the springs of our prayer life dry up. The Christian scholar must keep that personal relationship to the Living God alive, and then let his or her intellect freely explore all the realms of knowledge to which it is drawn. While our understanding and formulation of our beliefs may grow and change over time, as befits a pilgrim making their way toward the light, the certitude of our faith supplies an anchor that will not fail us.

CAILLIET'S DEVELOPMENT AS A SCHOLAR

Emile Cailliet, the early scholar.

It is possible to place Cailliet's major scholarly publications in three broad classifications: first, those which focus on cultural anthropology, magic and symbolism; second, writings which focus on Blaise Pascal and on the relationship of Christian faith and culture; and third, a smaller

6. Cailliet, *Journey into Light*, 56–58.
7. Ibid., 56–58.

group of more personal writings, often, but not always, growing out of more popular lectures he gave at various times or out of a period of reflection (especially during his retirement years.) As was discussed before, Cailliet's education was broad and helped to shape him as a scholar. He completed his undergraduate studies at the College of Chalons, at the University of Paris, in 1913. After his service in the First World War and a period of school teaching, he received an appointment by the French government as a research fellow at the University of Basel in 1919. From 1920–1923 he pursued additional graduate studies at the University of Nancy, where he earned his Master's degree. He also had opportunity to participate in the conducting of psychological research under the French philosopher and pioneer of experimental psychology, Marcel Foucault (not to be confused with the later well-known historian of ideas Michel Foucault), who would become the advisor for his doctoral work.

During his years in Madagascar, 1923–1926, Cailliet had occasion to use the psychological testing methods he had learned under Foucault, as well as field work questionnaires devised by noted Sorbonne anthropologist Lucien Lévy-Bruhl, in his extensive studies of the language and symbolism found in the oral traditions of the tribal peoples of Madagascar. This involved advanced study in the languages of these tribes, and Cailliet was awarded the official "Brevet" of Malagasy dialects by the Governor-General of Madagascar for his achievement in this area in 1926. Even years later, this major work "Géographie de Madagascar, avec productions photographiques, 20 figures et deux cartes hors seize couleurs, 243 pages, by A. Dandouan, Larose, Paris, 1922" was loaned to the War Department Army Map Service, Corps of Engineers, sometime during World War II.[8]

The results of his studies became his doctoral dissertation, *Essai sur la Psychologie du Hova*. The doctoral degree was awarded *cum laude* by the University of Montpellier in the south of France, and the dissertation became Cailliet's first major published work. The same year it was published, 1926, Cailliet emigrated to the United States to take up a position as a teacher of French at the University of Pennsylvania in Philadelphia. However, he kept up his French scholarly connections.

Having reported further data on his Madagascar research to the French Academy of Colonial Sciences, Cailliet was congratulated by Paul Doumer, President of the French Republic, at the session of April 17, 1929,

---

8. The usefulness of this work was acknowledged in a letter by Evelyn A. Walsh, Emile Cailliet Collection, Special Collections, Princeton Theological Seminary Library.

and the 1930s proved to be a particularly fruitful period for his scholarship. His *La Foi des Ancêtres: Essai sur les représentations collective des vieux Malgaches*, was published by the Société d'Editions Géographiques, Maritimes et Coloniales in Paris in 1930 and later reprinted in the official *Annales* volume of the Académie des Sciences Coloniales for 1933. In this same period he published in French a study of magic, shamanism, sorcery, witchcraft and modern spiritualism under the title *La Prohibition de l'Occulte*, which was also translated into English and brought out by the University of Pennsylvania Press in 1931.

At this point in his academic career, 1931, Cailliet moved from the East Coast to the West to teach at Scripps College, in Claremont, California. Applying his work on magic and symbolism to the literature of European Romanticism, he published *The Themes of Magic in XIX Century Fiction* in 1932. In the same year he was elected a fellow of the French Academy of Colonial Sciences. Around this time also he published with Professor Jean-Albert Bede of Princeton University a highly significant article on "Le Symbolisme et l'Ame Primitive" which used the thought of Lévy-Bruhl to examine the poetry of figures like Baudelaire together with the writings of other French Symbolist authors. In essence, the authors of the article proposed that the kind of pre-logical mentality, such as that found in the tribal cultures of Madagascar, is not lost to modern Western society, but is essentially recoverable through the work of poets. By the use of symbols and correspondences, the poet is able to re-capture an approach to experienced realities that more "civilized" forms of society too often overlook. The article made a deep impression on T. S. Eliot, for instance, who referred to it in his *The Use of Poetry and the Use of Criticism*. Eliot came to California and spent a day hiking in the mountains with Cailliet discussing some of these ideas with him. It was in part through Eliot's encouragement that Cailliet felt it could be valuable to develop the ideas on symbolism expressed in the article into a full-length study.[9]

In 1934, Cailliet was awarded the academic palms "for distinguished service in the field of letters" by the French government. The year 1936 saw the publication of his major study on *Symbolisme et Ames Primitives*, his book-length exploration of the meaning of symbols, of the Symbolist movement in French literature and of Impressionism in the world of art.

9. Emile Cailliet, handwritten draft of a letter to Julius Birge, Emile Cailliet Collection, Special Collections, Princeton Theological Seminary Library, Box 1, File 25.

It came out at a time of the celebration for the French Symbolist movement and was hailed by noted Sorbonne professor and literary critic Fortunat Strowski as "the most important contribution made to our understanding of symbolism during these celebrations."[10] At the same time Cailliet was appointed reader on Symbolism for the Publications of the Modern Language Association of America (PMLA). It was also in 1936 that Cailliet brought out a small book of reflections designed for young people just finding their way into wider society. Under the title *Le Service Social: Orientations Philosophiques*, Cailliet offered some thoughts on topics such as choosing a profession, enlarging one's social circle, the practice of self-discipline, the process of inner reflection, and the value of solitude and silence.

In the twenty years following his experiences in the First World War, which had so deeply affected him and spurred on his search for meaning, Cailliet had accomplished much as a scholar and thinker. He had become a Christian believer, but he was not yet satisfied. "All this notwithstanding," he wrote, "I was only half way in my quest for the ultimate meaning of personality. The same search had to be carried further into the realm of religion."[11] The late 1930s provided Cailliet a sabbatical opportunity from Scripps to pursue further graduate study, which he chose to do in France with the theology faculty at the University of Strasbourg. Upon the completion of his dissertation (*Mysticisme et "Mentalité Mystique": Etude d'un problèm posé par les travaux de M. Lévy-Bruhl sur la mentalité primitive*) in 1937, in which he carried out a critical exploration of the thought of Lévy-Bruhl, both its positive value and its limitations. Cailliet was awarded a ThD *summa cum laude*. The dissertation was so highly regarded by the Strasbourg faculty that they gave it the significant honor of being published in the official faculty series of the University. It *was* also during his Strasbourg sabbatical that Cailliet began gathering material for his next major project, a study of the life and thought of Pascal.

The early 1940s found Cailliet once again invited back to the University of Pennsylvania to teach French literature and civilization. Among his major published works from this period was *La Tradition litteraire des Ideologues*, a two-volume study of Voltaire, Diderot, Condorcet, and the French Enlightenment, with some attention to the influence of

---

10. Ibid.
11. Ibid.

their thought on Benjamin Franklin and Thomas Jefferson. As had been his custom for his many years in California, Cailliet also gave popular lectures and published more informal pieces. Among the latter were a little book on *The Life of the Mind*, published in 1942; and *The Beginning of Wisdom*, the Otts Lectures for 1946-1947 given at Davidson College in North Carolina. Both of these address his long-standing interest in the proper stance of the Christian scholar vis-à-vis the larger culture.

The first of these, *The Life of the Mind*, opens with a "Prologue" with the title "Occupying Oneself with the Abiding." Drawing on Goethe's *Conversations with Eckermann,* his *Tagebücher,* some material from Goethe's novel *Wilhelm Meister*, and other writings of Goethe, Cailliet sets forth the ideal of a "serene self-possessed life" which "will finally emerge in the light of the Divine, freely surrendering itself to God."[12] The first chapter of *The Life of the Mind* explores the proper role of emotion in our lives, and the need to balance emotion with thought for a full life. The second chapter delves more fully into the question, what does it mean to *think*? "*To think* implies in the first place the discarding of lazy routine . . . *To think*, in Latin, is *pensare*, which curiously enough gave in French two words: *peser,* to weigh, and *penser,* to think. *To think,* is, therefore, also *to weigh*; to weigh our words and our acts . . . Thinking, therefore, is a 'process of clarification.'"[13] The chapter closes with an appeal not to let our mind become closed prematurely, to imagine that the inner conversation which is thinking "can only be a monologue,"[14] but rather to "keep a house opened to the skies," open to the possibility that our thinking can also involve a listening for the voice of one beyond ourselves who can inspire our intellectual life and "make it whole."[15]

The third chapter, "Freedom Under Christ," presents the ways in which Christianity has contributed massively to the betterment of Western culture, "from agriculture to abstract sciences, from hospitals for the poor to temples built by Michelangelo and decorated by Raphael" (Chateaubriand)[16] to the development of popular education, the crusade for the emancipation of slavery, the ideals behind American democracy,

---

12. Cailliet, *Life of the Mind*, 25–27.
13. Ibid., 18, 25–27.
14. Ibid., 30.
15. Ibid., 32.
16. Ibid., 36.

and the "advancement of true liberalism"[17] with its respect for the person. "One of [Christianity's] first tenets is respect for the individual soul, and its very first duty is that of charity."[18] The fourth chapter speaks about the de-Christianization of modern education and society, and the fifth, the growth of philosophical skepticism and the retreat from Christian doctrine. The sixth and final chapter suggests there may be a reversal of this situation at hand, "that a long spiritual winter in the history of our western world is drawing to a close, as though the farthest point on some mysterious ecliptic had been reached and a summer solstice were at hand."[19] An "Epilogue," addressed to the Christian student, encourages that student to remain aware of the "tremendous amount of mystery" that exists in human life and in the cosmos, and therefore not to become arrogant: "Jesus never said, 'Blessed are the PhD's for they shall see God' but he promised that supreme privilege to 'the pure in heart.'... Between reason and faith there is no contradiction. Both come from God. Both find in God their ultimate goal ... As individuals we want to clarify matters for ourselves, remaining faithful to our convictions both as Christians and as Liberal Arts students, holding on with a firm grip to both ends of a chain whose central links are not all or even always visible to us."[20]

The Beginning of Wisdom explores some of these same themes in even greater depth. As Cailliet explains in a "Message to the Reader" at the beginning of the book: "This little book is patterned along the lines of the quest for true wisdom. Instead of dealing with generalities or abstractions, the author starts from the specific human situation of the cultured man of good-will ... [and] attempts to accompany the seeker through objections and problems until a right Biblical perspective is restored and the case for commitment is stated with singleness of purpose."[21] The first chapter, "Groping for Light," once again rehearses the Christian background of Western civilization: "The civilization of our Western world is Christian by birth and by right."[22] After reviewing how this sense has been lost in contemporary undergraduate education, Cailliet admits that

---

17. Ibid., 42.
18. Ibid., 38.
19. Ibid., 72.
20. Ibid., 74–79.
21. Cailliet, *Beginning of Wisdom*, 7.
22. Ibid., 11.

"organized Christianity" itself "has become a confusion of tongues."[23] The book goes on to explore "the challenge of naturalism" to Christianity, questioning on the one hand a too facile liberalism that sees in the Bible only "a monument of English prose" and is content to study the Bible primarily as just another piece of literature, but on the other hand also questioning a too narrow Fundamentalism, simplistically denouncing the legitimate attempts at critical and historical studies of scripture. Both, he feels, miss the mark.

The central chapters of *The Beginning of Wisdom* are focused on the issue of the Christian scholar and what Cailliet calls the "dilemma of Christian scholarship." Cailliet is willing to give genuine admiration to "the truly religious inspiration of Hellenistic metaphysics," in which he includes not only Plato's *Timaeus*, but also the Twelfth Book of Aristotle's *Metaphysics* ("the most restrained, yet the most moving hymn ever dedicated by the Greek mind to the One who moves all things through love"), the Seventh Book of Aristotle's *Eudemian Ethics* ("what a tribute it pays . . . to the divine in us") and other classical authors. However, he feels that the Greek and Hellenic strains in Western Civilization fail to take with adequate seriousness the notion of a Creator God active in history, which is the message of the Hebrew-Christian heritage. Drawing on such figures as Kierkegaard and Pascal, Cailliet makes a distinction between scientific matter, "which naturally becomes an object of acquisition to which the personal life of the teacher is accidental" and ethico-religious matter, "realities wherein commitment is the essential thing."[24] It is one thing to examine the Scriptures and questions regarding religion as a professional. It is something else to look at them "from the inside."[25] For the Christian, the "eternal question in connection with Christianity remains: What then shall we do with Christ?"[26] Acknowledging that we do not live in the same three-storied cosmos of the Biblical writers, we nevertheless "may not rewrite the New Tesatament documents and fit the picture more or less into our naturalistic frame." To reduce Jesus to a purely human figure, divorced from the "divine Christ " who is the revelation of the Living God is to do injustice to the plain testimony of the New Testament. "Whether we

---

23. Ibid., 29.
24. Ibid., 96.
25. Ibid., 99.
26. Ibid., 125.

speak in terms of a Life, of a Power, of a Kingdom, or simply of a religion, Christianity, in the end, can be defined only as Jesus Christ himself."[27] Within history, and within our own life-history, the Living God is "even now at work" in a redemptive fashion through Jesus Christ. "It is then our business to play our part in this redemptive drama, if we would abide forever. And," he adds," this is righteousness." Such an understanding of righteousness implies a new direction in life, "a conversion," which on the part of God is "a new creation" and implies on our part "a new birth." Such a conversion gives us even now a foretaste of eternal life. The believer learns that "just as he was once dead in the midst of life, he may some day be alive in the midst of death."[28]

Cailliet goes on in the closing chapters of the book to point out to the students that as we begin to walk in the light of the truth of Christian faith, as we begin to appropriate that truth to ourselves, we find that it is we ourselves who are being appropriated by the truth.[29] It is in "doing the truth" and not just talking about it, that the "truth comes and takes possession of us."[30] He gives suggestions of Christian biographies to read (e.g., Augustine's *Confessions* and the *Journal* of John Wesley) and books to study, such as Bunyan's *Pilgrim's Progress*, the *Imitation of Christ* (though he warns against a certain sense of "gloom and martyrdom" that pervades this latter recommendation), Anders Nygren's three volumes on *Agape and Eros*, Tolstoy's *My Confession*, and Robert Speer's *The Finality of Jesus Christ*. The book ends with a prayer offered by Samuel Johnson and the testimony of Boswell to Johnson's life: "Amidst all his constitutional infirmities, his earnestness to conform his practice to the precepts of Christianity was unceasing, and. . .he habitually endeavored to refer every transaction to the will of the Supreme being." Cailliet certainly includes both himself, the students he was addressing and the reader of his book when he prays that when "the twilight of our life turns into the Dawn which brightens and widens our uninterrupted vision, may Boswell's simple testimony to the life of Samuel Johnson be applied to our life also."[31] Cailliet's hope was that his honest probing of what it meant to

27. Ibid., 118.
28. Ibid., 141–42.
29. Ibid., 145.
30. Ibid., 146.
31. Ibid., 182–83.

be both a faithful Christian and a thinking person would "be of some help to the rank and file reader as well as to the 'intelligentsia,' often unfairly stigmatized by candid souls."[32]

CAILLIET AND PASCAL

Emile Cailliet's widest reputation as a scholar in the English-speaking world is especially tied to his work on the life and thought Blaise Pascal. In reviewing his own intellectual pilgrimage, Cailliet once wrote, "A decisive encounter with Blaise Pascal, the XVIIth century scientist, philosopher, and man of God, came as the revelation of one who truly incarnated the best conclusions that had forced themselves upon me"[33] Elsewhere he wrote that feeling the need to bring together the essential views he had been gathering, "I found in the encyclopedic and deep genius of Pascal an inviting principle of integration."[34] Cailliet had seriously begun to gather his material on Pascal while studying at Strasbourg. His first draft of his book on the life and intellectual history of Pascal was done in French. In the summer of 1943 he was invited by John Mackay, President of Princeton Theological Seminary, to give a series of lectures on Pascal at the Princeton Institute of Theology. He chose several chapters from his yet unpublished book, chapters which focused especially on Pascal and the Bible, as the central core of his lectures. These lectures were soon published by Westminster Press, with an introduction by John Mackay, under the title *The Clue to Pascal*.

Although thoroughly based in the best Pascal scholarship, as attested by the judiciously selected quotes from other Pascal scholars and the notes at the end of the book, the tone of the writing remains lively and picturesque, the sense of the living lecturer coming through. The first chapter begins with a geographic and historical review of the birthplace of Blaise Pascal in Clermont, France, and tells of his family background, including his relationship with his father, Etienne Pascal, and his early

---

32. Ibid., 7.

33. Emile Cailliet, handwritten draft of a letter to Julius Birge, Emile Cailliet Collection, Special Collections, Princeton Theological Seminary Library, Box 1, File 25.

34. Emile Cailliet, typescript notes for a "Research Project on the Emergence and Nature of PERSONALITY," Emile Cailliet, Special Collections, Princeton Theological Seminary Library, Box 1, File 25.

education. The second chapter traces Pascal's intellectual development, the encounter of his family with the Jansenist movement (essentially a strong Augustinian revival in the French Catholic Church of the time) and Pascal's growing acquaintance with and study of the Scriptures. Highlights of the chapter include a moving account of Pascal's deep religious experience on the night of November 23, 1654, as recorded in documents found only after his death sewn into the lining of his coat, and the dialogue between Christ and Pascal recorded in Pascal's *Mystère de Jesus* which climaxed in Pascal's words of consecration to Christ: "Lord, I give Thee all." Of the *Mystère de Jesus*, Cailliet wrote, "Let us simply say that every Christian should pause on Good Friday to read a few pages of the *Mystère* and then keep all those things and ponder them in his heart."[35] The third chapter looks more closely at how Pascal read his Bible, including a discussion of just which Bible Pascal was likely to have read, and explores Pascal's contribution in rendering passages from the Latin Vulgate into French. The fourth chapter considers Pascal's religious writings, drawing special attention to Pascal's vindication of Christianity in his *Pensées*, and also commending his letters on spiritual guidance and his *Short Life of Christ*. The fifth and last chapter explores the closing years of Pascal's life and examines the questions of the "saintliness of Pascal" and of the "anguish of Pascal."

The combination of deep scholarship and lively presentation in the *Clue to Pascal* led to its appreciation by a wide audience. After its U.S. publication by Westminster Press in 1943, it was brought out by the British Student Christian Movement Press and made one of their six yearly Book Club selections in 1944.[36] As the war drew to a close, Cailliet was able to bring out his full manuscript on Pascal, again published by Westminster Press, under the title *Pascal: Genius in the Light of Scripture*. The subtitle refers to the emphasis Cailliet placed on the influence of the Bible in the shaping of Pascal's life and thought. As with his shorter volume, this study widely received high praise, especially for making Pascal and the results of the best modern French scholarship on Pascal, better known to the English-speaking audience. The work continued to be in demand over the years and in 1961 Cailliet issued a new and revised edition of the work in the Harper Torchbook series under the title *Pascal: The Emergence of*

---

35. Cailliet, *Clue to Pascal*, 53.
36. Ibid.

Genius. In his new introduction, Cailliet tacitly acknowledges the most frequent criticism made of his earlier work, that he had perhaps too much emphasized his thesis about the role of Scripture in ordering all of Pascal's thought. ("It is one thing to say that the Bible is the primary source of influence upon Pascal, quite another to make it a principle which gives unity to the whole field of his thought," wrote one reviewer.)[37] Cailliet himself writes, "When the present work was originally published, I attempted to characterize Pascal's biblical viewpoint in the subtitle, *Genius in the Light of Scripture*. I have since realized that it held too static and too restrictive a connotation. Hence the new subtitle, *The Emergence of Genius*, which more adequately conveys the basic conception of the treatment at hand."[38] The text of the book is not only revised to take into account Pascalian scholarship between 1945 and 1960, but a new appendix gives an extended account and appraisal of that scholarship.[39]

In the years following the first publication of his Pascal manuscript, Cailliet also brought out two additional Pascal-related volumes. The first was an English translation of *Great Shorter Works of Pascal*, with an extended introduction by Cailliet and a translation of the selected texts by John Blankenagel. It includes a translation of the *Memorial*, the *Mystery of Jesus*, the "Prayer by Pascal Asking God to Use Illness to a Good End," and selections from Pascal's correspondence.[40] The second, and shorter volume, was a translation of Pascal's *Short Life of Christ*, again with Cailliet's extended introduction.[41]

THE CHRISTIAN APPROACH TO CULTURE

Along with his work on Pascal, Cailliet continued to reflect on the relationship between Christian faith and culture. A major outcome of this reflection was his book *The Christian Approach to Culture*, published by Abingdon-Cokesbury in 1953. After its publication, it became the primary textbook used by Cailliet in his course for Princeton Seminary

---

37. Duthie, "Introduction to the Torchbook Edition," in Cailliet, *Pascal: The Emergence of Genius*, 11.

38. Cailliet, *Pascal: The Emergence of Genius*, 364–74.

39. Ibid., 364–74.

40. Cailliet, *Great Shorter Works of Pascal*, 1946.

41. Cailliet, *Pascal's Short Life of Christ*.

students on "Introduction to Christian Philosophy." In writing to his publisher about this work, Cailliet stated, "Although I have published thus far some fifteen books, the present one occupies a place quite its own in my personal concern and commitment. A long experience of European and American campuses has brought to me an increasing awareness of the widening and deepening gap that separates the Church and the realm of culture—especially with reference to our Reformed tradition . . . While counseling anxious students I searched in vain for a satisfactory book on the Protestant approach to culture. . .*The Christian Approach to Culture* brings into focus some twenty years of research."[42] At the time of its publication the book received many favorable reviews. Among the most interesting and complete was that by the noted British evangelical, J. I. Packer, in the British Inter-Varsity Fellowship publication, *The Christian Graduate*. The review begins rather strikingly, "A great book is measured not by length but by breadth, not by the amount of thought it embodies, but by the amount it begets . . . If it makes [the reader] grapple with the problems it raises and rewards him as he does so; if it opens new perspectives which bring some order out of jumbles of loose facts, if it helps him to see woods he never could see for the trees—if, in short, it turns mere knowledge into wisdom—then it is a great book." Packer felt *The Christian Approach to Culture* was a book worthy of being ranked in this category and ended his review, "Nothing but good can come from the study of this book. I hope we shall see an English (i.e., British) edition of it before very long."[43]

Ranging as it does from prehistoric times, through the development of philosophy in the ancient world, through medieval scholasticism, the Renaissance and Reformation, the subsequent secularization of Western culture, the effect of Kantian philosophy, and on into discussions of Marxism and process thought, it is not possible in the space available here to give an adequate summary of the full contents of this book. Cailliet himself added a six-page typed "digest" of the book to his syllabus as a brief outline to help students work through the text, drawn from the Packer review. However a few points are worth highlighting, as the opening section, "The Christian Point of View on Culture," is one

---

42. Emile Cailliet, typed note to Sarah Frost, Abingdon-Cokesbury Press, October 3, 1956, Emile Cailliet Collection, Special Collections, Princeton Theological Seminary Library, Box 6, File 118-A.

43. Packer, "Christian Approach to Culture," 6, 12.

of the most complete presentations of Cailliet's own mature thought. In discussing the issue of Christ and culture, Caiiliet takes the position that to turn one's back on the world and its culture is not Christian, but a manifestation of Manicheanism, since it denies the goodness of the created order. Christianity must be brought into relation to culture. But finding the right way to do this may not be easy. There is a kind of biblical literalism, he maintains, which relies on a mechanical theory of verbal inspiration and which is really not useful in exploring the approach of Christian faith to culture. "No Christian worth his salt would come out today with the assertion, for instance, that in I Samuel 15 a genuine test of loyalty to God is to be derived from the command, 'Go and smite Amalek . . . and spare them not; but slay both man and woman, infant and suckling, ox and sheep, camel and ass.'"[44] Nor, he says, is it useful to simply draw up a list of all Biblical passages that seem to deal with a particular subject and place them side by side with no attention to chronology or cultural context. Nor can one simply accept some external authority, neither the pronouncements of a church hierarchy, nor a "majority vote" on what the texts say. Since the core of faith, in his understanding, is "that the living God was in Christ reconciling the world unto himself"[45] it is in the living witness of the community which confesses faith in this living God that becomes normative in Christian witness, from the people of Israel of the Hebrew scriptures, to the Body of Christ of the New Testament, to the early church as it formulated creeds such as the Apostle's Creed and the pronouncements of the ecumenical councils, down to the Confessions of Faith of our own day. This language of doctrinal statements should always be as correct as can be formulated at any given time, but it will always need to recognize its human formulation and the need to be reformulated in each new age and culture. As an example of such a statement, he gives in full the statement of faith drawn up by the Reformed Church of France in 1938.

Cailliet also points out that such an understanding means that Christianity itself can never be identified with any specific culture, including of course "Western" culture. "Such an equation would amount to idolatry and could well constitute a new aggressive form of cultural arrogance similar to that which has brought about the bankruptcy of

---

44. Cailliet, *Christian Approach to Culture*, 35.
45. Ibid., 48.

missionary endeavor in many parts of the world."[46] On the other hand, an extreme "Barthianism" is also an inadequate answer to the issue of Christianity and culture, in his point of view. He tells the story of an Episcopal bishop attending the 1948 World Council of Churches who, after hearing an address by Karl Barth, remarked, "If I believed that, I'd leave Amsterdam and go fishing. I would not bother to bait a hook or wet a line, but would set my skillet on the shore and start frying, grateful to God for undeserved blessings if a fish jumped in, admitting that as a poor sinner I was getting what I deserved if I went hungry."[47] Cailliet, trying to steer between a "theologism" which places all the weight on Biblical revelation, and a secularism that totally ignores it, finds himself in agreement with the "law of closeness of relation" described by Emil Brunner in *Revelation and Reason*:

> The nearer anything lies to that center of existence where we are concerned with the whole, that is, with man's relation to God and the being of the person, the greater is the disturbance of rational knowledge by sin; the farther away anything lies from this center, the less is the disturbance felt, and the less difference is there between knowing as a believer or an unbeliever. This disturbance reaches its maximum in theology and its minimum in the exact sciences, and zero in the sphere of the formal.[48]

With the early Christian apologist, Justin Martyr, Cailliet is willing to claim that "Whatever has been well said belongs to us Christians," and therefore the Christian philosopher can help "prepare the path of the man of culture toward the light" provided that the Christian philosopher is both humble about his or her own intellectual attainments, but is also qualified and prepared to speak in an intelligible way to the "person of good will" whom he or she is trying to address with the Gospel and lead closer to "that center of existence where we are concerned with the whole."[49] "While theology attempts to clarify the process according to which the light is being presented to the world," he writes, "Christian phi-

---

46. Ibid., 49.

47. Ibid., 54.

48. Brunner, *Reason and Revelation*, 383 as quoted in Cailliet, *Christian Approach to Culture*, 61.

49. Cailliet, *Christian Approach to Culture*, 62.

losophy should remain in the world without being of it, so as to prepare the path of the world toward the light."[50]

While we cannot cover here all of the varied topics treated in *The Christian Approach to Culture*, one other major theme deserves some mention. After a discussion of the nature of religion as seen through the lens of cultural anthropology, Cailliet goes on to introduce the notion of the "ontological deviation" in Western thought. A fatal turn was taken, he feels, when Greek philosophy, under Plato and Aristotle, began to confuse reality with intelligibility. This turn continued through Neo-Platonism and medieval scholasticism, and is present in modern day neo-Thomism. The Renaissance and the Reformation broke with this pattern, but the Reformation soon turned to a new scholasticism, and a secular science liberated from theological constraints went on to develop in a truly empirical direction, but without a theological orientation. Because western philosophy and theology moved primarily in the direction set by Parmenides, a philosopher of "Being," rather than Heraclitus, the philosopher of "Becoming," Cailliet feels they have lost touch with the dynamic personalism of the Biblical witness. In reading Exodus 3:14, for example, where God reveals to Moses a personal name, theologians have taken the passage to justify an identification of God with "Being." "He who was meant to be conceived of as *HE* WHO IS, became not only HE WHO *IS*, but an Absolute Self-contained Principle, the very thought of Whom—or Which—is sufficient to dry up the springs of prayer in the human soul. When he disclosed himself to Moses as I Am, the burden of his revelation was that he is not only the One Who *Is*, but the One Who says "*I*."[51] Modern scientific developments, Cailliet felt, have given lie to the idea of a static universe, and thus at least point to the possibility of understanding the universe in a dynamic manner more consistent with a true Biblical personalism, one which acknowledges a Creator God active in history and revealed in Jesus Christ, the Logos of the Gospel of John, who makes known the One who was at the beginning, and who reconciles the world to God.

After finishing this extended scholarly discussion of Christianity and culture, Cailliet felt the need to convey his ideas to a broader audience in a way that could reach them. "Such a massive work classified as 'schol-

50. Ibid., 78.
51. Ibid., 248.

arly,' and heavy with footnotes, might hardly be expected to reach a wide public," he wrote to his publisher. "What is needed at this time of crisis is a smaller, more direct book, the kind that I sorely needed myself when as a lad of twenty I began to wonder about the meaning of personality and its ultimate destiny—if any."[52] The result was *The Dawn of Personality*. It took him no small effort to carve out the time to write this book. "The plain truth is that I obviously did a little too much in recent months with the result that I was plagued by a writer's cramp for six solid weeks . . . As things go, *The Dawn of Personality* had to be written almost exclusively at night and in the morning hours while the author was otherwise carrying quite a load of 'current' work."[53] Centered around the basic questions, "What kind of place am I in?" and "What am I to do in this situation?" the book presented Cailliet's fundamental ideas about the human person, the personal reality of the Living God, and the meaning of authentic life. It is dedicated to "the American people, who so kindly took me in." It represented, Cailliet wrote to another correspondent, "the most earnest effort I have made since my Pascalian publications, to state for our day and age what Erasmus so beautifully called 'the philosophy of Christ.'"[54]

One further work, published toward the end of Cailliet's teaching career, was *The Recovery of Purpose*. Although not as well known as Cailliet's work on Pascal or *The Christian Approach to Culture*, it deserves a wider audience. It is not simply a repeat of Cailliet's earlier work, but marks a genuine advance in his own thinking about the issue of the relation of Christian faith and culture. It was published, in typical Cailliet fashion, with the intention of helping those men and women of good will "find their bearings," and "more proficiently proceed with the task of relating their efforts to proper ends." It shows his own willingness as a Christian scholar to continue to examine and reflect on his previous views, in order to be an even more faithful witness.

In the Introduction itself Cailliet speaks of the "many lessons Christianity needs to learn from modernity." "Modernity," he says, "may be said to have advanced farther and more efficiently in the knowledge

---

52. Emile Cailliet, handwritten draft of a letter to Julius Birge, Emile Cailliet Collection, Special Collections, Princeton Theological Seminary Library, Box 1, File 25.

53. Emile Cailliet to Mrs. Paul A. Burton, April 3, 1956, Emile Cailliet Collection, Special Collections, Princeton Theological Seminary Library, Box 1, File 25.

54. Emile Cailliet to James A. Pike, Emile Cailliet Collection, Special Collection, Princeton Theological Seminary Library, Box 1, File 25.

of nature, than Christianity in the knowledge of the Creator and his ways. Consensus of views is the criterion and aim in the scientific realm whereas confusion of tongues and bitter contention too often characterize Christian self-assertion in the theological realm . . . We no longer burn heretics, but a number of hardly veiled substitutes for the practice have been devised. Self-examination is in order on our part, together with a mending of our ways, if we expect to secure a hearing from those to whose condition we should address ourselves." The important division is not, in his opinion, between "evangelicals" and "liberals," but rather between those who "look back with nostalgic longings" and those who "look ahead in the obedience of faith," those who "hark back to ready-made solutions of ages gone by" and those who "look forward to ever more accurate and constructive patterns of understanding." "As it was said of old, knowledge begins with wonder. Those who claim to have knowledge in its once-for-allness rarely learn anything new. Should they perchance be confronted by fresh information, their impression likely would be that they had lost something. Their next natural move would be to expose as destructive the creative activity which threatened their peace of mind—a peace of mind in this case comparable to the peace of the grave . . . The Christian intellect should act as an incentive, not as an inhibitor."[55]

The opening section of *The Recovery of Purpose* treats the question, "Is there room for purpose in the scientific world?" A second section is more explicitly theological, discussing Karl Barth, Friedrich Schleiermacher and the concept of revelation, and particularly highlighting an understanding of God as the "Doer of the Unexpected." The third section attempts to establish points of contact between contemporary scientific outlook and a Christian conception of reality. It explores the question of anthropomorphism in theology and examines further the understanding of the concept of revelation. The last section lifts up the Promethean and tragic elements in so much current understanding of life, even among Christians, and contrasts this with a biblical and prophetic view of life and its purpose.

It is particularly here in the last section that Cailliet makes some creative moves in a way which goes beyond some of his previous formulations. He begins by boldly challenging "one of the most deeply entrenched views in theology today"—the contrast between the Hebraic

---

55. Cailliet, *Recovery of Purpose*, 12–14.

and the Greek heritage in Christianity. This "well-worn study in contrast ... may no longer be telling the whole story." Exploring the classical understanding of sin as *harmatia*, "missing the mark," as the term is used in ancient Greek drama, he points out that it is not to be confused with the New Testament understanding of sin. The classical view of a "tragic flaw," he writes, has "no room for the redeeming grace of God. Rather it leaves man to the sheer determinism of the nature of things moving on their own accord." The "genuinely prophetic and Christian notion of sin is essentially that of alienation from an all-loving God who truly grieves over an estrangement amounting to betrayal."[56] Yet his main concern is not to point out the difference between the tragic view and the Christian view in themselves, but to point to "the degree to which current evangelical views have been contaminated by the tragic view." "There is above all," he writes," an overemphasis on the *fatal* character of original sin understood as a *personal* guilt unavoidably inherited, together with its ominous implications. As if I had sinned in Adam, not as what I am, but as who I am! And there are those crude theories of atonement seemingly devised by Origen and brought into full expression by Anselm, according to which, only a blood ransom duly paid to God, conceived as a feudal overlord, can possibly break up the fatal determinism ... To all practical purposes the saving power of the Cross of Christ has been reduced to theoretical concepts accessible to our human infirmity and likely to betray their human origination."[57]

The next portion of his analysis looks at the classical concept of sin as *hubris*. This he feels is not adequately conveyed by the usual translation of *hubris* as "pride." *Hubris,* he contends, is more properly understood as referring to people "who are misled by wanting too much, even daring the impossible ... Their arrogant, intemperate ways are bound to bring down upon them the wrath of Zeus through the retribution of Nemesis."[58] The most dramatic account of *hubris* Cailliet finds in the myth of Prometheus. Zeus has become despotic and decided to destroy humanity and replace humans with a better race. Prometheus decides to defy Zeus, steal the forbidden fire, and bring it down from heaven to the mortals along with the secrets of the arts and crafts. "This is the essence of *hubris*, namely, a defi-

---

56. Ibid., 128–29.
57. Ibid., 128–30.
58. Ibid., 133.

ant transgression for the sake of some self-appointed achievement which may prove praiseworthy, yet is sure to release calamity... In arrogating to himself the prerogatives of Zeus, even for laudable motives, the heaven-storming hero has called down on himself a wrathful, divine retribution."[59] The tragedy lies in that the transgression seems to have been motivated by a virtue. The Promethean strain in humanity is both humanity's nobility and humanity's doom. Cailliet finds that the modern Christian insistence on sin as essentially pride "must be pronounced a Christianized version of the tragic view of *hubris*." It results in "the enormous amount of false humility which prides itself at not being proud" and the magnification of guilt complexes as the Christian "loses touch with the divine simplicity of the Gospel."[60] Cailliet finds the most exalted version of Christianized *hubris* in a theological approach which too strongly over-emphasizes the" wholly-Otherness of God." "Such a radical theological tenet is likely to call forth the Prometheus slumbering in every man of flesh and blood. To say that the finite is best instructed by the infinite is one thing. To assert that there is in the finite nothing that prepares it to approach the infinite is quite another thing, in fact, a terrible thing."[61]

Having shown that elements of the Greek tragic understanding of sin have also crept into Christian proclamation, Cailliet then makes his point that "interpreting the landscape of reality in terms of the either-Greek-or-Hebrew criterion has proved as irrelevant as it had already proved misleading." The result has been to set Christianity and modernity into irreconcilable opposites. "If to be a good Christian means to think Hebraically and accordingly to shun the Greek values revived by the Renaissance and nurtured by the Age of Enlightenment, men of culture will have none of it. If, on the other hand, modernity implies turning one's back on a genuinely biblical heritage, then evangelical Christianity will have none of that." Like Jerome, who "managed to rule out the three outstanding representatives of Latin literature at one blow" ("How can Horace go with the psalter, Virgil with the gospels, Cicero with the apostle?") or Tertullian ("What indeed has Athens to do with Jerusalem?"), Christians are too often led to the conclusion that they must reject modern culture *in*

---

59. Ibid., 134.
60. Ibid., 140.
61. Ibid., 141.

*toto.*⁶² With William Temple, he believes that what is needed in our time is "a Dialectic more comprehensive and more thorough in its appreciation of the interplay of factors in the real world."⁶³

Reaching the conclusion of his analysis in *The Recovery of Purpose*, Cailliet feels that "far from standing at opposite poles, both modernity and Christianity actually labor under one and the same delusion" and that this is linked to "Promethean leanings inherent in the tragic view and coming to expression in the classical sin of *hubris*."⁶⁴ What is needed in both is a conversion from the tragic, Promethean outlook (emphasizing the human revolt against God either positively, as an emancipation from superstition, or negatively, as human arrogance in refusing to be subservient to God) to the prophetic outlook with its insistence on God's ongoing care and concern for humanity, God's unfailing nearness to us and love toward us. This love is exemplified in certain Psalms, such as Psalm 139, in the prophets with their announcement of God's passion for righteousness and justice to prevail, in the Sermon on the Mount, with its emphasis on the care of the Loving Father which extends even to the lilies of the field and the fowl of the air, and in the great Pauline writings which declare such truths as "What shall separate us from the love of Christ? . . . I am persuaded that neither death, nor life, nor angels , nor principalities, nor powers, nor things present, nor things to come, nor height, nor depth, nor any other creature , shall be able to separate us from the love of God, which is in Christ Jesus our Lord." "These capital texts blaze the trail of light that so safely and triumphantly points the way . . . Modernity has been missing the mark . . . not so much because of a liberalism swayed by secular world views. But rather because of modernity's surrender to the tragic world view."⁶⁵ This view has given the modern person an understanding of the universe as one where human beings find themselves in a cold and essentially empty universe, over against which they stand.

On the other hand, Cailliet goes on, "current views of Christianity stand condemned on a par with the corresponding views in modernity. Granting that the story of the Fall in the Book of Genesis does suggest a biblical version of *hubris* as self-sufficiency or pride, the current insis-

---

62. Ibid., 144–45.
63. Ibid., 147.
64. Ibid., 161.
65. Ibid., 162–64.

tence upon its dramatic, fatal character pertains more to the tragic view than the prophetic . . . The reason sin has thus taken tragic overtones in evangelical circles today is that the dramatic building up of Satan as Ruler of a world of Darkness, standing on a par with God as the mighty opposite of God and his world of Light, has affected the more sober biblical view . . . What we have in the opening pages of the Book of Genesis is a vivid presentation of man's eternal plight—namely that one created to live in fellowship with God chooses to keep away from God . . . No cleavage, no irresolvable antinomy is at stake in this situation, no fatal necessity. The heavenly Father of his prodigal sons has overruled it in Jesus Christ . . . The fact is that our Christian circles today are plagued by attitudes of constrained self-debasement, which border more on the pathological than on the evangelical."[66] An overemphasis on the Ransom theory of the atonement and Anselmian satisfaction theology "simply propounds the tragic view . . . There is no doubt that it has alienated multitudes from the Gospel."[67] Too often the tone struck by evangelical Christian witness is one that "may hardly be said to contribute to the propagation of the Gospel . . . The *contemptus mundi* to which they bear witness no longer expresses that loosening from earthly attachments and ambitions, initiated deep within by the stirrings of divine love. It is no longer *contemptus mundi* in the hallowed, long-established sense. It has now literally become *contemptus* pure and simple, in the revived tragic context."[68] Truth, for Cailliet, in the prophetic meaning of the term, "is truth grounded in the reliability of God. This is why it is live truth, truth to be done by those who would know with certainty." Recovering a sense of the Presence of God at work in the universe, at work in human history, and at work in the very center of our lives gives a new orientation to life which "proves to be dynamic, uniquely power-giving. There is incalculable and unaccountable energy at work in it for the good of creation."[69]

---

66. Ibid., 164–65.
67. Ibid., 166.
68. Ibid., 168.
69. Ibid., 169, 178.

RETIREMENT YEARS AND RETURN TO SYMBOLISM

Cailliet continued a very active life in his earlier retirement years, including guest lectureships and preaching engagements. His book on the Young Life movement, written during these years, is a careful presentation of the history and ideals of the organization as well as a thoughtful critique with practical suggestions regarding the challenges it faced. His *Journey into Light* is a type of personal testament, summing up for the interested reader some of the themes over which he had pondered for many years in the course of his Christian pilgrimage. *Alone at High Noon* explores for a popular readership the themes of loneliness and solitude in life and the possibility for their transfiguration when we bring to them a daily practice of the Presence of God. Aside from these, one of the more interesting documents to come from the retirement years is Cailliet's own revisiting of his earlier work on Symbolism. The document was not meant for publication, and is an attachment to Frank Gaebelein's personal memoir of his friendship with Calliet, which he penned following Cailliet's death in 1981.

"In the late1960's," wrote Gaebelein, "I unwisely accepted an assignment to do the major article on symbolism for one of the multi-volume Bible encyclopedias. After checking authorities like Eliade, Langer, Tillich, Dillistone, Ramm, Ferguson, and others and doing my own thinking on the subject, I realized that I was in water beyond my depth. So I called my friend and told him of my predicament. He said he would send me some notes. Then in a few days a handwritten essay arrived, entitled, "Memo on Symbolism for Frank." With it was a note urging me to use its ideas but not to mention his name. Of course, I drew upon it and of course I referred to him by name. What he did for me was to solve my dilemma by giving me the catalyst that recharged my thinking and resulted in my completing the article." Without knowing it, Gaebelein realized only later, he had gone "to one of the fountainheads on the subject of symbolism."[70]

Only a single paragraph from this document has seen publication, as part of the tribute to Cailliet that Gaebelein wrote for *Theology Today*. That being the case, it seems appropriate to publish a somewhat longer account of it here:

---

70. Frank E. Gaebelein, typescript, "Friendship an Election of God—A Brief Memoir of Emile Cailliet," together with Emile Cailliet, "Memo for Frank," Emile Cailliet Collection, Special Collections, Princeton Theological Seminary Library, Box 8, File 159.

> What is a symbol? In my younger days I turned the matter in my mind and found no clear answer. Dictionaries and technical works only added to my confusion. They spoke of the symbolism of poets, but also that of impressionistic painters, of Hegelian philosophers, of cathedral builders, of mystics, prophets, mathematicians, chemists—and others too numerous to remember. I had begun to unravel a thread but the skein was tangled. I refused the Gordian solution. The reading of an article by the famous psychologist Ribot gave me a precious clue. To him the symbol had appeared with the origin of humanity. That was even its golden age. Since then it had retreated and weakened under the antagonistic pressure of rational thought . . . Thus began my long conversation with a strange world which on occasion took on the resemblance of a fairyland.[71]

Here Cailliet offers to spare Gaebelein "the tortuous itinerary which resulted," but mentions his research among the tribal peoples in Madagascar, where he tried simply to record the data presented to him "in a spirit of submission to fact." He modestly tells of the fine reception his work had received in France and mentions that even on "the other side of the Atlantic," a Yale professor was quoted as having said that Cailliet's book on symbolism "was the best thing he had ever done; that he should have gone on instead of turning to theology!"[72]

"From the symbol to the concept," Cailliet goes on, "there was an abrupt change. In this sense, the concept appears as a symbol which has been submitted to violence. . . The symbols formerly used to suggest such and such a state of mind to a fellow man have henceforth lost their living substance. Colorless, shrunken, classified, defined clearly and distinctly, they have taken on the aspect of intelligible concepts circulating in gradually expanded territories."[73] The translation of a symbol, with all of its living associations, into an objective sign, inevitably is thus accompanied by a certain loss.

> Can a symbol live again? Cailliet felt that it could. He gave the following examples: A man goes abroad, on board ship he passes another ship whose flag indicates Its foreign nationality. To him, that flag is an *emblem*. But let our traveler arrive abroad, experience isolation amid a new culture whose language he does not

---

71. Ibid., 7–8.
72. Ibid., 8–9.
73. Ibid., 11.

know—then suddenly upon turning a street corner, be confronted by the flag of his own country. His heart jumps in his chest. He gets all excited as old participations crowd into his mind. To him *this* flag is no longer an emblem. It is a *symbol*. In that symbol he is involved with his whole being.

Or take the case of a Roman soldier of old seeing the design of a fish—to him a sure *sign* that Christians have been around. It leaves him cold and starts him calculating. Later, one of the early Christians passes by and suddenly sees the fish. Immediately his heart pounds, his mind is filled with rich associations culminating in the longings of divine love. To him this fish drawing is emphatically *a symbol*.[74]

For Cailliet, what makes a symbol a symbol is "the sense of participation." Symbolic thinking is thinking "with ones whole body." We count the way we do because we have ten fingers. Space has three dimensions because our body has three dimensions. The "fully restored" person thinks with the "whole body's commitments." The important factor is "to maintain contact with the generative reality. This reality is our experience of life itself." The human being, at base, is "a symbolistic agent." Therefore, writes Cailliet, "Christians who know only too well the dangers of dilettantism, of the detachment of pure intellectualism should appreciate the recovery of wholeness implied in a genuine symbolism. Their life is rooted in a deep sense of participation with Christ. Their ministry is one of powerful suggestion aiming at creating or recreating in others this very sense."[75]

Reading through this piece, penned near the close of Cailliet's long and productive career as a scholar and written simply at the request of an inquiring friend, we can perhaps see some of the traits of Cailliet as a Christian scholar which made his work so penetrating to many of those who encountered him and his writings. First of all, for Cailliet the work of scholarship was not a detached strictly intellectual activity. Rather, he took up the scholarly projects he did out of a need to find for himself basic answers to fundamental questions about life and its meaning. He took up his projects, one by one, with the passion of his whole being and followed the trail wherever it led. Second, he took up his work not to gain some kind of fame or recognition, though a certain amount of that came his way,

---

74. Ibid., 12–13.
75. Ibid., 13–14.

but with an earnest desire to share the results of his research and thinking with those who were wrestling with the same problems he was, to perhaps be of some help to them as they sought out for themselves the way to life. He provided important keys to further his friend's article, yet told him not even to bother mentioning his name. Third, Cailliet presented the results of his thinking not as dogmatic assertions, but in a spirit of humility—as a ministry and as a testimony to his own living faith. A living faith, for Cailliet, was a faith that had accepted the "invitation to pilgrimage," to explore the mystery, to penetrate further and further toward that light of which the Scriptures were a witness, the Living God made known in Jesus Christ, present at the very heart of the universe, active in human history and in our own lives, seeking to reconcile us, and redeem us and invite us to participate in that life which is life indeed.

5

The Philosopher

A Christian Philosopher in a Theological Seminary

OVERVIEW

PHILOSOPHY IS THE MOST ancient of intellectual disciplines. In the fragmentary writings of the sixth century BC Pre-Socratics, philosophy, theology, and science are inextricably interwoven. Indeed attempting to apply these distinctions is an anachronism. What we know as science took a very long time to emerge, but thanks to Socrates, Plato, and Aristotle, by the fourth century BC a distinctive form of inquiry had come into existence that is recognizable by philosophers today as their discipline. The Wisdom literature of the Old Testament emerged over much the same period, yet, as is well known, its pattern of thought was quite different, prophetic, and exhortatory rather than analytic and explanatory. In Acts Chapter 17, the two mentalities encounter each other when Paul addresses the citizens of Athens, an encounter that starts a long-standing debate summarized in Tertullian's famous question: "What has Athens to do with Jerusalem?"

The Church has wrestled with this question from the first century of its existence. The philosopher Justin Martyr (ca. 100–165), a convert to Christianity, addresses it in his *First Apology* to the Roman Emperor Antoninus Pius, and in his *Dialogue with Trypho,* a notable Jewish figure. A succession of Christian thinkers have followed him in this endeavor, famously Augustine and Aquinas, whose influence on both theology and philosophy would be hard to exaggerate. In the course of this centuries-long debate, the relationship between philosophy and theology has fluctuated from close alliance to deep hostility.[1] At the present time, there is something of a *détente* between the two, facilitated by an almost total institutional separation. Philosophy's current home is in the secular university; confessional theology has largely retreated to the seminaries. There are occasional exceptions, however. Some major universities have schools of divinity, and a few seminaries have professors of philosophy among their faculty. The place of theology (as opposed to religious studies) in the secular university (if any) has received widespread attention, the role of philosophy in the seminary much less. The purpose of this chapter is to address that question, using the unusual position of Emile Cailliet as Professor of Christian Philosophy at Princeton Theological Seminary, and his reflections on it, as an *entrée* to these two questions: What role can philosophy play in a seminary education? What role should it play?

THE TEACHING OF PHILOSOPHY AT PRINCETON SEMINARY

Emile Cailliet's appointment as a member of the Faculty at Princeton Theological Seminary in 1947 had two notable features; he was the first layman to hold a full professorship, and he was expressly appointed to a chair of Christian Philosophy. This was the same Stuart Chair that had been founded in 1880, first held by Francis Landey Patton, a graduate of the seminary, subsequent President of Princeton University (1888–1902), and later still, first President of the Seminary (1902–1913). The founding title of Patton's Chair, however, had been different—"Professor of the Relations of Philosophy and Science to the Christian Religion," and between his tenure and Cailliet's, the title changed again, to "Stuart Professor of Apologetics and Christian Ethics." Under this description, the position was held by a number of individuals until Cailliet was named "Stuart Professor of Christian Philosophy." This remained the designation with the appointment of his successor, John Hick, but when Diogenes Allen was appointed in 1965, he was named "Stuart Professor of Philosophy" *simpliciter*. The qualifying adjective "Christian" had been dropped. Forty

---

[1] This history is described in the essay by Gordon Graham on "Philosophy" in the *Oxford Handbook of Systematic Theology* (2007).

years later and four years after Allen's retirement, the position became "Henry Luce III Professor of Philosophy and the Arts."

These changes in title may have resulted in part from internal administrative and financial concerns, as well as the personal preferences of the people involved. Yet they nevertheless reflect a more general uncertainty about just what the role of the philosopher should be in a seminary. It is clear that the original intention behind the establishment of the Stuart Chair was an apologetic one. In 1880s America, as in European culture quite generally, the advances made by the sciences were increasingly seen to be made at the expense of religion, and in particular Christian theology. In this post-Darwinian context, however, the precise role of philosophy was unclear, an ambiguity that the title of the Patton chair expresses. Was philosophy the discipline that could mediate between religion and science? Or was philosophy another of the intellectual competitors to which the protagonists of the Christian faith needed to respond?

It is not easy to say. At the time of Patton's appointment, the Presidency of the College of New Jersey was held by a philosopher—James McCosh—a Scottish Presbyterian minister and a Director of the Seminary. True to his own philosophical education at Glasgow and Edinburgh, McCosh was both an exponent and an adherent of "the Scottish Philosophy." In a book with that title, he traced its course from Hutcheson to Hamilton, and held that both empirical methods and realist metaphysics were distinctive of the Scottish philosophical tradition. He further held that the empirical method was fully in accord with Christian theism. It was this belief that underlay his endorsement of evolutionary biology, a matter that he famously debated with the Seminary's leading theologian, Charles Hodge. Empirical method and realist metaphysics, McCosh claimed, could form the basis of "What an American Philosophy Should Be" (the title of a late essay) as the United States came to assert its intellectual independence from Europe.

Taken as a prediction, he could hardly have been more wrong. The philosophy that came to be identified as distinctively American was the pragmatism of William James and C. S. Pierce. Though in some important respects a mutation of the Scottish Common Sense philosophy, which the Princeton theologians avowedly endorsed, American pragmatism was neither realist nor empiricist, and owed something to the New England "Transcendentalism" of Emerson and Thoreau. In any case, the principal rival to pragmatism in America's academies soon emerged as an Idealism that expressly rejected empirical realism. In the hands of someone like Josiah Royce, William's James's colleague at Harvard, Idealism was certainly allied to religion, but not entirely in ways consonant with orthodox Christian theology.

The benefactors of the Stuart Chair had Patton in mind before they made their gift to the Seminary. It is plausible to think that the debate between McCosh and Hodge played a part in their generosity, and their choice of a candidate. Their hope appears to have been that Patton's classes would arm young clergy in training for the Presbyterian Church with the intellectual weapons needed to combat the religious doubts that modern science seemed to prompt. Patton was not a philosopher, and the two books he had published established no scientific or philosophical credentials on his part. He was, however, an immensely eloquent speaker, and a reliable defender of conservative Protestant theology. We may conclude from this that his task was an apologetical one—to be a persuasive voice opposed to scientific atheism, and to bolster the confidence of his students. When Patton succeeded McCosh as President of Princeton University he lectured on Ethics, not philosophy, while continuing to give lectures on Theism at the Seminary. In 1902 he exchanged his Presidency of the University for that of the Seminary, and shortly after, William Brenton Greene, Jr., was appointed to the Stuart Professorship, then titled "Apologetics and Christian Ethics." The references to science and philosophy had disappeared, and so it remained for over forty years.

With the appointment of Cailliet, the reference to philosophy returns. All the previous holders of the Stuart Chair had been clergymen. He was not. Moreover, they had spent significant periods as pastors, and taught widely across all the biblical and theological subjects. Though a convert to Protestant Christianity, and in no way hesitant about his religious allegiance, Cailliet was first and foremost an academic. He had completed a doctorate in philosophy, and came to Princeton from the Wesleyan University in Connecticut where he was both Professor of French Literature and held an associated position in philosophy. The connection between the two lay with Pascal, on whose writings he was an established expert.

Scholarly integrity does not sit easily with apologetics. As Plato argues in several of his early dialogues, there is a deep difference between philosophy and rhetoric, between inquiring and persuading. Apologetics is primarily aimed at securing and protecting belief. Its purpose is to fend off attacks and restore the confidence of the person who already believes, not to inquire into what he or she ought to believe. Describing the apologist's task in this way need not amount to discounting or dismissing it. Apologetics, no doubt, easily degenerates into mere propaganda, but sermons, like political speeches, can have a valuable and important role to play in sustaining a community and channeling its energies in creative and productive ways. As Plato rightly saw, however, philosophy cannot play this role. Its distinctive nature is to take nothing for granted, but to probe and question the suppositions upon which thought and action rest. At the same time, so conceived philosophy too carries a risk—the risk of producing a paralyzing skepticism. Famously, David Hume wrestles with this issue in his *Enquiry Concerning Human Understanding* when he draws a distinction between "academical philosophy" and "skeptical philosophy."[2] The first maintains a spirit of critical inquiry without descending to the nihilism characteristic of the second. Hume's distinction is easy to draw, but much harder to sustain, and arguably, he does not succeed in doing so. But even if we could do better in this regard, there is a further issue to be resolved. Why would the education of clergy aim to turn them into academical philosophers?

CAILLIET'S VIEWS OF THE CHRISTIAN PHILOSOPHER

It seems plausible, in the light of his writings, that the title "Professor of Christian Philosophy" was suggested by Cailliet himself. Whether or not this is true, "Christian philosophy" and "the Christian philosopher" are concepts that he both employs and elaborates at considerable length. While still a professor at Wesleyan, Cailliet gave a lecture at Princeton entitled "The Path out of this Wilderness: A Charter for the Christian Scholar."[3] At the time of his appointment to the Stuart Chair, he gave a related lecture entitled "Outlines of a Christian Positivism."[4] In these two lectures he presents succinct versions of themes that were developed at much greater length in *The Christian Approach to Culture*, a book he published some years later.[5]

> 2. Hume, *Enquiry Concerning Human Understanding*, chapters 1 and 12.
> 3. Cailliet, "Path out of this Wilderness," 17–26.
> 4. Cailliet, "Outlines of a Christian Positivism," 28–37.
> 5. Cailliet, *Christian Approach to Culture* .

"The wilderness" to which the first lecture refers is one created by the tension between "those who hold an essentially Greek outlook" and "those who hold a Hebrew-Christian outlook." The distinction, and the tension, was nothing new, of course, but on Cailliet's reading the contemporary conflict between scientific inquiry and religious faith is a modern manifestation of the long-standing debate about Athens and Jerusalem. "The Christian scholar" he says, "must find a path out of this wilderness. A charter must be formulated which will allow him to remain in perfect good faith both as a Christian and a scholar."[6] He thereby sets his face against mere apologetics, "the old Athenian tradition where men were paid to argue for victory rather than for truth" as he puts it.[7] But how is this dual faithfulness to be secured? Like McCosh, and in the spirit of Pascal, Cailliet wholeheartedly endorses the aims and methods of scientific inquiry. By his account, however, once these have been properly understood, "one fails to see how . . . any real conflict could arise between a sober science and the Christian faith."[8]

At the present time the often shrill tone of exchanges between "science" and "religion" make this sound a very odd conclusion. But the adjective "sober" is crucial here. The indisputable success of science, and especially medical science, has given it an unprecedented "sway" over the "world of men and affairs." This has given scientists ambitions far beyond their true competence, while at the same time putting religious people on the defensive and forcing them to choose between "religious obscurantism and religious defeatism" (Cailliet is here quoting Reinhold Neibuhr). So the first step is to look carefully at the true nature of science. Three features emerge from such scrutiny. Science is at its most powerful when it focuses on getting results, and simply refuses to enter the realms of either methodological or metaphysical debate (which is not to deny that successful scientists often yield to this temptation). Second, these results, though immensely interesting and valuable, are always revisable. As Cailliet puts it, "Scientific truth is what remains at the end of the last cross-examination . . . What we call scientific knowledge now turns out to be a sort of temporary script, a series of clues about that which is, and the manner of its being what it is." Third, and perhaps most importantly,

---

6. Cailliet, "Path out of this Wilderness," 17.

7. Ibid., 21.

8. Cailliet, "Outlines of a Christian Positivism," 48.

"science is impersonal, colorless and neutral by nature." The "sober" scientist acknowledges the limitations that these three features place upon his or her activity, and when this is the case "the Christian philosopher has every reason to accompany his scientific friend."[9]

When "we become aware of the true scope and impact of an unassuming science"[10] we see that it necessarily has a slender grasp on anything properly called "reality." For all his brilliance, Newton ultimately came up with a "transcript" that Einstein showed to be temporary, and sooner or later Einstein's transcript will suffer the same fate. This is not to say that either was false or inconsequential, only that by the nature of the case, scientific "truth" is highly provisional. "To the scientist, truth is that which everyone has been given a chance to discuss and no one can discuss any longer for the time being."[11] More importantly, the colorless neutrality of science means that it has nothing to tell us about how to live our lives. This judgment includes history, psychology, economics, and all the other social sciences. By extension, science in this very broad sense has nothing to tell us about the human condition in which those lives have to be lived, or about the springs of action that motivate us, for ill as well as good. Yet these are realities no less than anything that physics, chemistry, or biology might describe and explain. Cailliet takes this to be one of Pascal's great insights, and finds the same thought behind Kierkegaard's wholesale rejection of the Hegelian System.

To think that science might teach us how to live is a profound error. Confusing evolution and progress is one of the many mistakes into which it leads us, a confusion that intensifies when the explanatory power of Darwinian biology is erroneously applied to human history. "Contemporary 'primitives' so called . . . are most gratuitously made to represent somehow the pattern of our distant ancestors. Yet . . . it seems that those of our distant ancestors who can be traced back with any certainty, were as intelligent as we are."[12] Evolution may have given human beings longer lives (on average); it has not made them any better at living them. Cailliet, at several times, quotes George Eliot's remark (in *Middlemarch*) that "We are all born in moral stupidity."

9. Ibid., 31.
10. Ibid., 30.
11. Cailliet, "Path out of this Wilderness," 22.
12. Ibid., 24.

Science has nothing to teach us about how to live, because none of the information it can supply us with addresses our *moral* stupidity. So what can? Cailliet's answer is Revelation—not truth that we ourselves have acquired about the Creation, but truth simply presented to us by the Creator. Revealed truth is indispensable in just this sense: attributing meaning to human history, including the history of science, is possible only if we presuppose an external purposiveness that will enable us to separate significant from insignificant events. Revelation tells us that "the Creator and Performer of redeeming acts directs the plot of history to a triumphant climax. This means that history is *oriented* as we have found the universe to be oriented"[13] (emphasis original). Without this orientation, time simply passes as an undifferentiated and hence meaningless flow. From a strictly temporal point of view, the rising and falling of whole civilizations is no more significant than the rising and falling of the tides. To make the world *our* world, in any real sense, requires existential truth, and, unlike scientific truth, this is not something that human beings acquire and accumulate by means of careful intellectual investigations stretching over millennia, but something dependent upon Revelation from the outset. To deny the availability of revealed truth, is to accept the Protagorean doctrine that "Man is the measure of all things," a doctrine that if not absurd, is ultimately nihilistic.

Revealed truth does not change, though our grasp of it may improve, and for the Christian, the source of that truth is the Bible. It follows that the Christian scholar is not one who dismisses the findings of science or denies its explanatory power, but rather seeks to assess the significance of its successes in the light of revealed truth. But if this is true of the Christian scholar in general, what distinguishes the Christian philosopher in particular? "It is the part of the Christian philosopher to restore the true perspective as he has been given eyes to see it." "Christian philosophy should remain in the world without being of it."[14] Cailliet makes these remarks in the course of clarifying the difference between the Christian philosopher and the theologian, and as they stand, their implications beyond that limited context are unclear. In *The Christian Approach to Culture*, however, he expands upon the theme. "The Christian philosopher ... realizes that his task is not to sit in judgment on anyone, but rather to appraise cultural

---

13. Cailliet, *Christian Approach to Culture*, 77.
14. Cailliet, "Outlines of a Christian Positivism," 36.

manifestations in their themes as well as in their deepest intentions with a view to renewal and rebirth."[15] The remainder of this chapter uses this remark as the starting point for an account of the role of philosophy in the seminary.

DISTINCTIONS BETWEEN PHILOSOPHY AND SCIENCE

Why does the Christian philosopher not sit in judgment? Cailliet makes this statement toward the end of a section of his book in which he is rejecting a certain kind of dogmatism. This dogmatism can be found in popularizations of Barthianism that oppose religious faith to ordinary knowledge, and suppose that what is known by faith can cancel or override the claims that science or history or psychology may make. While Cailliet thinks that Barth is not entirely without responsibility for this popularization, he does believe that it is "a grave misunderstanding to characterize the Barthian attitude as a revolt against reason." After all, he notes, it is Barth himself who observes that "the saying 'despise only reason and science, man's supremest power of all' was uttered not by a prophet, but by Goethe's Mephistopheles."[16]

The Christian thinker cannot reject or despise science, because it is an exercise of reason. It is not the only one, however. Philosophy is another, and quite unlike science in certain important respects. To begin with, philosophy cannot claim to produce truth even of the modest kind that Cailliet attributes to science—"that which everyone has been given a chance to discuss and no one can discuss any longer for the time being." Discussion is of the essence in philosophy, and a philosophical contention that "no one can discuss any longer" is as valueless as a piece of music that no one can play. Contrary to the ways in which philosophers sometimes speak, philosophical investigation never produces results. This lack of established result is shown in several ways. For example, where scientific and historical inquiry can produce findings upon which further work by others can be built, there is no conclusion a philosopher can reach that other philosophers cannot intelligibly question. The reverse side of this is that no philosopher needs to fear that another philosopher will anticipate the conclusion of a philosophical inquiry. There are rival philosophical

---

15. Cailliet, *Christian Approach to Culture*, 65.
16. Ibid., 56.

views, of course, but they are not in competition in the way that scientific research programs can be; there is no element of a race to get there first.

These differences between science and philosophy arise from what we might call the distinctive direction of philosophical thought. The experimental scientist builds theories, and offers explanations on the basis of careful observation. These explanatory theories are then tested by further experimentation. Philosophy too draws on observation. By contrast, though, these observations are empirical propositions of such generality that their truth needs no special investigation. The philosopher's interest is to uncover the presuppositions of beliefs that are widely accepted and that no one has much inclination to dispute. The aim, we might say, is not to build explanatory structures upon them, but to dig deeper into their foundations.

One ancient way of characterizing this difference is to say that philosophy is the pursuit of wisdom rather than knowledge. If this is right, a further difference emerges. Philosophy is inescapable in a way that science is not. One can go through the whole of life without knowing any physics or biology, but one cannot avoid philosophizing—albeit only occasionally and to a limited extent. Cailliet makes the point as follows:

> According to etymology, philosophy is the love of wisdom. Thus Pythagoras (sixth century BC) coined the word by calling himself a lover of wisdom, a philosopher. His reference was to both the quest for wisdom and the wisdom sought. In this connection, each one of us is a philosopher. Each one of us actually has an outlook on life, a world view of his own, which motivates him whether he realizes it or not. . . . Common sense, then, would have everyone realize that Christian philosophy appears whenever and wherever a Christian begins to think. The possible alternatives to this could only be either a thinker who is not a Christian at all, or a Christian who did not think at all.[17]

Everyday reflection is not philosophy, of course, only its starting point. Philosophy proper arises once the reflection is pursued in a sustained way, and reaches a certain level of generality. At the same time, philosophy does not stand in relation to everyday belief as science does. Physics replaces folk physics. That is to say, the explanations of natural phenomena that physicists devise render redundant the commonplace explanations that preceded them. By contrast, philosophy does not ren-

17. Ibid., 59.

der common understanding redundant. It both sharpens and deepens it. The point can be applied to Christian philosophy. This neither displaces nor replaces everyday faith, but deepens our understanding of that faith.

RELATIONSHIP BETWEEN PHILOSOPHY AND THEOLOGY

Does this not make philosophy indistinguishable from theology? This is an issue to which Cailliet is acutely sensitive, and it is on this point that he several times repeats his contention that "Christian philosophy should remain in the world without being of it."[18] We might express the difference this way. While theology attempts to systematize Christian doctrine in such a way that it avoids both the incoherent and the heretical, Christian philosophy aims to uncover what it means to be a Christian in the world. On this conception, cultural engagement is key to Christian philosophy. To quote Cailliet once more: "The greatest service that the Christian philosopher can render . . . is to bear witness to what he sees when he looks at the world of men and affairs in the light of faith."[19]

So conceived, Christian philosophy is not the servant of theology. This, certainly, is how it has often been seen, both in times past and more recently. To think of the relationship in this way is to endorse John Locke's celebrated description of the philosopher as an "underlaborer." In modern versions of Locke's conception, natural science is the master to which philosophy is underlaborer, and its role is to clear away the conceptual confusions that hinder the advancement of science. In the context of the seminary, of course, it is not science but theology that is the master—a conception with a considerable pedigree, as the medieval Latin tag *"philosophia ancilla theologiae"* (philosophy the handmaid of theology) makes evident. A good many contemporary philosophers are willing, and even anxious to endorse the service to science. Philosophy in the service of theology will find very few contemporary advocates amongst philosophers.

The principal reason for this is an anxiety that philosophy in the service of theology quickly loses its essential freedom to inquire because its investigations are subject to dogmatic limits. David Hume expresses this anxiety in his *Natural History of Religion*. Philosophy that is "apt to incorporate itself with a system of theology," he says, "will soon find

---

18. Cailliet, "Outlines of a Christian Positivism," 36.
19. Cailliet, *Christian Approach to Culture*, 65.

herself very unequally yoked with her new associate. . . . Will you set up profane reason against sacred mystery? . . . [then in time] the same fires, which were kindled for heretics, will serve for the destruction of philosophers."[20] Today, perhaps, philosophers have no reason to fear real flames, yet the heart of the objection remains. The conception of philosophy as either underlaborer or handmaiden makes it subservient to intellectual purposes other than its own. Since philosophy is a distinctive intellectual discipline, the philosopher, in whatever context, cannot accept such limitations with integrity. This means, among other things, that philosophy courses at a seminary cannot properly be restricted to those that are helpful to the study of theology.

THE VOCATION OF THE CHRISTIAN PHILOSOPHER IN THE SEMINARY

What does this imply? To find a valuable role for philosophy in the seminary it is essential to grasp at the outset that philosophy is an activity, an activity of mind rather than body or soul. The life of the mind is at its most vigorous and enriching when the business of thinking is required to meet high standards of clarity, consistency, and comprehensiveness. Secondly, meeting these standards is most valuable when engaged in thinking about the most fundamental aspects of human existence. Both of these conditions are distinctive of philosophy, summarized in an ancient formula as the pursuit of wisdom about the true, the good, and the beautiful. To teach philosophy is to stretch and invigorate the minds of students as they seek to arrive at clear, consistent, and comprehensive beliefs about these fundamental topics. All this, of course, is quite compatible with thinking that there is no special place for philosophical study in the seminary. Seminary students can receive the benefits of a philosophical education by taking university and college courses before, or alongside, their divinity degree. What further purpose is served by their taking them as part of that degree?

This question arises with special force for students in divinity schools located within universities—Chicago, Duke, Emory, Harvard, Vanderbilt, and Yale, for example—and for Princeton Seminary whose students may include courses taken at Princeton University in their program of study. Why then have philosophy taught within the seminary? To arrive at an

20. Hume, *Natural History of Religion*, 165–66.

answer in the spirit of Cailliet, we must forswear both the role of apologetics and *"philosophia ancilla theologiae"* and uncover what it might mean to be a "Christian philosopher."

It is an important part of Cailliet's conception of philosophy that it does not begin *de novo*, as for instance, French or physics might. Rather, philosophy develops an existing, if somewhat inchoate, "outlook on life." Teaching philosophy well, accordingly, begins by identifying the seeds of the outlook that students bring to their studies in seminary, not with a view of undermining or replacing it, but giving it is fullest, most coherent articulation. We may assume, of course, that in the case of seminary students, this "outlook" is importantly Christian. Given, however, that it is (as yet) elementary in its articulation, it follows that the task of the Christian philosopher is neither apologetic nor skeptical. The outlook is insufficiently articulated to make the apologetics inapplicable, and by the same token skeptical criticism is premature. Of course, the role of the philosophy teacher is not to provide students with a "ready-to-wear" outlook on life, Christian or otherwise, but to inspire students with the desire to make a start on a philosophical journey of their own

What is the form of that journey? If it is to be philosophical it must apprentice itself to the tradition of inquiry that began with the ancient Greeks. This means engagement with the major figures within that tradition irrespective of their religious persuasion—Hobbes, Hume, and Nietzsche no less than Aquinas, Berkeley, and Kierkegaard. If it is to be Christian, however, this philosophical engagement must be pursued within certain fixed parameters. These parameters are not to be confused with theological or doctrinal limits. They are neither expressly theological nor doctrinal. They are nonetheless fundamental to Christian discipleship. Among them we may include attributing special status of the Bible (though not any one account of that status), holding to the unique importance of the work and person of Jesus Christ (though not to any specific Christology), and regarding the liturgical and spiritual history of the Church as both valuable and informative (though without any one denominational loyalty). Stated in this way, we can see the distinctive character of philosophy in the seminary. It is enough for professors and students of philosophy at college and university to engage with the major texts and thinkers of the intellectual tradition they hope to master. It is enough for Christians *per se* to think and act within these parameters. The distinctive task of the Christian philosopher, both student and teacher, is to hold these two dimensions together in a creative tension. It is misleading, however, to call the outcome of this tension "Christian philosophy" because, as Etienne Gilson remarks, "the idea of Christian philosophy has no more meaning than 'Christian physics' or 'Christian mathematics.'"[21] Nevertheless, to employ a distinction Gilson also draws, the fact that there is no such thing as "a Christian reason," leaves the idea of "a Christian exercise of reason" intact, and hence a Christian exercise in philosophical reason.

What is distinctive about this exercise? Here we endorse Cailliet's contention that the answer lies in cultural engagement. Plato's early dialogues are fine examples of this kind of engagement. Before he set out on the more ambitious metaphysical theorizing evident in his later works, Plato, through the character of Socrates, approaches issues relating to truth, goodness and beauty by means of the Socratic dialectic. He poses questions to interlocutors who represent authoritative, received, or popular opinion, and by this dialectical process exposes the weakness of their position and thus the false confidence with which it is held. Though the characters interrogated are named individuals, the positions they endorse and attempt to defend are representative of broader cultural trends. In this way, Socrates' questions are really directed *Against the Self-Images of the Age*, the title of a collection of essays by another philosopher two thousand, five hundred years later—Alasdair MacIntyre.

In the Platonic dialogues, Socrates famously professes his own ignorance, contending thereby that he does not examine the views of his interlocutors with some other rival theory in mind. Nevertheless, he does bring, and cannot avoid bringing, a distinctive "outlook" to bear on his conversations—an outlook based on (among other things) a belief in the power of reason, a desire for better understanding, and a respect for the realities of human life and the human condition. There is no reason why such an outlook should not be extended to include the parameters of Christian faith. Something of this sort, it appears, is what Cailliet has in mind when he says that "the greatest service that the Christian philosopher can render . . . is to bear witness to what he sees when he looks at the world of men and affairs in the light of faith."[22] Conceived in this way, the Christian philosopher explores the contemporary worlds of politics, art,

---

21. Gilson, *Spirit of Medieval Philosophy*, 36.
22. Cailliet, *Christian Approach to Culture*, 65.

commerce, technology, religion, science, and so on with the aim of uncovering their "self-images" and subjecting those images to critical scrutiny in the light of both philosophical cogency and Christian faith. "The philosophizing Christian," Roger Mehl says in a book expressly devoted to the subject, "differs from all other philosophers in that he reserves for himself the right—and the freedom—to judge and test his own work by a criterion which is not philosophical, but dogmatic."[23]

It is important to emphasize that this further criterion does not operate as a limit on inquiry that puts certain subjects beyond inquiry. That is the fear that the expression "Christian philosophy" prompts in the minds of most philosophers. Rather it functions as an additional test and asks what we should think about (for example) democracy, modern art, scientific discovery, if there is truth in Christian revelation. Philosophical inquiry as such does not specify any particular attitude to the authority of the Bible, the person of Jesus, or the history of the Church. But neither does it forbid nor prevent us from asking what difference to philosophy a positive attitude to these things will make. The spiritual value of art, for instance, is a question in philosophical aesthetics that has special interest for the role for Christian art in a secular world, and secular art in the life of the Church. Similarly, the proper relation of religion and politics—a question extensively discussed in political philosophy has special interest for anyone who wants to uphold a social dimension to the Gospel.[24] It is here, finally, that we find the rationale for the study of philosophy in the seminary. Philosophical debate within these parameters can only take place profitably if subscription to them is shared. No one can reasonably expect them to be shared in the lecture halls and seminar rooms of a modern university. Conversely, no one can object to the assumption that they will be shared within the walls of a seminary.

It is of course the case that neither intellectual prowess nor academic accomplishment is a necessary ingredient of faithful discipleship. Indeed the simple-hearted may encounter fewer obstacles to faith in God than do the highly intelligent. But Christians who find themselves with an inquiring mind cannot wish it away, or suppress its activities for fear that their faith will be undermined. They have, indeed, a sacred obligation to bring

---

23. Mehl, *Condition of the Christian Philosopher*, 29.

24. These examples are drawn from two of the MDiv courses that Gordon Graham regularly teaches at Princeton Seminary, namely "Philosophy of the Arts" and "Political Philosophy and Public Theology."

their faith into conversation with the culture into which they have been thrown, by birth or other circumstance. Their task and their vocation, to repeat Cailliet is to "remain in the world without being of it." But there is a more individual dimension too, one that has to do with personal development and educational accomplishment. Philosophical understanding can sustain, and even generate, spiritual virtues. It does so in two ways. First, grasping the profundity and complexity of a philosophical issue ought to result in the humbling thought that the human mind is a glorious gift, not something of our own making, and contrary to the occasional aspirations of artificial intelligence, not something we could manufacture either. This gift of mind can be taken for granted. It can even be ignored. It can also be something we actively care for and enjoy. Philosophy is one mode of that intellectual care and enjoyment, a practical acceptance of the gift of mind. Second, because philosophical inquiry takes place on what we might call the edge of human thought, among its effects (as one writer has put it) is "making wonder secure."[25] That is to say, engagement in philosophy can awaken in us a keen sense of the astonishing power of the human intellect while at the same time giving us an equally keen sense of its limits. So considered, philosophy thus becomes a means by which gratitude and humility are instilled in us. Both are antidotes to *hubris*, the Promethean pride that is humanity's besetting sin. This is why, as it seems to me, in addition to its role as a medium for cultural engagement, philosophy can rightly claim a place in a seminary education. It also reveals what it means to *be* a Christian philosopher. This label properly refers neither to someone whose philosophical inquiries are confined by theological doctrines, nor to someone who happens to teach philosophy in a Christian institution. The person with a vocation to be a Christian philosopher is one who sees how philosophy can be an expression of Christian existence.

---

25. Drury, *Danger of Words*.

Epilogue

WHAT HAVE WE LEARNED about Cailliet as a man and as a Christian, teacher, scholar, theologian, and philosopher? How has *his* life changed ours—what is his legacy? Some have said that "one day Cailliet will stand in history with Calvin."[1] This may be hyperbole, but there is no doubt he was a powerful, though little-known thinker. The consensus is that Cailliet would most want to be remembered by his teaching, his writing and his family.[2]

THE MAN

Cailliet was a complex person. There is no doubt that the three formative events in his life were fighting in World War I, falling in love and marrying Vera, and becoming a Christian. His conversion to the Christian faith at twenty-three influenced every aspect of who he was as a husband, father, teacher, scholar and philosopher. The light of Christ illuminated him from within. His own journey into the light became a beacon for many searching for meaning and purpose. Following the model of Pascal, he was able to integrate science, philosophy, and theology into a holistic approach to life and scholarship.

Cailliet's national and cultural ties to France shaped and defined him. However, he was immensely grateful to Americans for their rescue of him during the war and spent the primary years of his life as teacher

---

1. Letter from Thomas Horace Evans (New York Medical College, Dept. of Anatomy), May 4, 1955, Emile Cailliet Collection, Special Collections, Princeton Theological Seminary Library.

2. Charles Mackenzie and Richard Oman interviews with Bartollas and Evans.

and scholar in the United States; he was truly a citizen of two countries. Teaching at four very different academic institutions reflected his versatility and the breadth of his scholarly interests and expertise. He had tremendous intellectual endowments and a photographic memory. The power of his personality and presence reached across cultures and disciplines to deeply touch many lives.

Although seemingly aloof, Cailliet had a tender heart for those close to him and a compassion for those marginalized by others. He had high standards and expectations of others but always challenged himself as well. He was a great man whose intellectual accomplishments deserved wider recognition during his lifetime than they gained. Although an intellectual, he was also a physical person who enjoyed mountain climbing, hiking, and later in life, taking long walks. Throughout his life, the companionship of his dog (of course, different ones) was dear to him.

THE BELIEVER

Cailliet, as a believer in Christ, was called by some a Christian centurion. He had used this term himself to describe one "who had but one concern—to do the Lord's will in joy and simplicity of heart. . . . It is a life of love and power, because it is a completely surrendered life, and therefore a life in line with the will of God. As such it abides forever."[3] He insisted on a personal relationship with God and the practice of early morning reading of a wide variety of books. His devotion was due in part to his piety and to his belief in all of our calling to be scholars and saints. The latter was more important than the former.[4]

Though Cailliet did not use the term in his writing, he implicitly held that the life of the believer is one of ongoing *sanctification*. Sanctification seems to be at the heart of what he discussed concerning the need to keep the fervor of one's faith, rejecting doubts and timidity. For him, we need to make the far-reaching statement of Augustine our own: "'Inquietum est cor nostrum, donec requiescat in te!' (Our heart is restless until it resteth in Thee!)"[5] Cailliet believed that what we need to do is abandon ourselves

---

3. Cailliet, *Beginning of Wisdom*.

4. Paul M. McKowen, Emile Cailliet Collection, Special Collections, Princeton Theological Seminary Library, Box 7, File 131.

5. Cailliet, "Christian Experience," 332.

to the will of God and abide in that will. What crowns that relationship is love—a love that emanates from God.[6]

Central to Cailliet's faith was the Bible, the book with the answer to the question, "'Who am I and what kind of place am I in?'" Cailliet asserted: "This question can only be answered with any degree of finality after the Bible [has] been brought out of a salvaged chest—to be lived."[7] While the reading of the Scriptures was central to Cailliet's devotional life, prayer also played a crucial role and was at the heart of his faith. Many people thought of him as a mystic. He always began class with prayer, and his prayers made quite an impression on those in his courses.

Cailliet had a profound Christian faith that touched the core of his being. Students believed that his effective Christian witness arose from his personal awareness of the Holy Spirit and the consistent time he took to communicate with God. His greatest influence lay not in his superior intellect, but in the discernment he received through daily commitment to Christ.[8]

It is clear that everyone who met Emile Cailliet had not the slightest doubt that he was a committed and devoted Christian to whom faith meant everything. His faith influenced not only his students, but peers and colleagues. There are a number of letters exchanged that reference Cailliet's witness for Christ and his holiness.

THE TEACHER

Cailliet's calling as a teacher may be his most enduring legacy. His influence through his students, who have spread around the world, speaks of how he shaped their personal Christian faith and vocation. He was named as one of the giants on the faculty, a professor with a massive grandeur.[9] His courses were powerful because his strong Christian faith shone through all that he wrote and taught. Students, years later, have testified not only to his exemplary qualities as a Christian teacher and scholar, but also to his character, calling him an "excellent human being."[10] For

---

6. Ibid., 334.
7. Cailliet, *Dawn of Personality*, 232.
8. WBM, letter to Rosemary Mitchell, December 2, 2009.
9. JRL, letter to Evans and Bartollas.
10. PCL, letter to Evans and Bartollas.

those who might still have had lingering agnosticism or only took philosophy courses from atheists in university, Cailliet as a brilliant Christian scholar, put the doubts to rest for these young seminarians who hungered for intellectual rigor coupled with strong personal faith. Cailliet gave his Princeton students an understanding of their faith and the Reformed Tradition.[11] On the other hand, for those who had studied science or the classics, they saw a sense of unity between their undergraduate and theological education that Cailliet's courses provided.[12] His teaching became "a personal encounter with the appropriateness of loving God with the mind as well as with the heart."[13]

His daughter's reflections on his legacy echo the importance of his teaching. "He would want to be remembered by his influence on his students, as he encouraged each student to find the direction he or she might take in their future careers. He believed that they must find the way but he encouraged them to choose."[14]

THE SCHOLAR

As a scholar, Cailliet's fame was primarily based on his outstanding lifelong work on Pascal, who was seminal in his own faith journey. His ability to interpret the profound philosophy of Pascal with true evangelical fervor is an enduring legacy. A thirst for knowledge and insights into faith illuminated by scholarship gave his students the gift of a liberal, evangelical theology. He invited scientific thought into conversation with Christianity and showed "an affinity of biblical cosmology with the modern Einsteinian cosmology."[15] Put another way, he had both evangelical piety and intellectual rigor. In fact, Frank Gaebelein called him an evangelical Einstein.

Cailliet's "best book," according to him, was *The Life of the Mind*. He wrote to his daughter that he put the best of himself into that book: "He would weigh his mind carefully and think what he should do. What

---

11. Donald M. Williams to Emile Cailliet, July 7, 1959, Emile Cailliet Collection, Special Collections, Princeton Theological Seminary Library.
12. DA, letter to Evans and Bartollas.
13. WO, letter to Evans and Bartollas.
14. Brunzie, letter to Evans and Bartollas.
15. Lemke, *Philosophy of Emile Cailliet*.

he should give up in order to choose well, etc. 'Thinking is the process of clarification,' he wrote. In *The Life of the Mind* certain chapters are to be eliminated, others adapted. These were controlled by *animus*, the brain, and *anima*, the soul. There was an inner conversation between the two, and it appears that *anima* won over *animus*."[16]

Cailliet focused on and was celebrated for his work in a wide range of academic subjects. An interesting feature of Cailliet's scholarship was not only his skill in crossing disciplinary lines but his field-based research that brilliantly revealed the heart of magic, the occult and religion. He was distinguished for his work on Pascal, research in Madagascar and for the Christian philosophy books and articles he wrote later in his career. Certainly the selection by the *New York Times* on December 4, 1955 of his *Dawn of Personality* as one of the two hundred fifty[17] outstanding books of 1955 was a singular honor.[18]

THE PHILOSOPHER

Cailliet did much to open theological students to the importance of philosophy as part of their education as future pastors, teachers, and scholars; he emphasized the significance of this discipline even to those entering non-church related vocations. He challenged them to develop their own philosophy of life and to see philosophy as a tool for raising questions to which theology might supply the answers. At the same time, philosophy was never to be viewed as purely instrumental but as a discipline that had a contribution to make in its own right.

In answer to Tertullian's age old question, Cailliet's life, writing, and teaching demonstrated that Athens and Jerusalem *do* have something to do with each other. He worked from a paradigm that philosophy and even science, to some degree, should be a part of theological education and attempted to integrate them into his own teaching. In fact, his most difficult challenge may have been "to break down the mythology of philosophy by

---

16. Brunzie letter to Evans and Bartollas.

17. Ten thousand titles were considered.

18. See box 25 of the Princeton Theological Seminary Library archives, Emile Cailliet Collection, for an entire notebook full of newspaper clippings and reviews praising this book.

showing its interrelationship with theology."[19] He was not lured by what was new or faddist in theology and especially at Princeton Seminary was not afraid to uphold the Augustinian/Calvinist tradition. He sought to place theology in social, cultural and academic contexts, while encouraging a Biblically-grounded study of Christian philosophy.

CONCLUSION

We trust that this modest volume may entice the reader to seek Cailliet's books and further understand his contributions in interpreting the Christian life. We conclude this book with the hope that in discovering something of Cailliet through these pages, the reader may be touched by this giant of a thinker—a complex man who was ultimately grounded in his love of Christ and desire to follow him with his whole heart, mind, and soul—into the light. We conclude with Cailliet's own words: "It now appears that if our journey was meant to be a journey into Light, it is because it was destined to find its climax in the glory of that glow [of Christ's love]. And, lo and behold, the whole Gospel is henceforth transfigured as we look through it in the Light that has now dawned upon us."[20]

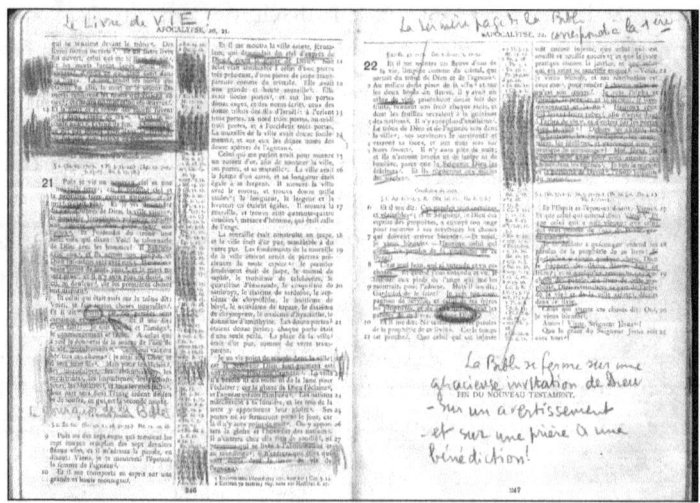

Emile Cailliet's *La Sainte Bible*, received from Vera Cailliet on December 17, 1917; Book of "Apocalypse" (Revelation).

19. Oman, interview with Evans.
20. Cailliet, *Journey into Light*, 109–10.

Emile and Vera Cailliet in later years.

Appendix A
Emile Cailliet Biographical Chronology

FAMILY

Parents: Adrien and Jeanne (née Courtin) Cailliet, Paris, France
Brother: Lucien Cailliet (May 22, 1891–January 3, 1985)
         Sailed March 2, 1915, from Le Havre to the United States with the French Army Band
         Citizenship: Naturalized US citizen on January 23, 1923
         Spouses: Valentine (married 1913); Vera L. Jeffrey (married June 23, 1946)
         Children: René, Marcel, Julie, Marguerite (with wife Valentine); Paul and Claude (with wife Vera)
         Profession: musician, conductor, composer, arranger

PERSONAL

December 17, 1894	Born in Dampierre, Marne, France
December 17, 1917	Became a Christian
April 23, 1937	Became a naturalized US citizen
June 4, 1981	Died in California, leaving his children, nine grandchildren, and two great-grandchildren

APPENDIX A
MILITARY

September 1914	Enlisted in the French Army, after the Battle of Marne during World War I
February 19–20, 1915	Wounded as a part of the 44th Infantry Regiment, Fifth Battalion of Sharpshooters
March–November 1915	Hospitalized at the American Field Hospital at Juilly, France
March 23, 1917	Released from the French Army

MARRIAGE AND CHILDREN

Wife: Vera Ethel Brabazon (June 1, 1896–March 9, 1969)

            Courtship and marriage: met Emile Cailliet in Germany, December 24, 1913; married Cailliet March 25, 1915

            Citizenship: Arrived in the United States on the Ile de France with Emile (who returned to accompany her) and their children in 1930; became a naturalized citizen of the United States February 23, 1940

Children   Hélène (Adcock) (July 17, 1916–June 14, 2001)

            André (June 16, 1919- June 8, 2006)

               Born in Chalon sur Saône, France

               Military service: Volunteered for the French Army in 1939 in WWII; captured and imprisoned in a German prison camp Stalag IX-A from 1940–1944 and later liberated by American troops

            Suzanne (Gardon) (born May 10, 1922)

            Doris (Brunzie) (born December 19, 1923)

EDUCATION

1913	College of Chalons, University of Paris, BA
1923	University of Nancy, *License ès-lettres philosophie*, MA

1926	Gouverner Général de Madagascar et Dépendances, *Brevet de Langue Malgache* (Malagasy language), Certificate
1926	University of Montpellier, *Doctorat-ès-lettres* (Humanities), PhD
1937	University of Strasbourg, ThD *summa cum laude*

PROFESSIONAL

December 1923–1926	Directed schools in Madagascar and did research for a PhD from the University of Montpellier
1926–1931	Assistant Professor, French Literature, University of Pennsylvania (Philadelphia, PA)
1931–1941	Professor, chairman, Department of Modern Languages and Literatures, Coordinator of Junior Humanities Program, Scripps College; Professor of French Literature and Civilization, Claremont Graduate School (Claremont, CA)
1941–1945	Professor, French Literature and Civilization, Graduate School of University of Pennsylvania (Philadelphia, PA)
1945–1947	Professor, French Literature and Philosophy, Wesleyan College (Middleton, CT)
1947–1959	Stuart Professor of Christian Philosophy, Princeton Theological Seminary (Princeton, NJ)

Appendix B

Account of the Wedding of Emile and Vera Cailliet

Cailliet, Vera Brabazon. *Froebel Gazette* 24 (February 1917).
January 31, 1917

Dear Old Girls and Present Students,

    I will try to give you a little description of my wedding. I was married in March, 1915, at the little Village "Mairie of Juilly," Seine et Marne. The bridegroom was a "Tirailleur Algérien," wounded, and under hospital treatment, with his left arm disabled from a German bullet. Present at the little ceremony were a French lieutenant who had his cheek disfigured, another officer who had a crushed foot, a native Arab with his right hand disabled, an English hospital nurse, the village schoolmistress, and the Mayor. I see I have omitted the bride, but you knew her well, some of you, Vera Brabazon, now Vera Cailliet. It was the ordinary French civil marriage, simple and impressive. With the Mayor before us reading the marriage law, and wearing the tri-colour scarf, and with the bust of the French Republic looking down on us, we promised each other fidelity. When our witnesses signed the register after us, it was pathetic to see our Arab trembling with emotion and unable to write his name alone with his left hand, especially as he had practiced doing so very diligently beforehand. The nurse who was there had to help him out by guiding his hand.

    After this we went to a hotel all together, and our guests drank to our health and happiness in champagne. Though there were unfortunately no members of our families present, we felt none the less great emotion at the joining of our lives together. Finally our guests left us to enjoy our 24 hours' leave together.

The next day I returned to Paris and my husband to the American Hospital at Juilly. But after a few weeks of lessons in Paris were finished I took rooms in the country near the Hospital where I went every day, or occasionally Monsieur Cailliet had leave to come and see me- sometimes he came without permission along the railway lines and across the fields. The Hospital, though beautifully fitted up and in a fine big park, was a sort of prison for him and it was under military authority too.

We spent the Summer thus and August found me in Paris giving lessons, where my husband joined me in September, a civilian once more, after having endured all kinds of severe electric treatment for his arm, without result; and now it is paralysed and is the cause of cerebral pains if he is overworked. He took a post at the "Ecole Commerciale" in Paris at first, but was obliged to give it up for the above reason; so we came here where we have less rush and he is teaching at the Ecole Professionnelle at Chalon sur Saône.

We have a darling little baby girl of nearly 7 months old now, called Hélène! Let us hope the war will be over before she can listen to and understand the story of our war wedding with a happy ending. I will now leave you, dear old girls and present students, wishing you heartiest good luck and perseverance and courage in your work in 1917.

Vera E. Cailliet

Appendix C

I Met the Huguenots

Cailliet, Emile. "I Met the Huguenots" (n.d.)

I vividly remember the day decades ago, when as a young man it was my privilege by the grace of God to journey through the Cévennes Mountains to the native Huguenot village as yet untouched by the hand of time. Let historians, psychologists, or Proustian novelists rave about libraries, search the mysterious play of memory, or brood over that which pertains to the recovery of the past. On that day I actually moved back through history, way back to the mid-sixteenth century, and met Huguenots of flesh and blood. Truly our God is the Great Doer of the unexpected!

JOURNEY BACK TO THE SIXTEENTH CENTURY

As often is the case, the circumstances that led to the great blessing were of a rather unusual nature. We had been invited to spend a week in a mountain cabin. Our little boy was taken ill. There was no doctor within reach. The only one known to the lonely folks scattered miles around, practiced in a distant village. Distant, that is, because it could only be reached through goats' trails across the mountain. And so I started out at the crack of dawn, with the small lad perched on my shoulder. Quite a demanding journey, I assure you. I finally "made it."

    A small surgical intervention being indicated, I left the boy at the doctor's until the following morning. As I walked aimlessly along the steep streets of the village, wondering where I could find a place to eat and sleep, a native Cévennol who had already seen me pass by, asked me if he could be of any help. This was said in a simple, unassuming way as if the occasion were a matter of course. Having heard my story, he opened the door of a house and introduced me to his wife.

The children stopped their games and stood up to greet the guest with an obviously inbred reverence. I was immediately taken upstairs to my room which must have been the best in the house—neat clean, with flower pots on the window sill. The evening meal would soon be served, I was told.

ORIGINAL MEANING OF THE NAME, HUGUENOT

As we now revert to our world of men and affairs,—and, pray, why should the transition be so keenly felt?—a reader may rightly remark: Was not the name, Huguenot, given to all the Protestants of France? Why, then, the suggestion that it essentially applies to those of the Cévennes Mountains?

Admittedly, the word, Huguenot, originally was a nickname which seems to have been popularized after 1560, and to have coined, not in the Cévennes, but in Touraine. There, in the capital city of Tours, the Protestants used to assemble by night, near the King Hugo Gate. A Catholic monk chose to play upon the superstitious fears associated with King Hugo, an evil spirit said to roam about after dark. The monk took advantage of the analogy, and said in a sermon that in doing likewise, the Protestants proved themselves to be the kinsmen of King Hugo; that accordingly they should be called Huguenots.

What matters is that when the mighty sovereign Louis XIV who at one time had subdued most of Europe, used every means of war and persecution to eradicate French Protestantism, a remnant remained, hidden away in the Cévennes Mountains, and as hard to break as their hardest rocks. The very setting of my opening story proved to have been the last bastion of the Camisards—the Huguenot peasants of the Cévennes—and that bastion held. Under the vigorous leadership of John Cavalier, teen-aged son of a local baker, they brought to naught the war of extermination waged against them by the mighty King in whose presence the continent of Europe had stood in awe. They never gave up, never entertained the thought of surrender. Those of their number who came to their end in the Tower of Constance of infamous memory, left engraved on the wall their one word motto, "*Resister*" (to resist). Some historians have chosen to single out for reproof the fact that this extreme Camisard version of the Huguenot movement was fanatical, and made much of tongues, prodigies, ecstatic prophecies, and even preternatural lights in the sky. My answer to this is that it is a much easier task to write academic history in the comfortable peace of one's study, than to resist unto blood in the power of the Holy Spirit. I have been fortunate enough to have acquired for my library a copy of the Bible edited by the pastors and professors of the Church of Geneva, published at Saumur in 1614. This copy bound in its original sheepskin hard cover, was originally a Huguenot family Bible. Its first entry in abbreviated French reads: "My father, born 1519, died 1560." There is evidence that the Book of Isaiah and the Book of Revelation were the most currently read—probably at the hour of danger. It does not take much imagination to think of the Book hidden away under a rock to be consulted in a few moments of respite. Pray God we could recover such spiritual hunger together with such a spirit of urgency!

There accordingly is ample justification for singling out for special appreciation the Camisard apex of the Huguenot movement. The ruling Pope of those days has vindicated this view for all times. Clement XI has exposed the Camisards as the "ancient Albigenses" having sprung from the same soil as those medieval "heretics" did! What a precious pointer, this, for the student of the distant origins of the Reformation, with special attention to the Huguenot movement!

THE WIDER CONTEXT

Following the lead this unexpectedly provided for us by Pope Clement XI, we do find as early as the eleventh century one of the roots of the Reformation deep in the soil of southern France, when the Albigenses reacted against the neo-paganism of the Church. They already felt the need to worship God in their own mother tongue. They proved so dangerous to the established Church, in fact, that Pope Innocent III ordered a Crusade against them. What that Crusade did, incidentally was to wipe out not only a "dissident sect", but a whole culture. Scholars will long ponder what might have become of that brilliant and most promising civilization of the province of Languedoc. Its center was Toulouse, where Counts were both poets and patrons of letters. Its language, the Limousine dialect, had become a beautiful literary medium. The war against the Albigenses can be said actually to have destroyed the learned and refined lyricism of the Midi. It proved to be a turning point in the history of the French language, literature and civilization.

It remains a fact none the less that the forerunners and later first adepts of the Reformation in France, for the most part were plain folk. It was only later that the nobility, the university, the judiciary, and the clergy itself, joined the movement. I think of such evangelical men as the disciples of Peter Waldo, the "poor men of Lyons," as they were called. They gave away everything they owned in order to have the Scriptures copied and distributed. Uniting with other Christians of similar vocation, they rejected the mass, purgatory, and the worship of the saints, in the name of the Apostolic succession. They became known as the Waldensians.

It now becomes clear that what came to full bloom in the Huguenot movement—henceforth, just another name for the French Reformed tradition—was a live evangelical tradition increasingly hemmed in by the Church of Rome. As early as 1512, i.e. five years before Luther broke with Rome, Lefèvre d'Etaples published his commentary on the Epistles of Paul, in which he proclaimed the great doctrine of salvation by faith. A 1509 edition of Lefèvre d'Etaples' Quincuplex Psalterium has been found in the Library of Dresden, covered with annotations by Luther. So, if there be affiliation between the French and the German Reformation, the priority in time appears to rest decidedly with the French. Later, in 1523, Lefèvre d'Etaples published the New Testament in the vernacular. Persecution was his reward. Nevertheless, he had broken ground for the cause of the Reformation. He had proclaimed not only the doctrine of salvation by faith, but also that of the supreme authority of Holy Writ. His translation of the New Testament was to be the starting point of Olivetan's work. Peter Robert, nicknamed Olivetan, a cousin of Calvin's was most influential in initiating his younger relative into the Evangelical faith. Olivetan's translation of the whole Bible, as revised in the eighteenth century, was to become the present Osterwald version, one of the most honored in the French language.

Investigate the names of the men who most influenced John Calvin, and you will have a splendid roll of the dignitaries of the French Reformation. In Paris, Calvin studied under the admirable Latinist Mathurin Cordier, the sixteenth century Lhomond as he has been called, an ardently pious soul consecrated to the welfare of his students. Calvin later called him to the Academy of Geneva. Then Calvin became acquainted with Farel, a disciple of Lefèvre d'Etaples, who had just arrived from Meaux, the center of the Bibliens, or men of the Bible. In Orleans, Calvin studied law under Peter de l' Etoile. How much this special education was to mean in the work of Calvin, we all know. In 1530 we find Calvin in Bourges, where he takes courses from the Hellenist Melchior Volmar in whose home he met a ten year old boy who was to remain his friend through thick and thin, namely Theodore Beza. Upon his father's death, Calvin went to Paris where he studied at the newly founded College of Royal Readers—now the College de France, and there he took Greek under Danes and Hebrew under Vatable. We may remember the Cop incident of 1532, and how Calvin sought refuge in the house of his friend, Canon du Tillet of the Cathedral School of Angoulême. Canon du Tillet's library contained three or four thousand volumes. There Calvin began his *Institutes* in the midst of friends. At Nerac we find another group centered around Margaret of Angoulême, or should we rather say, around the now prophetic figure of the centenarian Lefèvre d'Etaples. The latter announced to the Queen that Almighty God was about to recall him, adding that "he knew". He died the same night. Often as I have read the story, and even to this day, I am lost in admiration at the Biblical grandeur of that scene!

Calvin left Nerac fully committed. Remember how he renounced all his benefits; how, having been driven out of Basel after the Placards (Notices) incident, he worked out his *Institutes*. We must reluctantly hurry through a gallery of great and moving scenes: Calvin compelled by Farel in the name of the Living God to remain in Geneva; Calvin with Bucer in Strasbourg; his ministry to the Protestant refugees culminating in the Reformed liturgy with its grandiose Confession of sins; Calvin and his splendid creation of Protestant Geneva; Calvin and the Academy—a prototype of most of our institutions of higher learning. I wish space allowed at least a recitation of the great saga of a Christian learning remaining in close contact with the people; of its admirable contributions to agronomy, surgery, and the fine arts; above all, to the true spirit of democracy.

DEMOCRACY'S DEBT TO THE HUGUENOTS

The Reformers' exaltation of the infinite value of the individual soul in the sight of God singles out the Protestants as the promoters of a genuine democracy in the modern world. This is particularly true in the case of the French Huguenots. It was they who first developed the views opposing royal absolutism. What immediately drove them to oppose the king, to the point of advocating deposition, was of course the awful persecution visited upon them. This once granted, however, it becomes clear to the student of their writings on political philosophy, that they felt constrained by their deep conviction that the monarchial form of government was undesirable. Its centralized system had given rise to unbearable abuses. Exposing the dangers inherent in too highly concentrated a supreme power, the Huguenots went as far as to predict the ultimate destruction of the middle class which in every country constitutes the fundamental element of stability. That is to say that were they to reappear in our midst today, the Huguenots could pertinently ascribe a great deal of our political woes to our failure to have heeded their warnings nay, their characterization of true democracy under God.

Not only were the French Huguenots ignored, but they fell victim to a savage persecution which amounted to near-extermination. Of the 2,150 churches in existence in 1562, only 950 remained in 1598; only 760 in 1603. When, after the Revolution of Protestant faith was finally recognized in France, there remained only 171 Protestant churches in the whole country, 50 of which could not find a minister—ministers having been sent either to the galleys or into exile. Choosing expatriation and misery rather than recantation, 300,000 Huguenots left their native country; quite a number of them emigrating to America. 20,000 soldiers enrolled under foreign flags. A suburb of London and a whole section of Berlin were made up of French workers, industrialists and teachers or professors. There is something sadly ironical in the fact that Berlin was turned into a capital city mostly thanks to Huguenot immigration. The corresponding loss to France proved irreparable. Looking back at the sufferings of the Huguenots, at the purity, self-denial, honesty and industry of their lives, and at the devotion with which they adhered to religious duty and the worship of God, McFetridge writes: "We cannot fail to regard them as among the truest, greatest, and worthiest heroes of their age." To be pronounced "honest as a Huguenot" has since become a badge of the highest integrity.

THE AFTERMATH OF PERSECUTION

It has now for a long time been my conviction that the aftermath of the extermination of the French Huguenots has not sufficiently retained the attention of earnest, far-seeding historians. What the ferocious persecution finally amounted to, was the naked fact that the Church of Rome was not re-formed. A supreme attempt at correcting the resulting situation was made by the Jansenists during the seventeenth century. They too were defeated in spite of the gallant stand taken by Pascal on their behalf. Subsequently, worldliness, immorality, together with all the trappings of political craftiness, dominated the Roman Catholic clergy during the eighteenth century. Recent research—and I think here of such works as Daniel Mornet's scholarly study on the intellectual origins of the French Revolution—has shown beyond the shadow of a doubt, that the great French upheaval was originally directed, not at the throne, but at the Roman Catholic hierarchy. The lines were drawn, and the picture of conflict already set as early as 1750.

Consider further that the history of the last 170 years in many of its aspects may be construed as the aftermath of the great Revolution, various interludes of a few decades' duration notwithstanding, and formulate your own conclusions. As I have come to see it, the misery of our world today originated for a large part in the Roman defiance of the gentle promptings of the Holy Spirit. God was mocked and as a result "the grapes of wrath" now are coming to maturity. The fathers have eaten sour grapes, and the children's teeth are set on edge.

Could it even be that the shadow of the old Huguenots may yet be detected amid the darkness which is now spreading over Berlin? If so, this can only mean that the time has come for those of us who would be counted, to heed the roll call of true discipleship: Huguenots, Camisards, and all of you, Covenanters!

Emile Cailliet
Stuart Professor of Christian Philosophy
Princeton Theological Seminary

Appendix D

A Layman Among Ministers[1]

Emile Cailliet, LITTD, THD
Cailliet, Emile. "A Layman Among Ministers." *The Princeton Seminary Bulletin* 39.2 (1945) 4–10.

When I was called from my vacation by your President to give this commencement address, I was, fittingly enough, meditating upon Irwin Edman's widely read book entitled *Philosopher's Holiday*. To tell the truth, the title of the present address was inspired by the title of an isolated chapter from Edman's book, one likely to prick anybody's curiosity-"An Irishman among the Brahmins." To me this chapter presents a perfect preview of the scenes of holy impatience which may later unfold among our returning veterans as they once more go to college-or to Church.

George O'Connor has gone to his professor, who tells us the story, to ask whether a course of his in the philosophy of religion was "worth taking," or whether it was "just another course." Now listen to the amplification rendered by our eager young student: Does this course, he asks, "really give you new ideas, or do something to your old ones? Does it make you over, or give you a new world?" Having finally tried the course—and a seminar besides—, having tried even to enter into the necessary discipline of this intellectual life, young George one day decides to leave the college with the remark intensely expressed: "I can't stand it anymore, I don't see how you can. . . . The place is too confoundedly intellectual.

---

1. The Commencement address delivered to the graduating class of Princeton Theological Seminary, August 17, 1945.

All the intellectual words, but no ideas with life in them. Ghosts of the mind walking around the campus." Of course his professor sees him to be wrong, and he tries to make a case for his own philosophy of education.

As I read the story, however, I could not avoid thinking that even this distinguished scholar had not fully understood what the student was driving at. There was indeed much more involved in the case than the mere fact of academic regimentation admitted by the professor. The latter had missed the main point in the youngster's verdict.

How searching in this connection is the statement of Paul to Timothy concerning persons who are "ever learning, and never able to come to the knowledge of the truth." We have a name for such intellectuals: we call them *dilettantes*. For them speculations has become an end in itself: they *lend* themselves to all sorts of attitudes without ever surrendering to any cause whatsoever. Their playfulness borders on voluptuousness. We should not insist on this infirm state of mind, were it not so prevalent, though not always developed to the extreme. The progress of philosophy in stressing both the possibilities and the limitations of our human faculties has done much to encourage that skepticism we describe as "playful." The Greek work *skepsis* in fact means research, and research, like hunting and fishing, tends to develop into a pleasant occupation—with the difference that the hunter and the fisherman are as a rule interested in the result of their sport. Yet we know, do we not, that they would disregard the game or he catch, were it simply offered them for the asking.

Such "playfulness," combines in various degrees with a false objectivity and attended by a natural instinct for a sheltered life and the usual anxiety to be intellectually respectable, makes up a certain type of "academic" attitude which is, alas, widespread. Professor Theodore M. Greene of Princeton University seems to me to have happily defined this detached and essentially cowardly attitude, when he branded it "one of endless investigation and argument without decision or commitment—of never taking sides on anything, of never committing oneself to anything." In similar terms President John A. Mackay has denounced what he calls a life enjoyed on a balcony as opposed to a life of commitment on the road. If I sense accurately the feelings of our returning veterans—God bless them!—they will have but little patience with this variety of tight-rope acrobatics, which the mere academicians of yesteryear seemed to consider a pre-requisite to the granting of PhD degrees.

Kierkegaard would help us throw light on such tragic misunderstandings, as he draws a dividing line between scientific matter, which naturally becomes an object of acquisition to which the personal life of the teacher is accidental, and ethico-religious matter, realities wherein commitment is the essential thing.

In the same vein, Pascal had already laid down the principle that it was necessary on the one hand to restore to experimental science the naturalistic and rationalistic method which properly belong to it; on the other hand to restore the theology the authority that is its proper due. As we take this position three centuries after Pascal, however, it must be with the frank admission that a part of what Pascal classified under the heading of theology had now been claimed by new disciplines. Nevertheless the basic principle formulated by him it left intact. It remains truer than ever that, having safeguarded each and every privilege of the most exacting scholarship, we should reserve for "the mysteries of faith. . . . that submission of mind which extends our belief to those mysteries which are hidden from sense and from reason."

Kindly notice therefore—and this is important—that *scholarship is not at stake*. In no point is it being questioned in connection with our faith. Indeed the critical approach to the New Testament's literary and historical problems is as legitimate and proves as useful as scientific investigation in the realm of physics and astronomy. It is not condemnable in itself. The time has come for fundamentalists to realize that it is as bad to denounce the New Testament scholar as it was for short-sighted men in the past to denounce and condemn the system of Copernicus or to force the abjuration of Galileo. The fact is that we should in this connection carefully ponder Galileo's treatise on *The Authority of Scripture* defining the relations between physical science and Holy Writ. It is humiliating that a book need ever have been written on *A History of the Warfare of Science with Theology in Christendom*.

Scholarship is not at stake, but there is indeed a tremendous issue at stake. And it is on this very issue that the George O'Connors as well as the enlightened men and women of our day crave an authoritative message. In the words of Professor Theodore M. Greene, they expect both "decision" and "commitment," the two being inseparable. They may have read Kierkegaard and approved of what he says about "realities wherein commitment is the essential thing," but they want to make sure of such realities. They would probably, as we do, subscribe to the strong reservation made by Pascal as to "those mysteries which are hidden from sense and from reason," but they want to know whether such mysteries veil any deeper reality at all, or whether Voltaire, Thomas Paine, or W. E. H. Lecky are right in their denials concerning them. The issue is more or less clearly defined in their mind, *but it is there*, and in the last analysis it must be met with yes-or-no simplicity. No evasion, however clever, will any longer do. At this juncture the last word in intellectual honesty is called for.

II

This is more true today than it ever was. The returning veteran has seen his "buddy" fall at his side. He himself has repeatedly seen death face to face. He has to know whether Jesus Christ is truly the Resurrection and the Life, or whether, in the words of James Thompson in his *City of Dreadful Night*,

> None can pierce the vast black veil uncertain
> Because there is no light behind the curtain;
> ... all is vanity and nothingness.

It is very natural, then, that the less educated should turn to our great seats of learning for an answer. Alas, they are due for disappointment. It is not so much that college professors are the atheists they are said to be. Many of them are indeed religious people, but somehow they are for the most part careful to hide the fact. The late beloved Professor William Lyon Phelps tells in his *Autobiography* how he was invited to teach in a certain college and asked if he could keep his religion out of the class room. On telling this to President Dwight he laughed and remarked: "My own observation shows that college teachers who are religious never mention it in the class room; the pupils never find it out, whereas those who are antireligious impress their views on the students and talk about it constantly." We must admit the fact that for all practical purposes the naturalistic faith is nowadays the only one looked upon with favor in academic circles. College men are encouraged to carry over into their entire sphere of influence the rationalistic presuppositions of pure science according to which subject matter is depersonalized in order to become socialized. As they disregard the pertinent reservations made by men like

Pascal and Kierkegaard, it follows that their whole life seems to be based on the assumption that man is the measure of all things.

I wish I had time to uncover for you the pathetic cases of students going to their advisers under the pretext of conflict in their schedules, or some such trifle, but in reality looking for some opening in the wall of academic objectivity. Once in a while the Christian convictions of the advisers are revealed and then—what blessed encounter in the office now become a sanctuary wherein naked soul meets naked soul in the hallowed presence of the Saviour! Personal confessions give you an entirely new outlook on the campus and into the fraternities where the midnight oil often burns over prolonged religious discussions—as though God were to be found at the end of a syllogism! Again you hear about the student's friends, and people in town, and about the folks at home. The spiritual need of our age is progressively brought into the open, and looms larger than ever.

One thing is certain. That need is not being met in our school system, surely not in our great seats of learning, except in a semi-clandestine fashion, which proves altogether insufficient. It is true that, thanks to the splendid corps of chaplains who have risen up to unique opportunities, the need is now being met in the Army, Navy, and Air formations. While this situation is only temporary, I see great possibilities for the future. On the whole, however, the tremendous spiritual vacuum of our age calls for total surrender on the part of the ministry.

III

On this point I will abstain from any criticism. In the first place, who am I that I should feel entitled to judge? In the second place, criticism is hardly, if ever, constructive. Do not criticize me. Love me, and help me. Like Herodotus in his *History* I shall not dispute whether ancient tales be true, but will begin rather with those wrongs whereof I myself have knowledge. In the manner of Socrates, at the beginning of Plato's *Apology*, all I ask is that you take heed and mark whether what I say is just. Some of the commonplace suggestions made herewith are meant to meet the needs of the situation as I have learned to appreciate the latter.

What happens here and now is as solemn an occasion as can arise anywhere at any time, and should be considered most seriously by every one of us. As you are about to enter into your ministry, our living God has appointed a layman—a most humble, unworthy one—to lay bare in your sight the dire need of his sheep. In his name I would charge you, and you, and you, to make sure of his commission and of its nature and responsibilities. In his name I say to you that the ministry you are about to enter upon is going to be either the most unique opportunity that ever was under his high heaven—or the most terrible curse in your life and on the lives of the flock to be entrusted you. The question before you is not one of "more or less," but of "either, or."

Be not deluded into believing with current writers who force the contents of the Holy Book into categories foreign to its central message, that the God of the Old Testament was first "conceived of" as an awe-inspiring divinity finally to become in modern man's enlightened understanding an "invisible Friend" no longer to be feared. The plain truth is that fear as well as love enters into the revealed notion of that which is called "sacred." While it is true that we have in the Bible a progressive relationship culminating in the incarnation of the Son of God, nevertheless God remains, even and especially in the teaching of Jesus, the awe-inspiring Sovereign to be feared. Be God-fearing ministers! As such, rest assured that he remains from everlasting to everlasting, a Consuming Fire. It is still true that to fall into the hands of the living God is a terrible thing. Yield yourselves obedient unto him without striving, and live every moment of your ministry in the firm assurance that, in the words of Queen Ann, there is not one circumstance so great as not to be subject to his power, nor so small but it comes within his care. You may very well ponder therefore over the implications of your total surrender to his service.

From then on, like Abram, you will be living in tabernacles because you look for a city. Abram, let it be remembered, was nicknamed "the Hebrew" because, as the ancient Greek translation of Genesis expresses it, he was "the man from the other side." You will likewise no longer be *of* the world, but still *in* the world. This plain statement implies at the same time the sacred character of your ministry and the terrible hardships it involves. From the very outset men will look to you as to a man. We know only that which we are. Only they will be infinitely more severe to you than to any ordinary man, and as you are the man of God, whatever judgment they pass on you will reflect upon their view of our holy religion.

As I must be brief, restricting myself to bare essentials, what I have to say on this point will be readily summed up in three words—the first, work—the second, work—and the third also work. On the human level, which is where we must stand, I know of no greater curse to the ministry than that of laziness.

Visit every home represented in your congregation at least once a year. Let me cite to you as an example a good friend of mine who is a Methodist minister. While he set out in his ministry, being assigned to a village, he forthwith visited every house in the community except one—an awe-inspiring mansion evidently inhabited by the most influential people in the neighborhood. Finally one day, after a long prayer, he went to the door and knocked. As the door was being opened by an imposing gentleman, a big dog rushed through almost passing between the legs of our friend. The scared preacher, trying to regain his wits, just blurted out: "Excuse me, I did not know that the *other* dog would come too!" The gentleman of the house was amused. He smiled. Soon everybody joined in the conversation, and the whole household found their way to church.

Should you object to the pressure of time, then remember with Marcus Aurelius, that the greater part of what we say and do is unnecessary; and that, if this were only omitted, we should have more leisure and less disturbance. This applies to our thoughts also, for impertinence of thoughts leads to unnecessary action.

Pulpit preparation is a capital importance. It is hard for me to refrain at this point from making a few drastic statements, but I shall only remark that nothing is so painful to the churchgoer, and nothing more destructive of the respect normally enjoyed by a minister than the unprepared sermon. Paraphrasing Machiavelli's *Prince*, we would say that the best fortress a new minister can have is not to be despised by his congregation. The worst of it all is that the less prepared the preacher, the more he will talk, and the more harm he will do to himself and to the cause of the Gospel. Let me now give the example of the minister who played a great part in my own conversion. After days of preparation on one particular occasion, he was inspired in the prayer with which he began his work, to shelve the almost finished sermon and prepare another, doing it very thoroughly. The following Sunday, at the close of the service, after having apparently taken leave of every worshipper, he saw a woman coming out of the shadow into the aisle. She pressed his hand and gave him thanks as she declared her faith. She had come to church, as she thought, for the last time that Sunday, intending to commit suicide immediately after the service. To grasp the full impact of this minister's message and its effect on one lost soul among others, we should look into his own personal life. For during the last war he underwent a great spiritual struggle. He had lost his soldier son—a splendid boy whose letters were later to be released for the edification of Christians. His wife had died of a broken heart. As the remains of the son were to be brought back from the battlefield, a joint burial was decided upon for mother and son. Ministers from miles around offered their good services but were kindly declined one by one. During the entire week this bereaved man of God had hardly left his study. As you must have surmised, he was the one to officiate at the funeral. There, before two open graves, he proclaimed his faith in him who is the Resurrection and the Life. And this he did in an impeccable sermon. How many sheep were saved through the pastor that day, only God knows. Yet you will agree that on this particular occasion, our old French friend had some cause for not exerting himself.

Pulpit preparation implies that a minister never stops praying, studying, and reading. Reading in turn implies writing, and this leads me to think of our religious periodicals and of our book reviews. For they are a real issue to me, as I compare our Protestant journals with similar publications on display in university libraries. How many book reviews consist merely in a reproduction of the advertising material usually found on the flap of the book cover; thank God that *Theology Today* is bringing about a change in this situation. A great opportunity is yours, my young friends, in this extremely important phase of the ministry.

Underlying all the preceding considerations is the constant implication that the minister can exult in Paul's great motto: "To me to live is Christ." For the "realities wherein commitment is the essential thing," according to Kierkegaard's classification, those realities described by Pascal as the "mysteries which are hidden from sense and from reason," may be summed up in the expression *mysterium Christi*. Paul has just defined Christianity for us, as Christ himself—Jesus Christ, belonging to the category of the divine, indeed in a class by himself, and as such finally inexplicable.

You all know as well as I do, that when scholars have done their best—or their worst—and come to the beginnings of Christianity through the Gospels and the Epistles, through early collections of the savings of Jesus, and notes on his life possibly written in Aramaic, they must witness that this "Gospel before the Gospels" remains *the* Gospel. Therein, indeed, early believers have testified to the supernatural Being clearly pictured from one end of the New Testament to the other, and responsible for its unity. The early Church, as she stood praying to her unique, absolute, final, and cosmic Lord, who could say "Before Abraham was, I am," was truly a remnant. According to Gibbon, this remnant made the record that it did through its inflexible and uncompromising zeal. It remained separate and exclusive; it refused to *appease*, as we have now learned to put it. To the extent that conflict, nay, death, was willingly undergone so that Christianity might *displace* other religions, men were won to the living Lord through the living Lord. Gibbon further mentions as causes for the rapid growth of the Church the pure and austere morals, the union and discipline of the Christian remnant, the miraculous powers ascribed to it, and its doctrine of a future life. In his excellent book on *The Apostolic Preaching*, Professor C. H. Dodd of Cambridge has clearly shown that there was not deviation from the original content of the Gospel as found in 1 Cor 15:1–11: "Moreover, brethren, I declare unto you the gospel which I preached unto you, which also ye have received, and wherein ye stand; by which also ye are saved, if ye keep in memory what I preached unto you, unless ye have believed in vain. For I delivered unto you first of all that which I also received, how that Christ died for our sins according to the scriptures; and that he was buried, and that he rose again the third day according to the scriptures," etc. As the Passion narratives are now shown to have been among the first New Testament documents to be written down, the burden of the original message delivered by the Apostles was that of "Jesus and his resurrection," that of the redemption wrought by him as Lord and Saviour. This dynamic faith, releasing as it did the power of the triumphant Lord in heaven, was quick to generate and sustain Christianity in the mission field when there was not in evidence the grave question of "rethinking missions." It is such genuine faith which fills Churches in our day, such genuine faith which will surely fill *your* Church if *you* abstain from "re-thinking your ministry" on this basic, *sine qua non* point.

For this *is* the Christian faith. The Christ did not come to found one more religion better than others and comparable to them. He came as the self-revelation of the Father. He is all we know of God. Furthermore since according to Scripture the main function of the Holy Spirit is to bear witness of the Christ with our spirit, the Son is truly the God of men. You must therefore insist on what our admirable layman, Robert E. Speer, calls *The Finality of Christ*, which is the title he has given to his best book.

Let me ask from you as a very special favor this day, always keep that book on hand, right on your desk, near your Bible.

Do you not see, my friends, the world outside is groping for truth and *you are going out in the world with the final truth*. All other masters are only human masters. They must give way to your master, to the one Lord in whom all our questions are answered. In its original and authentic form, Christianity is incommensurable and unique, like the Christ. Such uniqueness, in fact, not only explains but necessitates the resurrection. The weakest point in David Hume's famous essay "On Miracles" is his central statement as to the impossibility of the fact that a dead *man* should come to life, because that has never been observed in any age or country. It reminds one of Richard Jeffries' *Story of a Boy* in its reference to the cruelty of Crucifixion, to the effect that "if God had been there, he would not have let them do it!" The whole point is that none other than God was there; and precisely because he was there, he could not stay there in utter defeat and shame. Therefore Paul's assertion underlies and undergirds your whole ministry: "If Christ be not raised, your faith is vain; ye are yet in your sins."

I say to you that if this is not your faith, your personal religion may indeed be beautiful and highly respectable among men, but it is not Christianity. You have no good news to proclaim to a needy world. Rather go and sell real estate! Waste no time giving lectures about the latest schemes of social improvement. Sir Thomas More's *Utopia* is to me one of the most boring things to read and suggests one of the most disappointing places to live in. Your message of the Kingdom of God owes no apologies to Bacon's *New Atlantic*, Campanella's *City of the Sun*, or to the idealizations of William Morris and H. G. Wells. I repeat that there is no question of more or less involved at this crucial point in the ministry; there is only a question of "either—or." At this very moment then, here and now, may you come face to face with our living Lord and not be found wanting. For you are going to have before you eager eyes and anxious faces—anxious, that is, according to the original text, expressive of division against self—a congregation of souls pleading to be made whole again. You cannot evade their quest. You cannot lie to them and to yourself Sunday after Sunday. In their name I ask you: Is this your faith? Is it?

If so, go to them with all you have because you have everything. What a glorious, comforting thing it will be indeed for you to take your place in a heavenly fellowship, carried forward by eighteen centuries of this Christian experience! To feel Paul, and Augustine, and Calvin, and Pascal, and Wesley, and an immense army of other great servants of the living Lord back of you! You will be one of them. You will speak their language because their experience is being repeated in your own, because it confirms your own, and your own is a confirmation of theirs. Oh, the glory of it all for you, a Christian warrior in the front line, backed up by such stupendous reserves and in the words of the old hymn, with the "Cross of Jesus going on before," with the Lord of Life ahead.

Appendix E

Where Would Jesus Be?

Cailliet, Emile. "Where Would Jesus Be?" (n.d.) (Subsequently published in the *War Cry Magazine* of the Salvation Army)

The famous question, "What would Jesus do?" has helped, and continues to help, a great many Christians in need of guidance. An emergency arises. You ask: what should I do? Well, at Sheldon's suggestion you can transpose your question to this: in my place, in the very same situation, what would Jesus do? A most helpful way of solving a multitude of problems: As I have watched for now thirty years the Salvation Army at work in many parts of the world, another question has been echoing in my mind, not one referring to emergency situations or anxiety as to what the right thing to do might be, but a question full of wonder and certitude that it can be answered, that it has in fact already been answered. It is the sort of question that has a reply clearly implied, as when a person, confronted with a perfect case of Christian love, exclaims: Have you ever witnessed anything more beautiful? Just so, as in humble admiration I see the Salvation Army blessing mankind today, I know the answer to the question: where would Jesus be?

Where would Jesus be? The question came to my lips some thirty odd years ago in France. Two lassies had just passed by on a bicycle. They were dressed in strange uniform, the Salvation Army uniform. I had never seen it before. So I looked on. But the two lassies had already alighted and were smilingly helping someone along the road. How wonderful was the joy radiating from their entire being: Where would Jesus be, but with them?

Nothing formal about it. Galilee all over again, as through some sudden shift of scene, except that there had been no bicycles in those days.

Truly, knowledge begins with wonder. I spoke to the two lassies. Later I saw their 'post.' Jesus' abode must have been something like that, insignificantly small, and yet giving one the impression that it was the threshold to Heaven. Christianity is nothing more complicated than this—Heaven breaking in on earth; a luminous transparency suddenly disclosed in the most commonplace of all human situations.

Some will object that this is imagination on my part, to which I would answer: but then, is not Jesus the greatest help, the greatest Gift from God to imagination? In Him God transcends our illusory world-view and brings us to the reality of the things that *are*. We also would see Jesus, for He is the very highest we know of God. Certain it is that in Him we actually get a glimpse into the Lord's high Heaven.

Now, I have nowhere experienced the feeling of seeing through to the very gate of Heaven, a sense of what I call heavenly transparency, so much awe I have in my contacts with the Salvation Army. So that, when I ask: "Where would Jesus be," if He still lived on earth, that is, I find my answer in the Salvation Army. For Christ is there, in the Army, under it, before it, behind it, over it and above it, if I may here adapt St. Patrick's famous hymn. That is why I love it. I love it, indeed, with the same kind of love I have for my Lord.

But it must not allow my enthusiasm to run ahead of my narrative. Sometime after I met the two lassies, I went to a mass-meeting of the *Armée du Salut* in a small city of the Huguenot country, in the Cévennes. The French Commissioner Albin Peyron was there with some of the best leaders of the Army. They had what many of the churches seemed to have lost, that unique blend of simplicity and depth which characterized the proclamation of Jesus in Galilee. Where would Jesus be, but there first of all? The risen Lord was in that meeting house. Let no supercilious student of the modern trend babble about mass-psychology, hysteria, or idly speculate on some "will to believe." Nothing of the sort was in evidence, only in earnest plea for souls on the part of the leaders, an almost utilitarian concern for safety on the part of those who were saved by the Spirit. Then did the Call meet the personal Need, and the personal Need, the Call. God and many came face to face. This was no longer the sophisticated twentieth century striving to spell learned things; it was Galilee all over again. One called to mind Zacheus rushing down from his tree and the man born blind groping for the pool of Siloam. The scene of that memorable service had the transparency of early Christianity. Our risen Lord was there.

Later I spent an evening at the fireside with the French Commissioner. I shall never forget it. Nor shall I forget the depth of those eyes of his, reminiscent of the expression of the seventeenth century Port-Roy lists as revealed in the portrait paintings of Philip of Champaigne. It has always been a source of wonder to me that the age which rediscovered the inner man in literature and philosophy should be rediscovered the human eye in its paintings. Commissioner Peyron's innermost being and commitment radiated through the thin face in its frame of beautiful white hair. Again, transparency. The Christ was there, gazing on me, through those eyes.

As I look back to that meeting across a quarter of a century, it seems to me now that I did most of the talking that evening. Salvationists have a way of "bringing you out." First the varnish comes off, and then follows the dirt. Some of the words I still hear because they stuck:

> "Too much sophistry, my friend. Christianity is simpler than that
> ... because it is the truth."
> I also need to go and wash at the pool of Siloam.

Recently a learned New York critic, commenting on my latest book *The Beginning of Wisdom*, called me "an evangelistic philosopher, that is, a contradiction in terms." How good it is to be called that! I knew then that I was on the right track, that Albin Peyron might be pleased with the "contradiction in terms."

Wherever I have gone, whether in Europe, in Africa, or in America, the Salvation Army has remained the Army I love. In its work, its gatherings, its personnel, I have found the same quality of transparency. It was one of the greatest joys, upon arriving in the United States, to find the Army so active in this land. When I lived in California, I served on the Advisory Board. I was invited to speak to the cadets of the Training College in San Francisco and have yet to find a more receptive audience. Where would Jesus be? I was bound to come across Him. And once I actually *saw* Him. It was during the depression at Pomona, California.

The occasion is unforgettable. The officer in charge at Pomona was a young captain, Paul Bodine by name. In his office one day, I was standing by when a ruffian came in. I say "a ruffian" and I measure my words. The man wanted a pair of shoes. As he spoke, almost jeeringly, he kept on munching an orange he had picked up on the way. Not even troubling to turn aside, he would spit out the debris straight ahead of him—seeds, rind and all—right into the face of the officer. A silent witness to the scene, I was getting "hot under the collar." The amazing thing to me was that the officer did not seem to notice anything wrong about it at all. On the contrary, he kept up an open, lovely smile and answered the ruthless queries as though they had come from the lips of a gentleman, and the plain little office were a select sitting-room. Obviously his concern was wholly and undividedly for his visitor. Certainly, the shoes would be ready; yes, and of such and such a type and size. Just the same, he would make sure once more, and put in a telephone call about them. When the fellow finally left, Captain Bodine escorted him to the door as though the man had been the President of the United States. Then, remembering my presence, the young captain spoke again:

> "What were you saying?"
> "But . . . ," I managed, "looked at yourself in the mirror and wipe your face."
> "What is the matter with my face?" he asked.

I explained. The ruffian had kept on spitting at him. His face actually was covered with dirt of the worst sort. As he suddenly understood what I meant, he smiled. I never saw a smile like that, in a glory of sputum. I *saw* the Christ through that face. Now you know: I actually saw Him. I was struck with awe.

By that time Captain Bodine had wiped his brow. Then, noticing my expression:

> "What is the matter?" he asked laughingly.
> "That man . . ." I tried to explain, "that ruffian . . ."
> "Oh," the captain commented, "that one was alright; we see far worse than that!"

Shortly afterwards I learned that a Salvation Army officer should never be mentioned without his wife. We went to a meeting where a number of souls were saved. A poor wretched fellow among others came forward, then was assisted for a long time by Mrs. Bodine. As we talked together after the meeting, she was crying softly. My wife inquired. Then Mrs. Bodine, tears rolling down her face, replied:

"Why, that poor man didn't even know how to kneel down!"

Where would Jesus be? The Christ was there, in that Salvation Army post. Under just such circumstances is His hallowed presence being disclosed with a luminous transparency all over the world today. Where indeed would He be, but in the driving rain at the street corners, waiting patiently near the drum, ever cheerful, feeding the hungry as they come out of the night, loving the unlovely, going out for those we call "the worst" and whom He lovingly calls by name?

Reader, my friend, have you lost the Christ? Then acquaint yourself with the Salvation Army post nearest you. You may find Him elsewhere, I know, but you are sure to find Him there.

Emile Cailliet
Stuart Professor of Christian Philosophy
Princeton Theological Seminary

Appendix F

The Mind's Gravitation Back to the Familiar

Emile Cailliet. "The Mind's Gravitation Back to the Familiar." *Theology Today* 15 (April 1958) 1–8. (Used by permission.)

The familiar setting constitutes for us the substantial reality to which we revert as through a law of our being. The substantial character of the experience is happily suggested in Coleridge's phrase, "palpable and familiar." And just as we are at home in the familiar, so are we likely to be homesick in strange surroundings. The experience recalled by George Pope Morris speaks to the condition of many of us:

> In other countries, when I heard
> The language of my own,
> How fondly each natural word
> Awoke an answering tone.

Natural words act upon us as do familiar names. Once more it took a poet to apprehend this deep affinity. Thus Shakespeare exalted the magic of names as familiar in one's mouth "as household words." The familiar gives us a sense of security in the midst of precarious circumstances, that is, of circumstances that call for prayer. And so, to revert to the safe haven of the familiar often turns out to be for us a mostly unconscious way of praying.

Where our treasure is, there will our heart be also. Because he so highly values the pearl of great price, the Christian is likely to experience more deeply than others, this gravitation of the mind back to the familiar.

There is something sacred about the familiar. This word "sacred" originally meant untouchable, as in the Latin dictum, *Res est sacra miser* (the miserable one is untouchable), where a primitive connotation is readily apprehended. The perennial character of such primitive views must be ascribed to a deep-seated misoneism, or fear of innovation. As primitives see it, to innovate is to expose oneself to the most dreadful dangers. A pertinent motto for the primitive landscape of reality could read, "Do not disturb."

As subsequent meanings of the word "sacred" come to light, it appears that the sacred object is no longer only the untouchable object, but further the desired, beloved object. In this connection our young people today may find it worthwhile to dwell on the tradition of courteous love as it developed through the twelfth and thirteenth centuries. I refer especially to the devotion of the knights of the Round Table to their lady in that state of near-worship which was then coming to fuller expression in the Virgin cult. It is historically true to say that the highest expression of human love originated in religious mysticism. And so, as we speak of the sacredness of the familiar we find ourselves treading on holy ground.

The reason I have insisted on this question of origin is that it helps us understand why we should respect views of long standing. They constitute patterns of sacred memories through which the soul perseveres in a wisdom unaware of itself. That wisdom we call tradition. It should never be lightly tampered with, still less allowed to become an object of ridicule. What may mislead many of us is that the deeper the roots, the better hidden they are. Conversely, the familiar becomes all the more sacred as its origins are lost in the night of ancient days. Hence the impression on the part of the faithful that things have always been as they are now found to be. The *status quo* accordingly may be felt to pertain to the very order of God. No wonder a religious fear is likely to be aroused at the thought that it might be disturbed.

One of the reasons some people are so hard on Fundamentalism may be detected in their ignorance of the distant origins of that position. Casting ridicule upon it is the natural reaction of detractors whose memory hardly goes further back than the year of 1909 when millions of copies of *The Fundamentals* published in Los Angeles spread over the Protestant world, preparing the way for the Christian Fundamentals League and the World's Christian Fundamental Association. Henceforth slogans take over, and the whole conservative position is easily dismissed amid catcalls and name-calling. The very name, Fundamentalist, is even currently abbreviated for the sake of brevity in final judgment. Whereupon the straw man supposed to incarnate the backward beliefs freely ascribed to him, is summarily disposed of. It is nevertheless a fact that he may have been an earnest evangelical Christian, as has often proved to be the case.

The plain truth is that the Fundamentalist attitude constitutes by birth and by right one of the essential aspects of the Reformation. This is stated in the awareness that men like Luther, and more especially the Renaissance scholar, Calvin, blazed the trail in more than one way to the modern attitude toward the Bible. What actually happened is that having opened the Scriptures to the laity, the Reformers were led by controversy to indiscriminately claim for the whole Bible an absolute authority henceforth substituted for that of the Church of Rome. Their theological interpretations of the book moreover remained controlled by the traditional *schema*. The main point is that the Fundamentalist's affirmation of the infallibility of Scripture originally was that of the Reformers. Were it only for this consideration, it should not be scornfully disparaged.

Sheer intellectual honesty would have us make a further acknowledgement with regard to this matter. As the Reformers opened the Book to the laity, an enthusiastic fervor greeted a Gospel now accessible in one's native tongue. Thus the Christian message was apprehended afresh in its pristine dynamism. A newness of life animated the Body of Christ. The fact to acknowledge further is that there comes to light at this juncture another striking similitude between Fundamentalism and the Reformation. Making full allowance for occasional cases of smug complacency and lack of charity on the part of some Fundamentalists, an uncontrovertible belief in the verbal inspiration of all Scripture today also generates the same enthusiastic fervor as of old, among the proponents of the ancient view. While many a sophisticated Christian feeds on an *Ersatz* diet of learned up-to-date disquisitions, Fundamentalists are out in every sort of weather ringing door bells. It is also a fact that Pentecostal sects hold the field in South America as well as on other continents where missionaries are at work. If it still be true that "by their fruit ye shall know them," what is to be the stand of many of us on the Day of Judgment?

Having thus attempted to do justice to Fundamentalism in the context of I Cor. 13, however, we must admit in the next breath, that ignoring to all practical purposes four centuries of cultural advances amounts to a serious declension. It is a terrible thing for Christianity to allow itself to be out of touch with the world of men and affairs which is its mission field. I recently directed a university retreat in the "Bible Belt." There I found myself confronted by a generation of students who had been "conditioned" against the evangelical message. A discreet inquiry revealed that in practically every case youth had been submitted to obsolete pressure methods of approach. It further appeared that quite a number of the younger instructors had already known a similar revulsion and, as a result, turned to Unitarianism. Moreover, currently available books had hardly proved a help. What purpose is ever served, may I ask, by reprint editions of obsolete theological dissertations, whose essential merit today is to act as tranquilizers for cases of religious misoneism? And yet a whole section of the publishing industry today is thriving on this business of warmed-over titles. What this means is that the vacuum which has naturally appeared during the last fifty or sixty years in the production of ultra-conservative Biblical literature, is being artificially filled. Conversely, as new manuscripts catering to the old stereotyped outlook may not get access to the wider cultural market, they worm their way into that late nineteenth century vintage of publications. The cultivation of obsolescence in this age of intense scientific progress truly has become an end in itself in a whole area of traditionalism.

Henceforth references to evangelism may be construed as labels of doubtful intellectual quality. This is particularly grave in the midst of a generation groping for trustworthy guidance. We are undeniably confronted at this point with baleful aftereffects of the mind's gravitation back to the familiar.

II

Let us now turn to a somewhat composite group of conservatives, quite a number of whom have achieved distinction in their own special field, yet equally concerned with an unswerving commitment to traditional interpretations of theology, they have chosen to be called "Evangelicals." In so doing, incidentally, they would seem to have claimed a monopoly on evangelical Christianity, and *ipso facto* revived the suggestion that any other construction put on the faith amounts to liberalism, and that liberalism is not Christianity. Many of us would take exception to all such suggestions of monopoly, however praiseworthy the intention behind them may be.

The real intention of these "Evangelicals," moreover, is hardly veiled by seeming concessions made in the hope that the day may be at hand when the old solution will once more come into its own. For this real intention is to all practical purposes conditioned by the mind's gravitation back to the familiar; in this case, back to the crystallized formulations of old. Should a man of good will suggest specific instances where the liberation of the natural sciences from the encroachments of an unenlightened theologism need not be duplicated in the case of the historical method painstakingly developed by the human sciences, the "Evangelicals" may temporarily agree. And yet their next move may well be to call him in for the sake of slightly "amending" his wording. This once done, however, it would readily appear that the mind's gravitation back to the familiar had run its natural course.

This is not meant to imply that "Evangelicals" agree among themselves. They do not, as even Billy Graham has had occasion to find out. Just as the most bitter disagreements are likely to materialize between neighbors across the fence, so the sharpest theological arguments originate among those conservatives who differ on minor points. Give them a rank atheist, and they will love him because he is "convertible." It is the minor dissident that arouses their ire. Meanwhile the children of this world pass by the island of discord, as an army would ignore quarrels among stragglers on the path of advance.

Billy Graham has done just that, yet in his own way. He has done it with bravery. I have in many respects reluctantly come to the conclusion that a great deal of controversy around him has originated in unconscious envy, if not professional jealousy, and this is particularly bad among servants of the same Lord. The fact remains, nevertheless, that to ignore obvious difficulties in no way disposes of them. Throw a problem out through the door, and it will reappear at the window. It is in many respects commendable to proclaim to a large gathering, "The Bible says ... and the Bible says ... ," as if nothing had ever happened since the days of the Reformation to affect the total picture. Yet the receptive listener who steps forward is likely to find out for himself sooner or later that even the India paper which bears the sacred text is no longer negotiable at face value. Not that the text itself has lost any of its significance. Quite the contrary. It commands higher value than ever before, and this, to the last word. It is merely that it has been identified as a dated and culturally conditioned human record of God's disclosure. Any profession of faith and statement of beliefs accordingly must proceed from both the account of events and meaning actually implied in them in a given social and cultural context. Any attempt to perpetuate the element of relativity which may have become involved in the process is bound to bring the one who makes it out-of-touch with the later age in which he lives, and moves, and has his being. Not only does such a situation prevent useful communication with contemporaries, but it interferes with the knowledge of God and of his design.

The mind's gravitation back to the familiar has this in common with the larger aspect of gravitation: to ignore or hide its existence does not prevent it from being there.

III

Our inquiry further brings us into contact with a rather likable group of Christians, conciliatory and ever ready to placate and mollify, yet withal anxious to hold on to the alloy of set ways of thinking. They are aware that the world in which they live keeps moving on and that there can be no turning back of the clock. While accepting as inevitable the inroads of the well established historical method into traditional interpretations, however, they are far from being wholehearted in their acceptance. In actual practice they welcome contributions likely to prove harmless while easing undeniable tensions. Yet they hardly control their wistful eagerness to have enough left of the old interpretations to carry on as usual. This is their way of not offending the congregation if they are in the ministry, or of professing Christianity with a tenable open-mindedness if they are in the now. In the course of conversations with inquirers, they proceed in the same spirit, ready to concede the seemingly unessential. But then, where is their frame of reference for essentiality? And so they essay a tentative give-and-take while holding on to what they cannot do without. In other words, they do their best to safeguard selected parts of their disintegrating profession, even while the facts which inspired it have been put in jeopardy. Their Christian conversation admittedly may be admirable in actual practice, as if they wanted to atone for the confusion of their ideas.

Eclecticism has often sought in activity, if not in activism, ways of creating unity among discordant intellectual views. This tendency is well known in schools of philosophy. It is also noticeable in ecumenical gatherings where participants of different theological persuasions come to realize that they can work together even in the face of unresolved tensions in matters of doctrine. Yet in a case where all such tensions come to light within the same individual person, it becomes obvious that a divided soul can hardly achieve that single-mindedness which makes light of obstacles encountered along the appointed way. Apart from a consistency grounded in a well-ascertained motivation, life is bound to be a succession of semantic nightmares in anguish and endless misery.

The mind's gravitation back to the familiar can never safely be taken for granted as a force in a component of forces. It must be squarely faced as a major source of disturbance across the path to maturity.

IV

New Christian currency has been issued in the world of thought since the days of the Reformation. It does indeed bear the same old symbols. More surprising still, these symbols would seem to command higher value today than they ever did, were it only because the realities to which they point now may be ascertained with more accuracy. This is new currency nevertheless, a currency devised to meet the changing needs of a new social and cultural environment which implies new ways of thinking. The mind's gravitation back to the familiar notwithstanding, we must as adults face the fact that it is not what we like to hear, read, or see, that constitutes the criterion of correctness, but the adequacy of our apprehension of the meaning and purpose of him who speaks to us. What matters in interpreting the Bible in particular is to apprehend and convey as accurately as possible the thought and intention of the original writer in his own situation.

Conservative Christians are right in insisting upon the wholeness of the Bible, and in holding on to every word of the precious record. The fact of the matter is that the historical method of studying the Bible is equally as insistent that it cannot possibly destroy a single word in that record. Its main concern is to find out what the words meant to say in the mind of those who used them. Once viewed in this light, the New Testament in particular bears witness to the actual preaching of the early Christian community. To construe it otherwise amounts to distorting it. To set it within the living context of the apostolic age that produced it, safeguards its genuine meaning for all times, including our own.

There always will be those who will ascribe to God the kind of thinking they would do, were they in his place. Ours is happily a simpler task, namely, to figure out what the Word of God who meets us in and through the Bible, actually says to us and expects from us. This we may safely do only in the measure as we counteract in his grace that ingrained tendency to gravitate back to the familiar. The Book of Deuteronomy (32:11) beautifully suggests the nature of the ordeal implied therein for a man of good will, as the Lord leads him:

> Like an eagle that stirs up its nest,
> that flutters over its young,
> Spreading out its wings, catching them,
> bearing them on its pinions.

We do need this divine stirring up of our natural propensities; yet we need not fear it as we trust ourselves to the protection of the everlasting wings.

Appendix G

This I Believe

Cailliet, Emile. "This I Believe." Lenten address at Scripps College (March 12, 1940).

I believe that thinking is a process of clarification. At this point I am overcome by the awareness of a tremendous amount of mystery in "man the unknown" as well as in the cosmos. With Pascal, I believe that "man surpasses man infinitely," and with the hero of Shakespeare, that there are more things in heaven and in earth than are dreamt of in our philosophy.

This however, does not mean that we should give up our philosophy, nor any legitimate method or instrument of investigation within our reach. Let my second article be the affirmation of my faith in all that we treasure under the name of a "liberal arts education."

Yet I believe that many a person in search of guidance will bear testimony to the fact that he did not see the Light after learned discussions with scholars who split hairs, but rather, it came through the inspiring example of a simple man who walked humbly with his God. Jesus never said "Blessed are the PhD's for they shall see God," but He promised that supreme privilege to "the pure in heart." He said also: "I thank thee, O Father, Lord of heaven and earth, because thou hast hid these things from the wise and prudent, and hast revealed them unto babes." I believe that we college people need to be constantly reminded of this, and in this manner to be warned against pride of intellect. And we should see a specific warning in the fact that there are more philosophers and theologians than holy men under the blinding sun of the Gospel. I for one, catch myself daily in the very act of enjoying the building up of a good case, where I should be doing a good turn in true charity and simplicity of heart. Indeed, God is not to be found at the end of an argument.

How could he be? Man is not to be the measure of all things. The error of naturalism is to pretend that he is, and to try to reduce everything to his own dimensions—a prejudice that implies the very negation of the supernatural, of the divine, of that which in man passes man infinitely. Indeed, reason is a God-given faculty. Between reason and faith there is no contradiction. Both come from God. Both find in God their ultimate end. Reason, however, has to work out its demonstrations from our knowledge of things material, the most remote from God in the order of perfection, the most inadequate effects of the first cause. Reason, therefore, cannot give us a satisfactory knowledge of God. In the hierarchy of the creation we are, as Thomas Aquinas saw it, on the borderline between the spiritual world and the world of sense experience, spiritual beings and yet engaged in matter, God inspired, yet restricted by the limitations of matter. Our supreme knowledge of God we receive through Revelation by Faith.

At this point, I am most conscious of the dangers arising from one's limitation to his own so-called illumination. Although I know that God speaks to His children, I know also that He does not rewrite His Bible for each one of us; nor does He rewrite Christian tradition. True culture, I once more assert, consists in taking stock of the past, in studying with intelligence and reverence the revelation handed down to us by great servants of God—among whom we find such philosophers as Plato, such poets as Dante, and the great religious thinkers that live on. It is, however, that unique source of revelation, the Bible, which remains for me the all-sufficient Word of God. That is why my gratitude goes out the reverent scholars, to the *men of God* who unfold the character and purpose of this record of facts in all its magnificence and purity.[2]

I firmly believe in the living Jehovah of the Bible, the God of Abraham, of Isaac, of Jacob; the God of Moses and the prophets. I believe that He finally and fully revealed Himself in the Person and in the works of our Savior and Lord Jesus Christ, who *is* indeed all He claims to be, and whose Gospel fully meets the need of a lost world. I believe as it is written in the Gospel according to St. John: "*If any man will do Hill will, he* shall

---

[2]. For an excellent first guide, see *Profitable Bible Study*, with an Annotated List for the first One-hundred Best Books for the Bible Student's Library. MA: Wilde, 1939.

know of the doctrine," whether it be of God or whether Christ spake of Himself. The willingness or unwillingness to take Christ at His word to me marks the dividing line between belief and unbelief.

I suppose that were I living in the Middle Ages, I would be writing a Sum under the auspices of the Church. But I happen to be living in the twentieth century, in an age of Liberalism, in an age also when human knowledge has become so vast in scope and so intricate in detail, that no one man can ever dream of even beginning to tackle such a task. Aware of this last fact, the Roman Catholic Church is reviving in neo-thomism the method and the spirit of conciliation that were found in Thomas Aquinas; and an army of Christian scholars are working on the type of sum that St. Thomas would want to write were he living in our day. We are thankful to the Catholic Church for this noble and most valuable undertaking and for the intellectual guidance that we derive from it. As an individual, I can only clarify matters for myself, remaining faithful to my convictions both as a Christian and as a liberal arts student, holding on with a firm grip to both ends of a chain whose central links are not all or even always visible to me.

My daily experience, however, convinces me that a process of clarification is going on from both ends. As a Bible student, I find myself greatly helped by the disciplines of scholarship; as a Liberal Arts student, I derive new understanding from my Christian faith. For me intelligence has now taken on a higher meaning, its true meaning, I think, namely the faculty to read. And reading has become easier as Light is shed on the books I read.

Still I only see "through a glass, darkly." My life may be likened to one of my hiking days, as I begin slowly to climb up through the fog. I know that the sun is shining up there somewhere, although a companion who has never seen it would find this hard to believe. And there are unmistakable signs, patches of white, now small and dim, then growing brighter and larger—unmistakable signs that sooner or later we shall emerge in a glory of luminous blue.

Appendix H

Courses Taught By Emile Cailliet at Princeton Seminary 1947–1959

See Princeton Seminary bulletin 1947 for a description of courses that he taught in rotation during his years there.

INTRODUCTION TO CHRISTIAN PHILOSOPHY

"Having cleared the way for presentation of revealed truth to a generation facing problems more complicated than ever before, this course aims at the formulation of a sane Christian outlook for our day. The great classics of science, art and literature are drawn upon as well as those of religion and philosophy."

Prescribed, the first year, 3 hours

HISTORY OF CHRISTIAN PHILOSOPHY

"A chronological approach to the fundamental issues faced by the Hebrew Christian mind throughout the ages. Constructive criticism of resolving formulations studied in their most outstanding representatives. Have thus clarified a well-rounded Christian outlook on life, the future minister is enabled to properly evaluate new literature on the subject, meet objections, counsel wisely and move cautiously in his own thinking. . ."

Prescribed third-year 3 hours
Prerequisite: Introduction to Christian philosophy

GREAT BOOKS IN THE LIGHT OF CHRISTIANITY

"An introduction to great books from the point of view of the Christian reader. The unique contribution of Christianity to our Western civilization is brought out; essential problems facing the Christian educator are formulated. Such authors as Sophocles, Aristophanes, Aristotle, Lucretius, Augustine, Dante, Thomas à Kempis, Cervantes, Shakespeare, Descartes, Pascal, Bunyan, Goethe, Kierkegaard, Hawthorne, Matthew Arnold, Dostoyevsky, Ibsen, and Claudel suggest the range of study. Assigned readings partially change from year to year."

Prescribed, second year for MRE candidates

THE PHILOSOPHY OF SCIENCE

"An objective consideration of the rise of scientific inquiry and of the resulting structure of human knowledge. Anthropology and the new frontiers of logic in the light of recent ethnological research. Elements of epistemology, the mathematical sciences and the sciences of nature. The laws of science and the laws of chance. The aftermath of mechanism. Inc. implications of the Heisenberg relations of uncertainty and quantum physics. The orientation of evolution and Max Planck's law of ethics. The unique opportunity of an uncompromised Christian philosophy independent of neo-Thomism and the contemporary world of science.

Elective, 3 hours, offered in alternate years

THE MAKING OF THE MODERN RELIGIOUS MIND

"The Roman Catholic Church and the validity of Christian metaphysics. Problems forced on the reform tradition from Descartes to Karl Barth. A constructive critical appraisal of the various solutions offered in our time.

Clarification of the philosophical implications of loyalty to a genuine Hebrew Christian tradition."

Elective, 3 hours

PASCAL

"An intensive consideration of the great Christian philosopher true to the best Augustinian tradition. The experiences which give rise to his life and work and commitment. The relevance for our day of his outlook on science and religion. Reading and discussion of selection from the *Shorter Works*, the *Provincial Letters* and the *Pensées*. Individual tutorial work for research."

Elective, 3 hours

THE CHRISTIAN PATTERN OF LIFE

"Introduction to the everyday practices of a sane Christian outlook on life. The disciplines of body, soul and spirit integrated as a whole. Relevance of Bunyan's *Pilgrim's Progress* for our day. Slow reading and analysis of this classic of the reform tradition. Nature and scope of the minister's reading and creative work. Devotional Classics in the Bible.

Elective, 3 hours

Appendix I

The Role of Seminary Education in the Secular Order

with Special Attention to its Cultural Aspects

Cailliet, Emile. "The Role of the Seminary in the Secular Order with Special Attention to its Cultural Aspects." (n.d.)

Time is so short and is so precious in fact at such a time and in such a place, that I shall not waste any of it in what the French call *précautions oratories*. I shall be direct and even blunt. What I have to say, moreover, I present in the form of a paper for the same motive as well as for the sake of more concision. Thus, ample room will be left for discussion.

I

The assigned subject is that of the role of seminary education in the secular order and the President wisely stipulated that it would be advisable to limit the consideration of the secular order to its cultural aspects. We immediately become aware that the problem raised is essentially that of Christianity and culture inasmuch as seminary education is concerned—an age old problem once more coming to a head in our midst at a time when Global Christianity and culture are threatened in their very existence. Because this is such a time of crisis, precisely, because we, as educators, are put on our mettle, we are likely to emphasize the immediate, that is, in education, theology; in theology, the Word; and in the Word the utter sovereignty and primacy of God. And it is well that it should be so.

This is neither the time or the place to pass a leisurely condemnation on Euripides' *Trojan Women*; Aristotle's identification of slaves with "living tools" in his *Nicomachean: Ethics*; still less on all that made the object of Thucydides' account of Athenian depravity. The pressure on us is such that Tertullian's dictum finds new echoes within some of our walls: "What indeed has Athens to do with Jerusalem? What concord is there between the Academy and the Church?—we want no curious disputation after possessing Jesus." I, for one, was sadly impressed by the rush of students to Miller Chapel to hear this and similar themes developed the other day, while the student body was so poorly represented at the triple Inaugural where four thoroughly prepared extremes were presented which brought up some of the most essential theological and cultural issues of our time.

What our young friends do not seem to realize is that the Tertullian dictum dear to such eminent churchmen as Bernard of Clairvaux, may be carried to extremes where preachers are made to share the fate of philosophers and other representatives of culture. Students may want to turn, for example, to the *Acts of the Nethermayne Congress of Calvinistic Theology* held in Geneva in June 1926 where it appears that the question was most seriously raised, only to be hushed in awe, as to whether a perfectly Sovereign God has any need of the preacher at all. The very relevance of churches, then, is at stake at this point.

Now, and to set at peace the minds of some of you, I am such a Calvinist myself that I should be quite willing to admit that God could do exactly that, and do away with the unprofitable servants that we all are. The fact is, however, that in the impenetrable secret of His decrees, He has chosen to use men, nay, to use the most unworthy instruments of His Sovereign Grace. One of the most glorious, spiritual achievements of the seventeenth century was the epoch-making renewal of the Port Royalist order. But how did this actually begin? The answer is, when a vagabond monk who was no better, if not worse, than the rank and file of his species at that time, preached in the worst style a sermon which happened to be heard by a sixteen-year-old romantic nun who used to spend the best of her time reading the novels of the day. Surely the ways of God are passed finding out.

This much is sure, God uses men, even the seemingly most unworthy, and through them actually calls ungodly people who had little or no thought of Him. Truly God is in heaven, and we are on earth; but Jacob's ladder remains nevertheless a busy line of communication. Moreover, exceptions—what we, in our infirmity see to be exceptions—should not blind us to the rule. And the rule is that the Savior Himself devoted the best of His time *preparing* His disciples. And in different ways God prepared Paul, just as He prepared giants like Origen, Augustine, Thomas Aquinas, and Calvin. Neither need we insist on the amount of committed thinking which gave us the Christology of the Creed. Such is obviously God's order. He does not need men; but for reasons known to Him alone, He uses men. Just as He uses secondary causes—and it is another obvious fact that He raise the best prepared men, great in faith and culture, at turning points of history. Nay, turning points in the history of Christianity and culture have as their most striking landmarks such Christian giants as we just named.

Here, then, is the first theme of seminary education: the Light going out into the world through the agency of well prepared Christian workers. Not only must they be prepared for their proclamation, but in the awareness that the Proclamation itself never takes place in a vacuum. The knowledge of anthropology is hardly second to that of soteriology. A mastery of essentials in the human science, *Geisteswissenschaften* is crucial on both counts.

But then, the Bible introduces us to another theme which Hebert brought out most effectively in his *Throne of David*—that of the Gentiles going to Sion, of the world going to the Light. The main trouble in this connection is that the world does not naturally turn in that direction. Hence, another aspect of the task of that unprofitable servant we call the Christian "worker." And while the theologian is mostly concerned with the former aspect, namely with the ways in which the Light goes out into the world, this second task, that is, the ways in which the world goes to the Light, is essentially that of the Christian philosopher.

Looking more closely into the matter, however, it soon becomes evident that the two tasks are inseparable. Just as the theologian must be a keen student of the human science, the Christian philosopher must be a keen student of the Word, his constant frame of reference. Precisely because he keeps that frame of reference constantly in mind, the Christian philosopher is in a position to point out the reason why such or such a pagan view of life and knowledge misses the mark. To illustrate, skepticism is to be ascribed to the elimination from the human scene of the primary truth, "In the beginning God". Or, to take other examples, while the stoic way may be aware of the greatness of man, he remains oblivious of man's inherent weakness, more especially of the weakness of his will. The skeptic, on the other hand, realizes the inadequacy of human faculties; yet he loses sight of the greatness of man. When eclecticism realizes that one system is right where the other is wrong, its immediate suggestion is to the effect that it would be sufficient to combine them in order to obtain the truth. But then, it further appears that such views can no more go together, because of their opposition, than they can subsist alone because of their faults. Pascal, who made this point so beautifully, rightly concludes that Epictetus and Montaigne clash and destroy each other in order to make room for the simplicity of the Gospel. Henceforth the Christian philosopher that he was could go to both the stoic and the skeptic and show a genuine appreciation of their real insights into truth—and this is Christian charity. Next he would show them how their contradictions were resolved on the higher order. Christian philosophy, then, is the Christian approach to philosophy. Only through such an approach does the human panorama and make sense. The Christian approach truly works.

II

It is at this juncture that the strongest objections appear, and we may very well circumscribe the surrounding area as the area of disagreement at the very center of a theological education: Have we, nor they, taken it for granted that there was continuity, homogeneity as it were, between Christian and non-Christian views? What, then, of the Fall and its aftermath; what of the stark realities of sin? Is not human nature a fallen nature, one corrupted to its very core? What other, if anything, is left of the original *imago Dei* in God's creature? If nothing remains, nay, not even the vaguest form of this divine endowment, where is the point of contact between the Creator and creature? Hence the central problem of theological education is the problem of communication which has been so, especially from Luther to Karl Barth through Calvin and Jansen. Only Karl Barth who, let us never forget, was strongly reacting against a shallow liberalism at a time of crisis, brought the issue to a practical deadlock. To wit, his much advertised controversy with Brunner.

I know that there are those who would object that Barth has made it clear that he was not responsible for the Barthians. I am not so sure of that. This first fact remains that a Barthian legend of utter irrationalism has been created, to the extent that lay philosophical periodical literature which you may find in the library, refers as a rule to Barthianism, neo-orthodoxy, Crisis theology as "the new Darkness"; and, the Roman Catholics helping our Reformed tradition is easily dragged in—thus, a time when the Thomists profess to have become the only true custodians of culture. I happened to have a long conversation with Dr. Louis Finkelstein of the Jewish Theological Seminary the day after a Jewish mother brought for a consultation with him, her own daughter who had been won over to the Roman church on the campus through neo-Thomanistic innuendoes. This is but one instance out of hundreds and thousands of how the Roman church is eager to use philosophy in terms of "vain deceit". It is sad that our Reformed tradition should choose such a time to be associated with irrationalism.

Objections would further insist, of course, that it is not so that Barth made his position clear as far as such implications are concerned. It is pathetic, to say the least, to see two great minds such as Barth and Niebuhr come to a deadlock at this point as was recently the case when each one blamed the other for having completely misunderstood things. To the point that Barth used the analogy of the popular game "Are You There?" One who is blindfolded strikes where the other is supposed to be, but the other was not where he was supposed to be—very much as in the case of an electron's velocity and position according the Heisenberg relation of uncertainty. A powerful suggestion forces itself upon one that the means is being taken for the end, and that theologians whose mainstay was supposed to be an existential sense of commitment, are actually fiddling while Rome burns.

Not so, a few will say, reminding one of Barth's resistance to the Nazi's. But then, suppose we turn to his consideration of the church between east and west ten years later. While a clear stand was advocated against the Nazi's, now neutrality becomes the unity of this present moment which partakes of what Barth calls, "the natural history of the world." Barth will have no part in what he sees to be merely "certain politically obscure and debatable opinions of the Western world." To him, the cold war becomes the expression of a conflict between oriental materialism and a most impure occidental capitalism. Between the two it is the duty of the Church to remain the Church. Only such a neutrality will allow the Church to resist both evils. An interesting thesis that and to some extent a valid one. But then, was it not equally valid in the case of, say, the United States versus Hitler? What then made it a duty for the Christian to become militant, if not that Nazism was a devilish form of neo-paganism? But so is the communism of Stalin. So are the ideologies of our time, once they are seen aright. If I may for once quote myself, it was my privilege to be commissioned by the American Philosophical Society to write for their series a rather bulky volume on the tradition of ideology. What impressed me most from the materialistic ideology of Lucretius down to the ideologies of our time, was the idolatrous character of all ideologies. In every case the Christian faith principle was being displaced by a more or less dangerous faith principle. The reading of such men as Koestler will amply illustrate the point with reference to communism. Admittedly Harry Truman does not say that this is our main reason for resisting Russia. But he should. This is a case of Christianity in dire peril. Only the Christian outlook on this whole situation will bring out this fact and, by the same token, cleanse our motives which admittedly need cleansing. We would further suggest that to bring such tremendous issues to the fore is one of the essential marks of a seminary education in our day. But where will you find a course on the making of modern ideologies?

In all fairness to Barth, we must admit that he is likely to become more human once he puts on his slippers. The fact is that when "the tumult and shouting dies," Barth's essential contribution of thought—apart from a much needed reassertion of God's otherness and sovereignty—will be found to have been that of a historian of thought. *Die Protestantische Theologie im neunzehnten jahrhundert* shows him as a remarkable historian and critic of our Western culture. His appreciation of the Eighteenth century, to begin with,—the Age of Enlightenment, mind you—his views on the significance of Rousseau, his full portraits of men like Kant to whom he owes so much, and Schleiermacher, to whom he owes no less, reveal what the man can do when he discards the system. I know of only one other man of whom this is equally true, the nineteenth century figure of Taine. "Barth en pantoufles" is also at his best when seen at prayer like you and me, in his recent treatment of prayer according to the catechisms of the Reformation. He even comes to dwell on the intercession of the saints to a God who wants to be God, and yet is not God without men—a God who *was* man in Christ Jesus.

And this leads me to the final confession of Barth's defenders. Barth has changed. Why, he has hardly done anything else. The fact is, I worry about having left so early this morning that I did not get the mail. Let this be a friendly way of bringing out what I see to be another danger in a seminary education today. To say that Barth has changed is as much as saying that he has extended the scope of his readings, especially in philosophy, although the philosophical scaffolding is now being taken down, (Dr. Metzger would do well to look into this matter of acknowledging one's indebtedness to philosophers). The best approach to Barth as I see it, may be a chronological survey of his readings. Thus we are kept on the *qui vive*! Barth very well knows that a great man is one who forces others to study him. But then, Barth uses so much paper and change, so swiftly and so radically at times—in spite of what *The Christian Century* professions of faith may say on the matter—that keeping pace with him becomes well nigh a full-time job. And, mind you, there are students who make it a full-time job to the great distortion of their cultural equipment. This is the price one has to pay for neolatry. If you allow me the expression, I should say that to follow the metamorphosis of Barth comes close to the theological equivalent of baby-sitting.

III

The former moderator of the Presbyterian Church USA told me the other day that he was alarmed by what he saw to be a deepening gap between seminary education and the Church. Could it be that, in a way, we are too progressive in our teaching? I mean by this that our teaching takes our students not only to the frontiers of our own research, but to the very battle line where the truth of tomorrow is being tried in the fire? I, for one, should welcome such a criticism. My own experience as a student always showed me that the teacher who eagerly proceeds with a genuine research project can hardly be dull. He stimulates and challenges. But then, this is said chiefly with reference to advanced graduate studies. We should never forget that a seminary is first and foremost a professional school where time is hardly found for bare essentials. Besides, many of us are likely to take too much for granted on the part of the students. Once you correct papers, and discover what was made out of your fine points, you feel like making new resolutions. This is especially true in these United

States where college schedules and programs are so uneven and so different. This fall, we were entertaining a group of Juniors in our home. The conversation turned to the Jesuit order. Then I brought up the fact that the Jesuits were the Order of the Counter Reformation. A Junior, who has thus far majored in electricity, interrupted and asked "what do you mean by reformation?" A *quid pro quo* followed in the course of which it appeared that the man had never had even a public school course in the general history of the period. He had never heard of the religious wars of the 16th century, etc. Should we turn down such candidates? But then, there are so many instances of such men having answered a genuine call, sometimes at great cost, and finally made good. The most immediate solution then, is to put first things first, and be willing to go through the drab routine of fundamentals.

It is noteworthy, moreover, that ministers will carry back to their churches the method of the seminary—and even some of the lectures. Then a gap will be opened between the minister and his congregation somewhat in the likeness of the one which was said by the former moderator to separate the seminarians from the Church.

Again, just because you and I get engrossed in our own theological position, we find ourselves stressing it, the more so, sometimes, as we know it to be challenged in the next room. No personal disloyalty is implied to be sure. Our president himself has openly said that he does not want our Princeton education to be "a badge that you wear on your lapel, but, rather, a banner which you unfold ahead of marching troops". Having just made my own *mea culpa* as a teacher, I feel free to point out that possibly the over-optimism of the classroom is carried across to the presidential office. For again, the president's statement—just quoted admittedly only expresses an ideal; yet, one which presupposes that the students, individually and as a group, have the equipment, the way and the means of judging what a pertinent philosophy of our Reformed tradition should be. Some may, others have not, quite a few seem to be all at sea. Once more, we must recognize, however reluctantly, that a seminary is essentially a professional school which recruits widely from the most varied fields; and that taking one's stand in the midst of Apostles, Church Fathers, theologians, and philosophers, between, say, Paul, Augustine, Aquinas, Calvin, Kant, and Barth, presupposes wide and well-digested reading based on the rock foundation of a solid classical culture.

A symptom that we all take too much for granted is that students are always asking for a "bull session," "question period", that new societies are being brought into existence where professors are asked to make a long story short and tell briefly "what this is all about". Meanwhile the Library is hardly crowded. A sound seminary education should take such realities into consideration. It is a fact, moreover, that the possible height and breadth of an edifice is predetermined by the depth and strength of its foundations.

What has just been said implies further and for similar reasons that a minimum consensus of opinion should be reached within the faculty. How can we expect students to thrash out the differences resulting from a great variety of points of view if we ourselves are unable, nay, do not even attempt to do so? I, for one, hoped that the foundation of the Faculty Club meant that this all-important task was at long last to be seriously undertaken. But this has hardly been the case thus far. This is said with due appreciation of pioneering work done during this first year. After all we have hardly begun.

There is finally, the tremendous question of bridging the gap between the Seminary and the lay world, our mission field. What was said at the outset of the main task of both the theologian and the Christian philosopher—who are to become one and the same man in the minister—will suffice to suggest the importance of a practical approach to this all important problem. Hair-splitting on the epistemological issue will no longer do, as those who testify will who know by experience the actual bearing of such issues on the life of the average church and community. The theological student should ultimately and in due time gain some insight into such issues, at least enough to remain aware of them within the framework of a well-defined Christian and cultural pattern. There is evidence that this seminary has already become aware of the urgency of a Christian approach to the great cultural and economic issues of the day. Yet we, as a group, must also work towards such a goal. Here, once more, the Faculty Club could help, more especially if its basis were widened so as to admit colleagues from the University and even representative citizens of the community. This I do in the awareness that I have hardly scratched the surface of such a tremendous subject.

Bibliography

BOOKS

Alexander, Hartley Burr. *Truth and Faith: An Interpretation of Christianity*. New York: Holt, 1929.

Cailliet, Emile. *Alone at High Noon: Reflections on the Solitary Life*. Grand Rapids: Zondervan, 1971.

———. *The Beginning of Wisdom*. New York: Revell, 1947.

———. *The Christian Approach to Culture*. Nashville: Abingdon-Cokesbury, 1953.

———. *The Clue to Pascal*. Philadelphia: Westminster, 1943.

———. *The Dawn of Personality*. Indianapolis: Bobbs-Merrill, 1955.

———. *La Foi des Ancêtres: essai sur les représentations collectives des vieux Malgaches*. Paris: Société d'Editions Géographiques, Maritimes et Coloniales, 1930.

———. *Great Shorter Works of Pascal*. Translated with Introduction by Emile Cailliet and John C. Blankenagel. Philadelphia: Westminster, 1946.

———. *Journey into Light*. Grand Rapids: Zondervan, 1968.

———. *The Life of the Mind*. New York: Macmillan, 1942.

———. *Mysticisme et 'Mentalité mystique:' étude d'un problème pose par les travaux de M. Lévy-Bruhl sur la mentalité primitive*. No. 36. Paris: Librairie Félix Alcan, 1938.

———. *Pascal: The Emergence of Genius*. 2nd ed. New York: Harper & Brothers, 1961.

———. *Pascal: Genius in the Light of Scripture*. Philadelphia: Westminster, 1945.

———. *Pascal's Short Life of Christ*. Translated with Introduction by Emile Cailliet and John C. Blankenagel. Philadelphia: Westminster, 1950.

———. *The Recovery of Purpose*. New York: Harper, 1959.

———. *Le Service Social: Orientations Philosophiques*. Paris: Les Presses Universitaires de France, 1936.

———. *Symbolisme et âmes primitives*. Paris: Boivin, 1936.

———. *Why We Oppose the Occult*. Philadelphia: University of Pennsylvania Press, 1931.

———. *Young Life*. New York: Harper & Row, 1963.

Drury, M. O'C. *The Danger of Words*. London: Routledge & Paul, 1973.

Dunn, J. C. *The War the Infantry Knew 1914–1919: A Chronicle of Service in France and Belgium*. London: Abacus, 1991.

Gilson, Etienne. *The Spirit of Mediaeval Philosophy.* Gifford Lectures 1931–1932. New York: Scribner's, 1940.

Hume, David. *Enquiry Concerning Human Understanding.* Edited by Peter Millican. New York: Oxford University Press, 2007.

———. *The Natural History of Religion.* Edited by J. C. A. Gaskin. New York: Oxford University Press, 1993.

Mehl, Roger. *The Condition of the Christian Philosopher.* Philadelphia: Fortress, 1963.

Ménégoz, Eugène. *Réflexions sur l'Évangile du salut.* Translated by Walter M. Horton. Paris: Sandoz et Fischbacher, 1879.

Ménégoz, Fernand. *La Certitude de la foi et la certitude historique, étude sur la problème du fondement de la vie religieuse.* Basel: Fincke, 1906.

———. *Gebetsproblem im Anschluss an Schleiermachers Predigten und Glaubenslehre.* Leipzig: Hinrichs, 1911.

Psichari, Ernest. *A Soldier's Pilgrimage.* London: Melrose, 1917.

———. *Le Voyage du Centurion.* Translated by E. M. Walker and Harriet M. Capes. Paris: Louis Conard, 1916.

Reed, Fanny. *Reminiscences Musical and Other.* Boston: Knight & Millet, 1903.

ARTICLES

Black, C. Clifton. "Remembering Otto Piper." *Princeton Seminary Bulletin* 26.3 (2005) 310–27.

Cailliet, Emile. "The Book That Understands Me." *Christianity Today* (November 22, 1963) 10–11.

———. "Books and the Book." *Christianity Today* 4 (December 1964) 3.

———. "The Christian Experience." *Theology Today* 2.3 (1945) 330–31.

———. "The Christian Scholar." *HIS* (December 1949) 35–46.

———. "Emile Cailliet: The Book That Understands Me." *Eternity* 25.7 (July 1974) 21–22.

———. "The Human Quest for Truth." Annual Lecture in the Humanities at Wheaton College, October 20, 1961. *Faculty Bulletin of Wheaton College* 25 (Winter 1962) 12–15.

———. "An Inquiry into Symbolism." *The Personalist* 17 (Spring 1936) 157–67.

———. "A Layman Among Ministers." *Princeton Seminary Bulletin* 39.2 (1945) 4–10.

———. "The Literary Mind and Religious Responsibility." In *Spiritual Problems in Literature*, edited by Stanley Romaine Hopper, 261–79. Institute for Religious and Social Studies 21. New York: Harper, 1957.

———. "The Mind's Gravitation Back to the Familiar." *Theology Today* 15 (1958) 1–8.

———. "Outlines of a Christian Positivism." *Princeton Seminary Bulletin* 42 (1948) 28–37.

———. "The Path out of this Wilderness: A Charter for the Christian Scholar." *Princeton Seminary Bulletin* 40.4 (1947) 17–26.

———. "Personal Religious Experience." *Religion in Life* 19.3 (1950) 381–88.

———. "Prayer and Certitude." *The Princeton Seminary Bulletin* 49.3 (January 1956) 13–19.

———. *Proceedings of Anniversary of the Inauguration of Graduate Studies at the University of Southern California* (1935) 165–72.

———. "A Scholar of Good Will Gets a Hearing." *Princeton Seminary Bulletin* 44.3 (1950) 29–32.
Cailliet, Vera Barbizon. *Froebel Gazette* 24 (February 1917).
Gaebelein, Frank E. "Friendship an Election of God—A Brief Memoir of Emile Cailliet." *Theology Today* 40 (April 1983) 55–57.
Hewitt, Arthur W. "The Story of Emile Cailliet." *The Christian Advocate* 120.28 (July 12 1945) 819–20.
Horton, Walter M. "The Theology of Eugène Ménégoz." *Journal of Religion* 6.2 (March 1926) 175.
Jones, Robert. "Keeping the Faith." *The Paper* 3 (June 21–25, 1981) 1–2.
"Lucien Cailliet." In *Baker's Biographical Dictionary of 20th Century Classical Musicians*, compiled by Nicolas Slonimsky. New York: Schirmer, 1997.
Ménégoz, Eugène. "Symbolo-Fideism." In *Encyclopedia of Religion and Ethics* 12, edited by James Hastings, 151–52. Edinburgh: T. & T. Clark, 1908–1926.
Oman, Richard J. "Emile Cailliet: Christian Centurion." *Princeton Seminary Bulletin* 5 (1984) 33–37.
Weber, Eugen. "Psichari and God." *Yale French Studies* 12 (1953) 19, 31.

DISSERTATION

Lemke, Steve Warner. *The Philosophy of Emile Cailliet*. PhD diss., Southwestern Baptist Theological Seminary, 1985.

REVIEWS

Cailliet, Emile. Review of *Christianity and Existentialism* by J. M. Spier. *Religion in Life* 23 (Winter 1953–54) 152–54.
———. Review of "Darkness Over Broadway." *Eternity* 8.3 (March 1957) 12.
Cotton, J. Henry. Review of *The Christian Approach to Culture* by Emile Cailliet. *Interpretation* 7 (October 1953) 489.
John, Ralph C. Review of *The Dawn of Personality* by Emile Cailliet. *The Pastor* (October 1955) 36.
Packer, J. I. Review of *The Christian Approach to Culture* by Emile Cailliet. *The Christian Graduate* 7 (1954) 6–12.
Schinz, Albert. Review of *The Theme of Magic in Nineteenth Century French Fiction* by Emile Cailliet. *Revue D'Historie Littéraire de la France* 40.4 (1933) 601–2.

UNPUBLISHED PAPERS

(Located in the Emile Cailliet Collection, Special Collections, Princeton Theological Seminary Library)

Cailliet, Emile. "I Met the Huguenots" (n.d.)
———. "The Role of the Seminary in the Secular Order with Special Attention to its Cultural Aspects." (n.d.)
———. "The Tasks of Christian Philosophy" (n.d.)
———. "This I Believe." Lenten address at Scripps College (March 12, 1940).

———. World War I War Diary" (January 8-February 28, 1915)
———. "Where Would Jesus Be?" (n.d.) (Subsequently published in the *War Cry Magazine* of the Salvation Army)

Authors

CLEMENS BARTOLLAS

Clemens Bartollas is professor of sociology at the University of Northern Iowa. He taught at Pembroke State University from 1973 to 1975, Sangamon State University from 1975 to 1980, and the University of Northern Iowa from 1981 to the present. He has received a number of honors from the University of Northern Iowa, including Distinguished Scholar, the Donald McKay Research Award and the Regents' Award for Faculty Excellence.

Dr. Bartollas is an ordained Presbyterian minister and for the past twenty years has been the stated supply for the St. Paul Presbyterian church in Washburn, Iowa.

He has published forty books and many articles and papers. He is best known for his works on juvenile institutions, juvenile justice, juvenile delinquency, and adult corrections. He has also written several biographies.

He holds a BA from Davis and Elkins College, a BD from Princeton Theological Seminary (class of 1961), an STM from San Francisco Theological Seminary, and a PhD in sociology, with a special emphasis in criminology, from The Ohio State University.

ABIGAIL RIAN EVANS

Abigail Rian Evans is a scholar-in-residence at the Center for Clinical Bioethics at Georgetown University Medical Center and theological associate at Fairfax Presbyterian Church. She is also Charlotte Newcombe Professor of Practical Theology emerita at Princeton Theological Seminary, a professorship she held during her years at the Seminary from 1991 to 2009. During her tenure at Princeton, Abigail also served as Chair of the Practical Theology Department and Director of the Field Education program.

Earlier, Abigail was the Founder and Director of Health Ministries for the National Capital Presbytery in Metropolitan Washington DC. She previously served as the Director of New Programs and Senior Staff Associate at the Kennedy Institute of Ethics, Georgetown University; Chaplain of Columbia University; Synod Executive; pastor of churches in five states; and Presbyterian missionary in Brazil. She is an ordained Presbyterian minister.

Dr. Evans has published over fifty-five books, articles, book chapters, and reviews and spoken at over three hundred different universities, medical centers, graduate schools, community agencies, and churches here and abroad.

She has a PhD in Philosophy and Bioethics from Georgetown University, an MDiv from Princeton Theological Seminary; a Diploma from Escola de linguas e orientação, Campinas, Brazil, and a BA from Jamestown College.

GORDON GRAHAM

Gordon Graham is Henry Luce III Professor of Philosophy and the Arts at Princeton Theological Seminary in Princeton, NJ. He previously held positions in philosophy at the Universities of St Andrews and Aberdeen in Scotland. He has published extensively on philosophical aspects of art, ethics, politics and religion, and his most recent books include: *Evil and Christian Ethics* (Cambridge University Press, 2001); *The Re-enchantment of the World: Art versus Religion* (Oxford University Press, 2007); and *Theories of Ethics* (Routledge, 2010). Dr. Graham holds an MA from St Andrews University in Scotland, and an MA and PhD from Durham University in England.

KENNETH HENKE

Kenneth Woodrow Henke is an archivist on the Special Collections staff of the Princeton Theological Seminary Library, where the Emile Cailliet Manuscript Collection is housed. He is a member of the Academy of Certified Archivists, and previous to his position at Princeton, served as the T. Wistar Brown Fellow at the Haverford Quaker Archives and the Charles E. Peterson Fellow at The Philadelphia Athenaeum.

www.ingramcontent.com/pod-product-compliance
Lightning Source LLC
Chambersburg PA
CBHW070321230426
43663CB00011B/2190